SQUEEZE IT
TILL THE
EAGLE GRINS

HOW TO
SPEND,
SAVE,
AND
ENJOY
YOUR
MONEY

SQUEEZE IT TILL THE EAGLE GRINS

Scott Burns

DOUBLEDAY & COMPANY, INC.
GARDEN CITY, NEW YORK

To Wendy

ACKNOWLEDGMENTS

You can't write a book without help. Chauncey Bell and Mike Fenlon, both of Arthur D. Little, Inc., provided advice and information, as did Jim Lyon of Neville, Rodie, and Shaw, and Scott Curtis. Christine Mattson and Mary Gilleece helped in putting the final manuscript together.

But I owe the most to my wife, Wendy, without whose constant encouragement the book would never have been completed, and to my sons Jasper and Oliver, to whom I owe, like all parents, a world.

Grateful acknowledgment is given to the following:

The Complete Guide to Winning Poker, by Albert H. Morehead. Copyright © 1967 by Loy Morehead. Reprinted by permission of Simon & Schuster, Inc.

"Cost of Car Operation," from *The Automobilist.* Reprinted by permission of the Automobile Legal Association.

"Distribution of Consumer Units by Amount of Wealth." Reprinted with permission of the Federal Reserve Fund, Washington, D.C.

"The Economics of the Coming Spaceship Earth," from *Beyond Economics,* by Kenneth Boulding. Copyright © 1968 by the University of Michigan Press.

"Good Living Begins at $25,000 a Year," May 1968, thirteen bar graphs from the article "How the Rich Differ," May 1968, Cardamone Associates; data source. W. R. Simmons & Associates Research, Inc., courtesy of *Fortune* magazine.

"Influence of Various Provisions on Effective Rates," from *Individual Income Tax,* by Richard Goode. Reprinted by permission of The Brookings Institution.

"Mortality Rate," from *Best's Flitcraft Compend.* Reprinted by permission of A. M. Best Company, Inc., Morristown, New Jersey.

"Rates of Return on Investments in Common Stock" (Merrill, Lynch, Pierce, Fenner & Smith, Inc.), Chicago Graduate School of Business.

"Table of Mathematics of Investment," from *Johnson's Investment Company Charts,* 1968 edition. Reproduced by permission of Johnson's Charts, Buffalo, New York.

"When All Taxes Are Counted" (December 9, 1968). Reprinted from *U. S. News & World Report.* Copyright 1968 U. S. News & World Report, Inc.

"The income-tax schedule climbs progressively as income grows," from *Economics: An Introductory Analysis,* by Paul A. Samuelson, 7th ed. Copyright © 1967 by McGraw-Hill, Inc. Used by permission of McGraw-Hill Book Company, Inc.

*If I ever get my hands on a dollar again, I'm
gonna squeeze it and squeeze it till the eagle grins.*
—from the song "Nobody Knows
You When You're Down and Out,"
by Jimmie Cox.

CONTENTS

How "hard" economic pragmatism pre-empts "soft" justice. History of federal income tax, exemptions, deductions, credits, and effective tax.

SECTION II

How?

Meaningful considerations. Experience. The cash vs. proforma account. Financing, depreciation, and insurance.

Money saved by spending. A house is a man's best friend. Popular myths vs. return on investment. Tax savings, amortization, and appreciation. The effect of leverage. Another viewpoint: the cost of financing in constant *dollars. Government-supported arbitrage for the wealthy. Break-even time, turn-around costs, effective government subsidy vs. income, imputed rental value as untaxed investment income. (Appendix D)*

Birth of a salesman. Why he will sell you anything. "It Costs You Nothing." What insurance really is. The cost of the guaranteed return; comparison with other returns. Calculation of retirement needs. Present value, discounted value, computations. (Appendix A)

The Xerox story. Spectrum of investment return. Return on common stocks. Relation of savings, income, and rate of return. Necessity for common-stock investments. Effects of inflation. Varieties of stockholder experience. How much your time is worth. The broker's office, the broker, his customers, his information. Games played by both parties. The switch to mutual funds. Reading the earnings report. Computer leasing as exam-

SECTION III

Why? . . . A Larger Perspective

ILLUSTRATIONS

AUTHOR'S PREFACE

"Inflation" is a word with an elusive meaning. It can be grasped only through cumulative experience. The anxiety and, finally, terror that the experience evokes is ill-expressed by the statistical series published so regularly by the Department of Labor. The past five years have witnessed an inflationary pace that has educated all of us. Understanding inflation is no longer the exclusive province of the mature and the elderly. It is one understanding that has crossed the Generation Gap.

This is being written only a few days after President Nixon declared wage and price controls. There is much shouting. Many threats. And counterthreats. And commentary! So much commentary!

Milton Friedman, the conservative monetarist, comments that wage and price controls are all right but not very effective, enumerating some of the infinite ways that will be found around them.

Ralph Nader comments on the favor to Big Business in the measures (the largess of the investment credit) and to the regressive nature of wage controls.

Several Labor leaders have accepted the new measures as a personal stab in the back.

All of which does little more than verify Abraham Lincoln's wisdom. Indeed, you *can't* please all the people all the time. Both Friedman and Nader are accurate in their comments. And Labor, if it hasn't been stabbed, can offer bruises that indicate a powerful kick. But there is something more in wage and price controls, something that many of us, in our elation at some dramatic action, have overlooked.

What we have overlooked is an admission of managerial bankruptcy. Inflation has been the constant companion to our commerce and economic life for more than a quarter of a century. It has staggered, crept (hiding behind socialism, perhaps?), and finally, worked itself into a brisk trot. In the process it has impoverished many of the elderly, deprived the young, and instilled a sense of futility in the mature.

Now, in one catalytic act, *we have admitted that all the sophisticated means at the disposal of the government are impotent against inflation.* No one can foretell the consequences. Meanwhile, we have won a ninety-day reprieve. It can be extended, perhaps several times. But several times is not forever. The fundamental problem remains unsolved.

The Phillips curve illustrates this fundamental problem; it shows us that inflation and unemployment are inversely related. We can eliminate Intolerable Inflation at the expense of Unacceptable Unemployment. And vice versa. The Nixon Game Plan was an attempt to find the political optimum in this relationship. It failed.

In a very real sense, the Phillips curve is the New Frontier for Industrial Society. It is the boundary of our future, the cutting edge of our economic experience. Every conventional economic weapon has been brought to bear on this barrier. None has broken it. Now what we have failed to do with finesse we attempt by fiat: wage and price controls. Once the controls are removed, inflation will resume. Perhaps, with luck and a good deal of unemployment, we will reduce the rate of inflation to a mere 3%. That still means that it will take a dollar and thirty-five cents in 1982 to buy what now costs a dollar.

We need a fundamental change in economic policy. Robert Theobald has suggested that only a redistribution of income will end the inflation/unemployment bind: I believe he is right.

Ironically, the events of the past decade have not widened the distribution of income. The top 20% of the population still control about the same proportion of national income as they controlled ten years ago. Indeed, there has been little change for more than three decades. While the cost of welfare programs has risen astronomically, the rise has been inadequate in relation to the benefits that have accrued to the wealthy and well to do. The tax reform of 1962 brought little real relief to the middle-class family; the tax reform of 1970 was, and is, a farce. Together the bills brought the marginal tax rate on the highest income group from 90% to just over 50%, while providing only minor adjustments for the bulk of the working population. What small benefits that were found in the federal tax reforms were more than lost in the constant spiral of state and local taxes, principally sales and real-estate taxes, which are the most regressive of all taxes. Finally, in spite of noble plans and voluminous reports from Washington, the housing shortage remains, largely because of high, inflation-caused, interest rates.

Housing is the primary route to the acquisition of assets. For 90% of the population, the accumulated equity in a home represents almost 50% of their net worth. Since the investment media available to the small investor have, by and large, controlled returns which are inadequate in the face of inflation, the net effect of the past decade has been to put more money with less purchasing power in the hands of the middle class, and limit, if not close, the avenues that allow one to accumulate modest wealth and equally modest security.

The only thing that has had a liberalized redistribution is unemployment.

A fundamental change in our economic policy requires a fundamental change in our employment policy.

Involuntary unemployment still carries the same penalties as voluntary unemployment, yet it is synonymous with price stability in all the major industrial countries.

The absurd results of our refusal to make the necessary changes can be read in the choice of tools for stimulating the economy. In dropping the federal excise tax on automobiles, the President hopes to both better the competitive position of American small cars vis-à-vis foreign imports, and stimulate the sale of automobiles, thus creating more jobs. Unemployment will decrease at the immediate expense of more pollution and more pressure to build more highways, and at the long-term expense of randomizing the landscape beneath varicosities of macadam and concrete. Surely that is too great a price to pay for our incapacity to align our values with an economy and society so constituted that it cannot employ all its members and maintain its stability.

In the chapters that follow I have tried to offer some advice on how to deal with an inflationary environment that will be with us for some time. We can learn to fend for ourselves as best we can. And we can change a world in which the real scarcities are of reason and compassion.

Scott Burns

Cataumet, Massachusetts
August 1971

"I said before that the higher mathematics of poker is not very important. It doesn't help a player much to know the chances of being dealt a straight flush or a full house or even a pair. Yet, most of the published tables of poker probabilities are confined to that kind of information.

"It does help to know the odds against improving any particular hand. Memorize these odds. At the very least, they will tell you when the pot is offering you good odds on a speculative play."

From *The Complete Guide to Winning Poker* by Albert H. Morehead

Poker players know the odds of the game. They know that of the 2.6 million possible poker hands in a normal deck, only forty are straight flushes.

Life is also a game; it differs from poker in that you know the rules of poker when you sit down to play and you can drop out whenever you please. *We* can't drop out, but if we know the odds we can play the game better. And if we don't like the odds, we can change the game.

SQUEEZE IT
TILL THE
EAGLE GRINS

INTRODUCTION

This book is about being middle class. Our immediate concern is to see what money really is and to learn how to live with it so that we may avoid the experience of living without it. It is also about how most Americans will die destitute, in poverty, or at best suffer a precarious old age, unwitting losers in a game with very unfavorable odds.

The median income of Americans over age sixty-five is $2116; almost seven in ten have incomes under three thousand dollars per year.[1] The word for their condition is *Poverty*. They are not slackers. They worked through the Roaring Twenties, suffered the Great Depression, manned overtime shifts and accepted rationing during World War II, educated their children, and presided over an economy that quadrupled during their working life-span.

Yet they are grotesquely poor. Only a fool could argue that 70% of the American population is composed of improvident ne'er-do-wells seeking handouts. Most of these people are Middle Class: they have worked hard and long. Obviously, they lost the money game. The same penurious fate may await *us*.

Few people would play poker if rewards accrued only to a single hand. This is precisely the case in the money game. While the common lot is to draw a pair or less, only a royal flush wins. The absurdity of basing the values of a society on a rare occurrence is seldom discussed. Alternatives are impatiently cast aside as "impractical." We continue playing a game with few winners and many, many losers.

Not long ago, a small wave of scandal passed through the oil industry: someone realized that the odds in the extravagantly advertised gas station giveaway games were ridiculous. They were. Lawsuits followed. The odds on winning ranged from minuscule to infinitesimal. Some of the contests were designed to virtually preclude winners.

Still, many people bought a particular kind of gas because

they were hooked on the related contest. They never considered the odds. If they *had* considered the odds, they wouldn't have played.

We don't consider the odds against winning the money game —perhaps because we don't dare. It is, after all, "the only game in town." Even if we have doubts about the worth or chances of winning, we know that it is a vast improvement on losing. So we play the game.

Reading this book will not make you rich. Nor will it turn you into a stock-market wizard or real-estate tycoon. But it *will* help you play the game better and relieve some of the pressures and worries as we search for a better game, one in which we can all be human beings.

This is not the book I started several years ago: my original intent was to produce a helpful economic primer by directing an otherwise rather useless numerical compulsion. The trouble with having a compulsion about numbers is that it makes you aware of how *arbitrary* they are. One can discuss a column of seemingly direct and absolute quantities in countless ways; depending upon the preconditions one sets (or discovers), inequities become just—even charitable—and absurdities become rational.

Understanding requires that we ask "Why?" as well as "How?" "How?" is a pragmatic question. Applied to personal economics in its most degenerate form, the word produces lists of major outlets for day-old bread in the fifty largest cities, cost-effective comparisons of beer and scotch, protein/fat ratios for various cuts of meat, calendars noting the annual best-price sale-times for particular consumer goods, and tips on how to make bed sheets last longer. The answers are intrinsically depressing because they tend to further propagate the already intolerable reduction of human life to dollar measurements.

For the vast majority of Americans, "How?" is a pressing question. *How* to make ends meet? *How* to pay all the bills? *How* to get a new car? *How* to send the kids through college? Depending upon one's income, it can press by the year, month, or moment. But we are all pressed. The differences are of degree, not substance.

"Why?" for the poor and the middle class is a luxury dropped in the expedient necessity of answering "How?" Worse, the question may be politically irrelevant.

We are Nowhere Men, ninety-seven-pound weaklings humiliated on the Beach of Life. Some escape humiliation by emulating Charles Atlas. The experience of failure is the life theme of those who remain behind.

Speaking for myself, I have some misgivings. I'm not sure I *want* to escape. More particularly, I am not certain that I want to become strong so that I might humiliate my former peers. Neither do I wish Failure to characterize my life. I would rather unite with other weaklings and *change the beach.*

Political relevance may seem unrelated to personal economics —but the only way to change the inequities, absurdities, and hardships created by our social organization is to *make* a conscious relationship between the two. Unless we do, revolution— or moral bankruptcy—is inevitable.

If we are to avoid an intellectual retreat from our social problems, we must examine the apparent "why?" of our system. If the numbers in the money system are arbitrary, we must examine their relation to one another. Regardless of its apparent arbitrariness, each system has logical implications that affect the quality of human life.

The current unrest is a product of our inertia and indifference to justice. We read about the ghettos and shake our heads sadly, much as mother used to do about "the poor people in China." Meanwhile we congratulate our white God for his grace. Without it, we might have been born in Watts.

We cringe from any recognition of self in ghetto inhabitants, more because they are poor than because they are black. We congratulate ourselves on our Prosperity and, better yet, our Prospects.

Yet the real difference, in the end, is one of degree, because we are only slightly less dispensable. (The current recession has painfully educated many engineers and scientists to their relative dispensability.) What a minority experiences from birth to death, we—the majority—will experience at age sixty or sixty-five. All our Prosperity and all our Prospects come to nothing.

Little time is devoted to thinking about being old. At times we are forced witnesses, but most often we avoid the reality altogether. Many who think about becoming old regard it as a period of escape—from change, from responsibility, from anything we would like to avoid.

But there is another "old"—a bitter old, an old in which the kind patina of time is revealed as a painful varicosity.

> At the corner store in a slum, the grocer resented my youth. "You want to know what it's like to be old?" he asked. He got an open two-pound coffee tin from under his counter and hurled the thousands of pennies it contained across the counter. "That's what it's like! Every month ends like this—a banquet of pennies!"

Old age isn't Golden at all. For most Americans—seven out of ten, maybe for us—old age will be little more than the arthritic pursuit of forgotten pennies.

My own wants are simple: I want to be a reasonable human being, to love and be loved, to share the experiences of life with my wife and friends, and pass a world of increased possibilities on to my children.

All but the last are vaguely possible—difficult, but attainable in some form, to some degree. I think I would settle for less love and reason—even less experience—if I felt proud of what we may pass on to our children. But I do not. Worse, I fear our congressmen may be shot by less-temperate, less hatefully "reasonable," men before they can read our belated, well-intentioned letters.[2]

The examination that follows is broken into three parts. In the first section we ask "What?"—What wealth is. What security is. What money is. What affects money.

The second section asks "How?" How we spend our money and how we should spend it. The analysis in this section is more abstract and involved than the "How To" variety of advice on personal finance, but it is these chapters that provide the most directly useful information and illustrate some of the problems posed in the first section.

The third section asks "Why?" It examines our institutions and the manner in which their power is directed, poses problems less immediately tangible than those posed in the first two sections, and attempts to formulate some tentative answers.

Close examination of the answers to these questions and the numbers that evoke them provides the most effective instruments for seeing the face of our keeper.

SECTION

I

What?

1

HAPPINESS IS
ELIZABETH TAYLOR'S
DIAMOND

Most of us are so caught up in the daily round we don't have time to ponder the meaning of money. But we do have occasional visions of what wealth is. Wealth is Elizabeth Taylor's diamond, Stirling Moss's heated toilet seat, Paul Getty's oil wells, Howard Hughes's purchase of Las Vegas, HIS and HERS airplanes at Neiman-Marcus, or a Degas hidden behind the dining-room door. It can also be a thousand-dollar raise, a new dishwasher, a car with power windows, tickets to a world-series game, or a smile from the mortgage officer at the local bank. Whatever it is, it's something we don't have. We may be a horse, check, or aging relative away from it, but it hasn't really arrived.

For some people, it never comes, because this year's definition of wealth is more refined than last year's. Like immortality or the end of the rainbow, wealth is something always sought and never found.

We *KNOW* some things about wealth. It lends its holder Power and a certain pre-emptive Status. We want it; but not too desperately—at least if we are middle class.

We also *know* that wealth, like masturbation, leads to insanity. (Even here it provides certain advantages: it's much more fashionable to stay at McLean's or the Menninger Clinic than in a state hospital.) Though there has been no research on the subject, everyone knows that the mere possession of too many shares of IBM is a hazard to genetic tissue, a probable reason for the stock-piling of vice-presidents in banks.

We like to think of the rich as different from ourselves in some deep, essential way. Lacking other goals, we can always aspire to the next rung on the economic ladder. We can aspire to the unseen top of the ladder, because it is more relevant to our real associations with wealth. In our hearts we know that wealth is magical: when one is wealthy, all life glitters with the crystalline clarity of fantasy. Unseen hands move and manipulate distant worlds; the flick of a flaccid ear buys a Rembrandt. Doors open, tables wait, traffic stops, and—oh, the excruciating joy—all women and parking places are ours!

Veblen once wrote that the rich exhibited their domination by conspicuous consumption and that the great mass of human beings lived out their economic lives in conscious or unconscious emulation of the rich. Perhaps the thesis still applies in limited cases, but it now seems that the rich are guilt-ridden and inconspicuous. With the possible exception of classics majors at Harvard College and certain other aberrant groups, the wealthy in America are conspicuous only by their absence. For the most part, they are as invisible as the poor; they have disguised their Solid Gold "Other America" to look like anodized aluminum and are infiltrating the ranks of the defenseless middle class— lower, if you judge the life station of the hippie subculture by its habits of consumption.

A survey of the top 2% of the population by *Fortune*[1] magazine came to some surprising and disappointing conclusions. "The upper-income American," *Fortune* says, "uses his extraordinary income for ordinary purposes. His desire is comfort, his goal security, his diversions passive and innocent. He buys the same things that anyone else buys, but he buys more of them and usually chooses models with the most buttons and gadgets. He is neither adventurous in his spending nor a taste-maker. The country club satisfies his modest social ambitions." It seems that Hemingway was right. The rich do have more money. But that's about all. One might think (or wish) that an income of twenty-five thousand dollars a year would cause some basic change in life-style, would create the magic divide that we aspire to cross.

The statistics show that there is no such change. They don't collect works of art (the Corporation does). Nor is there a constant crowd of Senior Executives hovering around the doors of J. S. Inskip awaiting the delivery of a new Rolls or queuing up at Harry Winston's to buy a rock bigger than Liz's—let alone installing, in the manner of Hugh Hefner, a bathtub on their private plane. Such activities are eccentric.

On the whole, while they may wander through Georg Jensen's or Tiffany's with more temerity than the 98% of the population not so fortunate, they are a rather uninspired group. They still shop at Sears, Roebuck (which isn't even *upper*-middle class), carry life insurance (a bit more), buy mutual funds (hedged, perhaps), and cook hamburgers on the outdoor grill.

A more careful view of their spending habits indicates that although this small group controls 12% of the national income, or about $50 billion, it fails to dominate any major consumer market. Although 60% own dishwashers, their demand constitutes less than 15% of the total market. The same applies for practically everything else—as the following graphs from the *Fortune* study indicate. (Ironically, inflation is already visible in these figures. In 1968 $30 per week was deemed a significant dividing line for food purchases!)

The difference, if any, seems to lie in the comfort margin. Sending kids through college isn't a terrible sweat, TV sets aren't bought on installments, and vacations are taken somewhat farther afield than Lake Cumquat. Their buying habits indicate that they are just as interested in buying tinsel as gold and diamonds—but they will pay more for it.

If material wealth is different in *degree* rather than in *kind* as one ascends the pinnacles of power and position, then where is the magic of wealth?

We know from daily reminders in the press that we are the richest nation on earth—an incredible, unending cornucopia of wealth and goods. We have automobiles, refrigerators, dishwashers, dryers, washers, air conditioners, and TV sets by the millions. We also own countless radios, electric meat carvers, lawn mowers, home freezers, sailboats, surfboards, power toothbrushes, and a deafening glut of hi-fi equipment and telephones.[2]

Everything, in fact, seems to be coming up injection-molded roses. The diversity of our enterprise is such that we also produce a good deal of pollution, crime, highway fatalities, coronaries, ulcers, addicts, and suicides. It would appear that everyone listened to Eisenhower's 1959 recession admonition to "buy any-

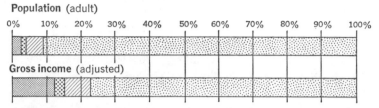

ILLUSTRATIONS I-A
How the Rich Differ

Sailboat

0%   10%   20%   30%   40%   50%   60%   70%   80%   90%   100%

Foreign travel *(between 1962 and 1966)*

Home remodeling *(in the past year and worth at least $1,000)*

Grocery bill over $30 a week

Imported wine *(served more than 4 glasses in week before survey)*

Country club *(with golf course)*

 $25,000 and over $15,000-$19,999

 $20,000-$24,999 $15,000 or less

thing"³; we seem bent on totally indiscriminate creation and consumption.

Quantities, unfortunately, are not conducive to learning or understanding. They can be impressive—but ultimately they are a bore, because we are all aware of the money and material wealth the United States has produced. Somehow it is difficult to relate numbers such as one trillion to the proverbial price of beans.⁴

We may be unwilling to confess a desire to keep up with the Joneses, but most of us are at least curious to know what they are doing. When the Joneses live next door in a house very similar to ours and suddenly buy a new car and a color TV set, and install a swimming pool in the back yard, all in the same month, we become not only curious but slightly indignant.

For a time, we are content to speculate on the sources of Jones's new wealth:

1. Jones got a raise.
2. The family collects Green Stamps and Raleigh coupons.
3. His kids forage for returnable soda bottles.
4. His wife takes in laundry.
5. Mrs. Jones wasn't really collecting for the United Fund last spring.

Explanations such as "Jones has just increased the national consumer debt by $4.3M" do us no good. Relief is nowhere in sight, because we know that Jones is a numskull. It can't be that he is doing something right. We must be doing something wrong.

From such situations are born ulcers, hypertension, and budgets that would make the meanest social worker look like the Last of the Big Spenders.

We might relieve the pressure by examining what the collective Joneses are doing, but this leads us back to the statistical trail. Averages, in their curious way, tend to become absolute rather than relative. Like Heidegger's "One" tyrannizing over the existential spirit, they rob us of identity. Worse, no one likes to think of himself as average. Even if we admitted to being "average" or "average, above average," the financial problems that beset us are in no way mitigated by the fact that they are "average" problems.

So where are we? Averages and quantities of things do us no good, and wealth, if it is statistically comprehensible, still remains a vague and ephemeral thing.

Perhaps the conscious equation of wealth and goods is erroneous?

Perhaps the lush ads in the Sunday magazine section have been leading us astray? Perhaps a high per-capita dishwasher count bears little relation to wealth? The voluminous statistics *do* indicate that the American Mother Hubbard has more electric can openers, vacuum cleaners, nail filers, and hair curlers stuffed away in her cupboards than her counterparts in other countries —but is this a reflection of wealth or an indication of some mad mechanical predisposition?

The ads suggest that true elegance (and therefore wealth) is yours with the simple purchase of a continuous-feed ⅓-horsepower disposal unit, but the glossy-paper image conflicts with the grinding reality. Once installed, the gloss fades and the perpetual carrot of wealth advances to the next contrivance of technology.

I do not mean, here, to begin another diatribe against dishwashers, automobiles, and the pressures of Madison Avenue. That particular road has been well traveled, is depressingly familiar, and leads nowhere. But it is alarming to observe the equation of the above items with the existence of wealth.

Michael Harrington could just as aptly have described his Other America as the Used America; a tour through the nearest ghetto[5] would reveal that the ghettos are, in truth, the wealthiest areas. Where else can you find automobiles casually abandoned in the streets and garbage cans filled with appliances? Not in Scarsdale or Grosse Pointe! The ghetto landscape is a surreal collage of yesterday's dreams of wealth. It is bursting with broken automobiles, bent washing machines, creaking refrigerators, and the shattered remnants of last year's fantastic TV plastic toy.

If we are to *be* wealthy, we must know that our material life-style is safe from anything but a malicious Act of God, and that we have the Power to enforce and protect that life-style from all unwanted disturbance. This is wealth as it exists with all its political, social, and psychological ramifications.

Very few Americans can, under this definition, consider themselves wealthy. Very, very few. We buy the artifacts of a "wealthy" existence, but keeping them is a constant worry. As long as we believe that tomorrow will be better, we can continue to play the game; should the cards change for one of us—or all of us—those precious artifacts of ease and comfort would be quick to disappear. If we once mistake the artifact for the state of wealthy grace it represents, we commit ourselves to a particular way of "buying" a better tomorrow.

We are secure because our material possessions symbolize the power to consume; our power to consume insures full production, and full production insures full employment—which brings us, round robin, back to the power to consume.

Defenders of the system are bound, at this point, to say that, regardless of the pressures that evolve from such cyclic relations, the United States is the richest and most powerful nation on earth. The system has produced the most incredible bounty of material goods ever seen; the middle-class Nowhere Man has more physical power at his disposal than most of the pre-medieval Popes. Indeed, on a relativistic basis, we are a marvel, provided only that one give physical power priority over equity, social justice, and spiritual growth. With dog food at thirty cents a can, many of us spend more on our dogs than the per-capita income allows for humans in the impoverished nations of half the world.

What the defenders argue is palpably true. Yet, if one must argue on a relativistic basis—without regard for what might be the *best* conditions for humanity—then one must also admit that relativistic considerations must be made within the relevant bounds of a cultural system; otherwise, one is obscuring the discussion by asserting a false objectivity.

When we discuss America and American goals, we are begging the question if we contrast the residents of Appalachia with the Ekes of Africa. The important matter is whether or not we, as a nation, have lived up to our unique stated purpose: "life, liberty, and the pursuit of happiness."[6]

The last decade has documented our failure to reach our stated national purpose and the difficulties of attaining liberty or pursuing happiness if one is crippled by poverty. Statisticians, economists, and political scientists still debate, in the manner of medieval scholars, the number of people who live in poverty on the head of the American pin. Estimates range from 15–40% of the population. Most of the estimates use dollar amounts to define poverty and then extrapolate the human costs as a by-product. The only trouble with this approach is that it relies on quantitative change. It assumes that more is better, that a sufficient number of dollars is an adequate index of "life, liberty, and the pursuit of happiness."

What we must ask is not how much money we all need to: (i) survive, (ii) prosper, (iii) bloat. But what *conditions* of life and relations are necessary to insure optimum functioning of our political and economic system?

Ferdinand Lundberg, author of *The Rich and the Super Rich*, and long-standing critic of our present system, defines poverty:

For my part, I would say that anyone who does not own a fairly substantial amount of income producing property or does not receive an earned income sufficiently large to make substantial regular savings or does not hold a well-paid securely tenured job is poor. He may be healthy, handsome and a delight to his friends—but he is poor. By this standard at least 70 percent of Americans are certainly poor, although not all of these by any means are destitute or poverty stricken. But, as shown in the 1930's, Americans can become destitute overnight if deprived of their jobs, a strong support to mindless conformity. As a matter of fact, many persons in rather well-paid jobs, even executives, from time to time find themselves jobless owing to job discontinuance by reason of merger, technical innovation, or plant removal. Unable to get new jobs, they suddenly discover to their amazement, that they are really poor, and they also discover by harsh experience to what specific conditions the word "poverty" refers. And even many of those who never lose their jobs often discover in medical and similar emergencies, that they are as helpless as wandering beggars. They are, in fact, poor. In such eventualities the man of property is evidently in a different position. He is definitely not poor.[7]

By Lundberg's definition, the poor of Mr. Harrington's Other America are no more than the top of the iceberg. The poor have neither assets nor income. Nor, we might add, are they in any position to acquire either. The middle class enjoys an income, but has immense difficulties in acquiring assets. What assets they do have, moreover, are maintained at the expense of income. "No tickee, no shirtee" describes the condition of most Americans perfectly. The wealthy, on the other hand, have both assets and income. The degree and extent of their security rests in large part on what portion of their income their assets produce.

The foreseeable future, however, does not contain a trust fund for every American. Nor would such a circumstance be acceptable to the value system we support. If we can't all be wealthy, then perhaps we can settle for one of the psychic artifacts of wealth: security.

Security, the precondition of liberty (political and otherwise) and the pursuit of happiness, is the guarantee of economic sufficiency when one has lived out his economic usefulness by virtue of either retirement or obsolescence.

The reasons for this definition will be pursued in Section III. For the moment, however, it should suffice to say that, even by this modest definition, most Americans are poor. Our Social Security and unemployment-benefit systems are grossly inadequate, and the investment realities of daily life are such that few Americans have the capacity to provide for their economic future.

Just as Lundberg suggests that unearned income from capital is immensely more secure than earned income from labor and that the security of one's sustenance is the true measure of wealth or poverty, we may also distinguish between different types of wealth. Some forms of wealth are *productive* and *growing*. Other forms are *consumable* and *wasting*—such as automobiles, dishwashers, and refrigerators. Yet it is just such "wealth" that leads us to call America "rich!"

According to the *Survey of Financial Characteristics of Consumers,* made by the Federal Reserve Board in 1966, 60% of the "consumer units" of the United States have assets of less than ten thousand dollars, while 83% have assets of less than twenty-five thousand.

FIGURE I-B

Distribution of Consumer Units by Amount of Wealth, December 31, 1962

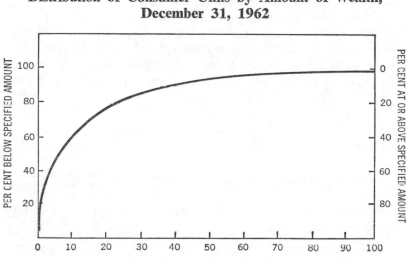

AMOUNT OF WEALTH IN THOUSANDS OF DOLLARS

These sums, while considerable, represent little more than the usual collection of worldly goods, home ownership, and the beginnings of an investment program. Clothing, household appliances, furnishings, an automobile, a small savings account, etc., are all that most Americans ever amass. Certainly, this is an inadequate base for an independent existence—particularly when most of this meager collection can disappear after a brief hospital stay or loss of employment.

We are probably blessed that not all Americans have the capacity (or desire) to follow an entrepreneurial career and amass great fortunes. Moreover, if more people were so capable, and desirous of achieving this end, the rewards wouldn't be nearly as handsome.

For the bulk of the American populace, life is an interminable battle, lost for some at birth, to amass enough wealth to pass through the winter of their lives in reasonable grace. Since some 70% of all Americans over the age of sixty-five live on an income of less than three thousand dollars a year, it is a foregone conclusion that most Americans lose that battle.

Other cultures, lacking entirely the technological sophistication of ours, reward, respect, and revere their aged. Regardless of the dimensions of their life accomplishments, the aged in such cultures have the security of knowing that their waning years are reasonably protected from humiliating want. Their value will not be measured by a productivity index.

Few Americans can claim the same. With the exception of a few incompletely absorbed cultural minorities, most of the Americans who can make such a claim are rich. And I mean Rich in the most conventional, mundane, crass way.

If wealth escapes definition by withdrawing to the labyrinth of human values, perhaps we can track it by examining the common denominator of all wealth, the alpha and omega of industrial society—Money.

2

WILL THE REAL
ROOT PLEASE
STAND UP?

Money is a technology devised to perform the role of translating ono kind of service into another.
—MARSHALL MCLUHAN

A. Systems

Depending upon your political or moral frame of reference, money can be the root of all evil, evil can be the root of all money, or, if one is given to ontological labors, roots can be the evil of all money. Debating which is which is the substance of political conventions, religious sermons, and intellectual meetings. To become a party to such debates, however, is to ascribe *moral* qualities to money and subscribe to the personification—and ultimate deification—that money has attained in our society. Money, by way of this personification, has become the collective unconscious of Industrial Man. Since we are proudly self-defined as Homo Economicus, our medium, money, has indeed become the message.

According to Webster, money is "something generally accepted as a means of exchange, a measure of value, or a means of payment." No mention of moral constitution, membership in the Hall of Great Gods, or anything of the sort. Those varicose nannies who posed as English teachers were right: you should read the dictionary.

As Marcuse, Fromm, and Norman Brown tell us in any number of words, we live in an increasingly abstract world. Symbols are everything. There is no Frontier. We do not trade bearskins for corn; we trade dollars for cars, and our time and thought for dollars. Pastoral dreams are pleasant things, but it remains that if the world is to be fed and if we are to provide the material goods most of the world aspires to, we must continue dividing the labor further and further, *ad nauseam* or *in reductione ad absurdum,* whichever you prefer, until we are, at best, several stages of diminishing reality away from anything real and palpable.

Anxiety grows easily in this kind of atmosphere. So does alienation, anomie, and all the other things everyone is writing about. At a certain point, crass reality rather than abstraction is the source of dissonance. The existence of ear wax, navel lint, and underarm odors seems at war with our notion of Love. We watch our job progress not by seeing countries tamed, or cattle raised and marketed, but by judging the size and arrangement of our office windows and the veneer of our desks. Minutiae become the major determinants of existence, and the parameters of progress grow increasingly obscure.

Analysts track all statistical variables: the Dow Jones as a function of hemlines, virility as a function of horsepower and comfort-and-convenience options. Security is a five-day deodorant pad. Happiness is a new washing machine. Love is a new Plymouth. Power is a worn Brooks Brothers shirt. Eventually, the relationship of any one thing or feeling to another is so tenuous that we begin to feel a certain absurdity in our existence. Impacted somewhere in this dense maelstrom of dream projections, quasi realities, and wish fulfillments, there is some key to the verisimilitude of our experience.

The only thing that seems universal in all our transactions with the world is the dollar. We reach for it as a source of Salvation.

That this should occur, reflects the disconnection discussed above and the fact that what was defined and created as a necessity of our economic existence also has value in our personal life. Money is very real. Money is ultimately real. It is our touchstone with Reality. Given a sufficient quantity of money, only Reality is impossible. The gates of Hell swing open for the man without money. But for most of us, our daily intercourse with money produces neither agony nor ecstasy, but . . . Prudence.

Misconceptions about money are perpetuated by the vast majority of books on personal finance and the advice columns in the daily newspaper. Such writings generally have what might be called an inquisitorial stance toward the economic problems of existence. We are exhorted to "stretch dollars" and "pinch pennies" as a means to the noble end of Saving Money. Interest becomes the pecuniary equivalent of feeding the five thousand, and the quarterly dividend from AT&T is as coveted as the last gold star on the Sunday school regular-attendance medal. The sado-pious imagery of money only serves to point up that it is terribly symbolic, volatile stuff—not the hard, reality-measuring, penultimate that we are inclined to feel it is.

The word "feel" is very important. Even the Federal Reserve Board has been known to "feel," and a regular reading of the financial page of the daily newspaper will show that the fluctuation of stocks, bonds, and store inventories is used as a gauge for reading the emotional health and mood of the nation.

MEXICAN VIRUS KEEPS THE DOW JONES RUNNING

Whatever qualities we ascribe to money, constancy is not among them.

Scientists and engineers scare us when they talk about the "systems approach." If you happen to be one or the other, pat yourself on the back and feel blessed. You have a head start on the only method for making money comprehensible.

The systems approach began when Galileo announced that our planet is not the center of the universe and that the earth revolves around the sun. Since then, we have worried about multibodied problems, Coriolis forces, rotating/translating co-ordinate systems, and a lot of other things that keep Keuffel & Esser producing new slide rules.

In addition to putting a permanent dent in our collective human ego, Galileo opened the door for modern physics and worried Einstein enough to make him overcome his difficulties with grammar school arithmetic and produce the Theory of Relativity. Practically no one understood it, including the United States Government, but a way was found to use American Know-How, and the theory's implications have borne a variety of radioactive fruit we have all been worrying about ever since.

In the less-awesome world of economics, relativity meant that nothing meant anything except in relation to something else. Since the inception of that idea, the nation's adding machines, slide rules, and commentators have been trying to relate everything to something else and have always found that something else is really a function of some other something else(s) until, finally, we couldn't even remember it all.

But we did discover "systems."

The only problem is that if nothing means anything except in relation to something else, which in turn means nothing in relation to everything, we are worse off than when we started. Hence, the frequent use of the word "feel" in the day-to-day economic commentary of the newspapers.

Given that something means anything or nothing only in relation to something else, we can begin assembling an intelligent notion of how it all works by putting something, anything, nothing, and something else in a box and seeing how they affect each other. By defining limits to what we see, measure, and attempt to control, we have created a "system."

The United States is a system. Our unit of exchange, universal within the limits of the system, is the dollar. Each nation has a universal means of exchange within its system boundaries. Anythings, nothings, and something elses that affect the value of our somethings within the system are: inflation, taxation, liquidity, productivity, and employment.

In relation to the world, the system of the United States is a subsystem. Although the dollar is the de facto medium of exchange among countries, the theoretical means of exchange that allows one nation to relate to another is gold.

Since national subsystems may change in relation to one another within the boundaries of the world system under the influence of the preceding something elses as well as of ideologies, components of the subsystem (people, corporations) may protect themselves against adverse change within their system by relating to the world system. If I expect the dollar to be devalued, I can protect myself by exchanging my dollars for another currency before the devaluation and then re-exchanging after the devaluation.

The famed economist Lord Keynes earned much of his own living and enhanced the fortunes of King's College by indulging in just such manipulations and speculations. The "Gnomes of

Zurich" also indulge. Speculators trade pounds for silver or gold, francs for marks, and somethings for anythings. This feverish and often fruitless activity is justified in the holy name of Liquidity, which is, ironically, the Cornerstone of International Trade.

The closest most of us get to such esoteric speculations is the exchange of dollars for francs and *Métro* tokens at the American Express office in Paris, or discovering that someone has slipped a Canadian quarter into our change at the local drugstore.

Most of us, however, are concerned only with dollars, and perceive the relative change in the dollar with respect to our needs through taxation, inflation, and liquidity. We perceive taxation most directly in the difference between our actual salary or wages and the amount we take home. We sense inflation when we take the money remaining and discover that we can buy less with it this year than we could last year. And we perceive liquidity when we discover that it is much more difficult to sell a used couch or washing machine than it is to sell a used car. Although

FIGURE II-A

The Leaky Bathtub (Why some people never take a bath)

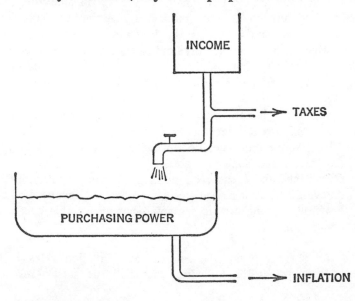

the washing machine may be worth a great deal to us because it washes clothes, we cannot recover its worth, because the market for such equipment is very small when it has been used.

Although most of us assume the dollar is pristinely constant, it is, in fact, very much affected by the three factors above.

Liquidity is rather more difficult to illustrate and has bearing on our expenditures in a less-than-specific quantitative way. Although the hamburger we buy in the market is worth a dollar to us, it is worth less to others we might try to sell it to, because people are unorthodox and, therefore, suspect sellers. Although the hamburger will be well worth the dollar we spent for it in terms of our full stomach if we eat it, we are at the mercy of the market if we wish to exchange it for our dollar.

For the moment, we will expand on the obvious. The relationship between dollars in and dollars out may be expressed in the following manner:

$$(1-\text{tax bracket}) \times \text{Interest rate} - \text{inflation rate} = \text{net gain or net cost}$$

Since inflation is the same for everyone, the real variables are interest rate (paid or received) and tax bracket in analyzing the disposition of any quantity of money. By setting the equation equal to zero, we can determine the *break-even point* for saving or borrowing. If the equation works out to zero for our tax bracket, we know that borrowing will have no net cost for us and that saving at the given interest rate will produce no net gain.

Ex.: Given an inflation rate of 3%, interest rate of 6%: The break-even point for borrowing is a tax bracket of 50%. Above that rate, borrowing is profitable (!); below that rate it has some net cost.
Conversely, the break-even point for saving is also 50%. Above 50%, saving results in a net constant dollar loss; below 50%, saving produces a small but measurable constant dollar gain.

The difference between the interest and inflation rates is a more or less constant 3%, indicating that the "true" cost of money (wholesale) is 3%. Additional interest is compensation for inflation.

This has some interesting implications for periods of heavy inflation. As inflation increases, the net cost of borrowing decreases for everyone, the break-even point drops, and it becomes increasingly *profitable* for the upper brackets to borrow. This, of course, assumes that one has a constant stream of income (insured by the tax-bracket requirement) to justify the interest cost. It also assumes that all people have equal access to all money markets,

GRAPH II-B

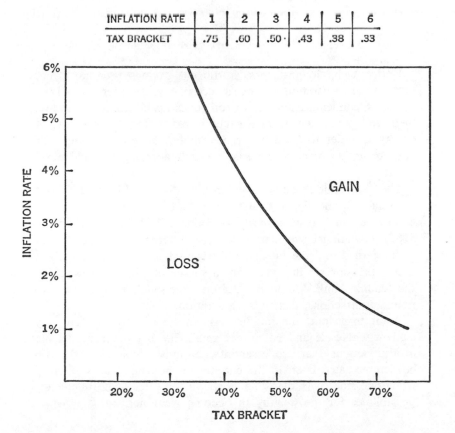

INFLATION RATE	1	2	3	4	5	6
TAX BRACKET	.75	.60	.50 ·	.43	.38	.33

an assumption that is demonstrably untrue. In practice, corporations and wealthy individuals control the flexible and responsive portions of the money market. Although the inflation rate for 1969 was 6%, and the bond-return rate is almost 9%, as predicted by the *Fortune* data, the going rate in the mutual savings banks and other institutions that cater to the middle class is between 4% and 6%, the amount being a function of the committed duration of the deposit. If we plug these values into the preceding equation, we find that saving can be a disaster.

$$(1-.20)\ 6-5=-.2\%,$$

or

$$\$1,000_{68}=\quad \$950$$
$$+60\ \text{interest}$$
$$-12\ \text{taxes}$$
$$\overline{\$998\ \text{net constant dollars}}$$

Under such circumstances, a diligent savings program is, at best, a demonstration of one's constancy of character. Like Sysiphus, condemned forever to roll rocks up hills and then watch them roll down, the average saver is expending a good deal of energy in order to tread water. Certainly, there is no danger of any corruption or crass material rewards accruing to such moral diligence.

The same middle-class saver, paying 9, 10, 11, or 12% on personal, automobile, or chattel loans, will find that the cheapest money he can borrow is mortgage money. And that will come at 8%. The rational explanation for the difference between the interest earned and the interest paid is that saving is essentially a retail operation for the saver, but a source of wholesale money to the lending bank. Moreover, Volume, the bitch goddess of economic transactions, demands recognition.

As it turns out, the middle-class investor/borrower can only lend at wholesale and borrow at retail; he can never participate in transactions that are essentially entirely wholesale.[1] As will be demonstrated later, in the chapter on housing, the wholesale/ wholesale side of lending and borrowing creates some interesting possibilities for the wealthy to become wealthier.

Obviously, the deck is stacked in favor of those with quantities of money, be they corporations or individuals.

It is also obvious that there is more than one way of accounting for how we fare on any given transaction. Most of us, if we indulge at all, add our numbers the wrong way. There are reasons for this.

B. Measuring

Most of us developed a disdain for accounting and budgets at the Saturday afternoon matinee. There in the theater, surrounded by our restless peers, eating popcorn, removing our first teeth in the secretive darkness and losing them before they could be preserved for the pillow, we learned that the Accountant, or Keeper of the Budget, was a coward. Always neat but never handsome, suspiciously neuter, this creature of deliberate meagerness never did more than impotently raise an ink-stained and desiccated hand against the Bad Guy. He forced the Free Spirit of the Plains, the All-American Cowboy, to fight his battles for him. Shane never saw the pro forma from the Whispering Gulch Savings Bank. Indeed, he refused to perceive the relation between the balance of the statement and the relative prosperity of the town. Roy Rogers and Lash LaRue were beyond such considerations.

And *we* want to be. The only problem is that Lash LaRue never had a house, let alone a mortgage. In spite of the fact that our mortgage payments are as regular as the phases of the moon, we still tend to reject the idea of budgets because they represent something limited, restrained, and Uncool. For some, the budget is positive evidence of God's disfavor. Like the early Christian who disclaimed his faith to avoid the lions, keeping a budget reveals a skepticism about the ultimate arrival of the Second Coming in Lauderdale.

Many people have no choice; to survive, they must transform their faith in the future into an evangelical crusade to save the dollar. The daily newspaper and the local library are full of such tomes and columns, all devoted to a pathetic concentration on the real and palpable. Budgets, for some people, are evidence of guilt and show the need for penance. The instrument becomes a machine for displaying the sins of the past rather than the hope of the future.

A budget that serves only to record the past is a waste of time and energy. In all likelihood, it serves a function that might be eliminated by regular visits to a psychiatrist.

A budget is a kind of clock. It helps us to see the relation of the present to the future. It should help us plan for the future and enjoy the present. Although the notion may be repugnant to that portion of our mind we left at the Saturday matinee, a real budget should be an instrument of *communication,* because it is a standard for a family to measure its wants, needs, and current capabilities against. It can also be a measure of risk.

The best form of budget is the one you create yourself, because it will, to some extent, reflect your personality. For the moment, a working budget will have to involve a ledger, files, or some system of sorting your checks. In the not terribly distant future, electronic banking will replace the need for any tedious adding and subtracting of bills and categories, because your local bank will function as your accountant.

For a nominal charge, several banks offer a computerized service. Most of them work in the following manner: the customer names the categories of his expenses and income; each category is given a number which is tied to his bank account; all checks are then annotated with the category number of the expense and may be broken into several categotries for one check. The monthly statement summarizes all expenses in each category and calculates the percentage of all expenses each category is of all expenses, by the month and for the year to date.

At the moment, the service is used more by small businesses than by individuals, but its usefulness is so obvious that it is difficult to think of the service remaining in such limited use. In any case, the oncoming development of the "cashless society" will necessitate elaborate systems of notation. The American Banking Society, an organization known more for its ponderous perception of banking realities than its visionary projections, has estimated that by 1977, 87% of all checking-account transactions will be handled electronically.

At this writing, numerous banks are unifying statements, and electronic transfers are being experimented with in Long Island

FIGURE II-C

JOHN AND MARY TEMPESTA 12/29/70

ACCT 149–081   MIDTOWN
BRANCH #4

		THIS MONTH			YEAR TO DATE		
ACCT	DESCRIPTION	# ITEMS	$ AMT.	$ %	# ITEMS	$ AMT.	$ %
	EXPENSE ITEMS						
1	HOUSE PAYMENT	–	–	–	–	–	–
4	HOME IMPROVEMENTS	–	–	–	–	–	–
8	HEAT	–	–	–	–	–	–
9	ELECTRICITY	–	–	–	–	–	–
11	TELEPHONE	–	–	–	–	–	–
14	MISC. HOUSE REPAIRS	–	–	–	–	–	–
17	CLOTHING	–	–	–	–	–	–
22	FOOD	–	–	–	–	–	–
24	HOSPITAL INSURANCE	–	–	–	–	–	–
30	HOSPITAL	–	–	–	–	–	–
35	DENTIST	–	–	–	–	–	–
38	DOCTOR	–	–	–	–	–	–
40	LIFE INSURANCE	–	–	–	–	–	–
45	VACATION	–	–	–	–	–	–
50	ENTERTAINING	–	–	–	–	–	–
51	RECREATION	–	–	–	–	–	–
60	ALLOWANCES—CHILDREN	–	–	–	–	–	–
73	EDUCATION	–	–	–	–	–	–
79	CONTRIBUTIONS—CHURCH	–	–	–	–	–	–
90	MISCELLANEOUS	–	–	–	–	–	–
99	BANK SV. CHG.	–	–	–	–	–	–
100	SAVINGS	–	–	–	–	–	–
-A-	TOTAL GENERAL EXPENSES						
	INCOME ITEMS						
423	SALARY	–	–	–	–	–	–
470	INTEREST—SAVINGS	–	–	–	–	–	–
500	DIVIDENDS—INSURANCE	–	–	–	–	–	–
504	DIVIDENDS—STOCK	–	–	–	–	–	–
511	TAX REFUNDS	–	–	–	–	–	–
520	TRUST INCOME	–	–	–	–	–	–
-D-	TOTAL GENERAL INCOME	–	–	–	–	–	–
	BANK FEE** ——						

and Delaware. "Electronic bankruptcy" may become a common event in the next decade. Banks will undoubtedly have to expand customer services into the accounting area if for no other reason than self-defense!

Ultimately, we will receive a monthly bank statement of all transactions. The end result; little cash, and constant surveillance of our expenses—and an easily kept budget, provided only that we are reasonably mature human beings. Maturity, in this case, is knowing what is possible and what is impossible, a definition anyone can live with quite happily, provided only that he has grown beyond secret wishes for infantile omnipotence.

All of us, however, will have many opportunities to experience bankruptcy between now and the glorious day that banking's omniscient Big Brother is on line, discovering our financial indiscretions in nanoseconds. Surviving the credit-card barrage is an achievement akin to Ulysses' resistance to the sirens; even though credit cards are no longer sent unsolicited through the mails, they are so easily obtained that we seldom consider what they are costing us, for the temptation is to use credit when it is available. Otherwise-prudent human beings, who would never consider committing themselves to an 18% interest rate, collect credit cards with little or no consideration of how much they are likely to pay for the convenience of carrying the card should they decide to delay a payment.

Finally, never forget that *cash* is always faster and more convenient than credit: Have you ever seen a dollar bill jam a cash register the way credit slips sometimes jam credit-card machines?

As the preceding chapter intimated and the discussion in the following chapters will elaborate, the disposition of our income is a rather complicated affair, in which dollars no longer available for immediate spending are still valuable to us. Some dollars buy more than others.

Most of us think of money spent as money gone. We almost never analyze our spending (read budget) in terms of investment, and if we do, it is usually in the most narrow sense of seeing how much of our income is invested in income-producing securities or savings accounts.

In a very limited and shortsighted way, the approach is real and prudent. Food, though we may enjoy eating it, is certainly not an expense that might be called an investment. At least, no one has found an interesting use for its form when recovered. Likewise, smoking, drinking, and most consumption seem totally unrelated to the idea of investment. For the most part, they are.

In careful fact, however, our expenditures cover a spectrum that ranges from pure consumption to pure investment. The continuum that bridges the two extremes becomes visible when we realize that many returns are in *services,* not dollars.

The visibility of the continuum is diminished by the fact that most of our investments that provide a return in services also require additional income to operate or maintain.

A washing machine, although it is an expense when purchased and consumes electricity and water in performing its services, is still an investment, because it is providing us with a service that could be evaluated in directly economic terms.[2] Location in the home assures us of direct access at any hour of the day or night without the need to battle for a parking spot at the local laundromat. Presumably, since a washing cycle costs less than five cents at home, the purchase of a machine is a capital investment because it costs more to wash away from home; the diminished direct and indirect costs are the measure of our return on investment.

Even if such investments require no additional income to operate or maintain during their service lifetime, most of them, more often referred to as practical necessities, ultimately waste away into something the garbage men refuse to remove. Rather than see them as investments, we see them as expenses—inconveniences that get in the way of enjoying the weekend.

A less debatable investment, which we will discuss in greater detail later, is a home. Although few have the capital available for this purpose, some people take a return on investment in the form of shelter by buying their home outright. Although some costs are still associated with living in the home, the owner is better off by the difference between the amount he would have to pay if someone else owned the house, and what it costs him. Even if a home is financed, the owner is receiving his return *in services* in proportion to the amount of equity he has invested in the house. An interesting extension of this theme is the summer or winter vacation camp. By converting the major portion of one's vacation expense into shelter expense, vacation expenses become tax-deductible interest and real-estate taxes. Moreover, since the owner has the option of renting the property, he still has the option of receiving his vacation in the form of services or in the form of cash, which he can reconvert into a vacation in some other place.

Enthusiasm for this notion can be disastrous if carried to extremes. Close examination reveals that some consumer investments (e.g., shoes) are more in the nature of commitments. Not only is the return on investment realizable *only* in the form of service (unlike the house or summer camp), but it is totally illiquid. No matter how desperately we might need money at some later date, it is highly unlikely that we could sell our shoes—or the rest of our clothing. In fact, there is a direct relationship between liquidity and form of return. The more a consumer investment commits us to a *service return,* the greater the lack of liquidity. Conversely, the more readily the consumer investment return can be realized in cash form, the greater the liquidity. We can do anything we like with the interest from a savings account or the dividend from our AT&T, but a dishwasher can only wash dishes, and a car can only drive us from A to B at the speed traffic will allow.

A Hungarian acquaintance once told me of the dramatic exception that proves the rule above. His most vivid memory as a child was of the frenzy that gripped people as the Russians approached and the Germans evacuated, at the close of the Second World War. People ran in panic through the streets and then tried to barter the family silver for a gallon of gasoline. Although silver is virtually a form of currency and a type of investment, only the paramount *service value* of gasoline—motive power—had any value. In circumstances of survival, only service return has value. In a society in which service return is diverse and survival is virtually assured, security is adjudged a function of the degree of freedom one has in utilizing return on investment. Money, obviously, is the most secure.

The fastest method for accumulating assets while maintaining a standard of living is to combine service return with investment return. This combination is the crux of middle-class experience.

Where the project of the wealthy is to place capital so that it will produce a large and safe stream of income, the project of the middle class is to direct income so that it accumulates as capital. Much of our consumption may be likened to watering the desert.

For most of us, the security of money must be given a lower priority than immediate consumption and service return. In this dilemma lie the need and usefulness of budgets. If we divide our expenditures into the following four categories: Immediate Consumption, Service Return, Immediate Savings, and Long-Term Investment, and cross them with the more-orthodox categories of spending, we find that most categories of expense cannot be isolated to one form of return.

RETURN	FOOD	CLOTHING	TRANSP.	SHELTER	INS.	SAV.	VAC. HOME	VAC.
Immediate Consumption	*	*	*	*			*	*
Service Return	*	*	*	*			*	
Immediate Savings		*				*		
Long-Term Inv.				*	*	*		

We can play around with these categories a good deal, our emphasis being a product of our personal priorities. Public transportation is Immediate Consumption. A private automobile is a Service Return. If the automobile happens to be an antique, it might also be considered a Long-Term Investment. Many people collect antiques to accomplish the same ends. I know of one man who has been an art collector all his life. Now in his late sixties, he is making his first investments in the stock market and selling some of his art collection. During all the years of his working life, he realized a visual Service Return on his investments, certainly a far greater value than the mediocre etching on a dividend check![3]

Immediate Consumption and Service Return are categories that determine our present standard of living. That this standard is maintained by our constant labor requires some form of Immediate Saving as a buffer between our living standard and the possibility we will lose our source of income by virtue of sickness, accident, or company bankruptcy. Obviously, this saving cannot be in the form of antique furniture, automobiles, or housing, because such objects also produce a Service Return; our living standard would be reduced by their sale. We need cash.

Different experts suggest different levels of Immediate Savings. Some suggest that half a year's earnings are necessary. By this definition, virtually all of America is living on the edge of economic disaster. We probably are. But such considerations are rather beyond conclusion. What each man must do is estimate the security of his position and weigh that against what he (in family conference) estimates to be pressing consumption needs.

As indicated previously, the diversity of human interest is such that almost anything can become a form of Long-Term Investment. It is also obvious, however, that more people will be interested in obtaining the cash return on my AT&T shares than will be interested in acquiring the Service Return on Grandma's international spoon collection, precious though it might be. Some investments are more arcane and eccentric than others.

Ultimately, our economic problem is a playback of the Grasshopper and the Ant fable. The Grasshopper has fun while the Ant saves for the cold winter. The Ant "wins" because winter (the end of our productive life) is inevitable. Moreover, technology is lengthening our student spring while shortening our working summer. (A more exhaustive examination of this problem will be found in chapter 8.)

The problem is solved rather simply by maintaining an adequate income to meet both needs: current consumption and retirement investment. Ironically, however, incomes are increasingly tied to standards of consumption by employer dictation rather than personal discretion, precluding adequate saving until one has reached an income level that only a minority of working Americans are privileged to receive.

We can respond to this dilemma in two ways: we can take a hard pragmatic look at our spending patterns, and we can attempt to minimize our tax expenses while overlapping Service Return with Long-Term Investment.

3

THE TAX MAN

When the first individual-income-tax bill was passed in 1913, it allowed for a tax of 1% on the first $20,000 of taxable income and progressed to 7% of all income in excess of $500,000.[1] Some people thought the tax was ruinous.

The coverage of the federal tax has since been broadened so that it is now virtually universal. Only paupers and a few of the very rich escape it.

FIGURE III-A

The income-tax schedule climbs progressively as income grows:

(1) NET INCOME BEFORE EXEMPTIONS (BUT AFTER ALL DEDUCTIONS)	(2) PERSONAL INCOME TAX	(3) AVERAGE TAX RATE PER CENT $[=(2)\div(1)]$	(4) MARGINAL TAX RATE $(=$TAX ON EXTRA DOLLAR$)$	(5) DISPOSABLE INCOME AFTER TAXES $[=(1)-(2)]$
Below $ 1,200	$ 0	0	0	1,200
2,000	112	5.6	14	1,888
3,000	260	8.7	15	2,740
4,000	418	10.5	16	3,582
5,000	586	11.7	17	4,414
10,000	1,556	15.6	22	8,444
20,000	4,044	20.2	28	15,956
50,000	16,460	32.9	50	33,540
100,000	44,460	44.5	60	55,540
200,000	109,972	55.0	69	90,028
400,000	250,140	62.5	70	149,860
1,000,000	670,140	67.0	70	329,860
10,000,000	6,970,140	69.7	70	3,029,860

AMOUNT OF FEDERAL INCOME TAX TO BE PAID AT DIFFERENT INCOME LEVELS BY A CHILDLESS COUPLE, 1966. A bachelor would pay more; a large family less.

In theory, the federal income tax is progressive. With marginal rates (the rate at which the top increment of additional income is taxed), ranging from 14% to 70%, the tax would appear to be progressive indeed. The fact that a man can pay 70% taxes on his income above $200,000 does not mean, however, that he pays 70% of his gross income in taxes. In fact, he will very likely not pay the effective rate (see chart), because much income is excluded from taxation by virtue of exemptions, deductions, or special allowances.

FIGURE III-B

Influence of Various Provisions on Effective Rates, Taxable Returns, 1960

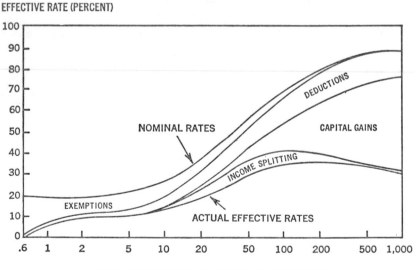

EFFECTIVE RATE (PERCENT)

TOTAL INCOME (THOUSANDS OF DOLLARS, RATIO SCALE)

When taxes that aren't even nominally progressive are taken into account—such as state, local, sales, and excise taxes—the *total* burden of taxation shows itself to be remarkably even.

Figure III-c
When All Taxes Are Counted:
Who Gets Hit, How Much
(estimates based on latest studies of tax trends and tax loads)

ANNUAL FAMILY INCOME	TOTAL TAXES PER FAMILY* (ESTIMATED AVERAGE)	TAXES AS PERCENTAGE OF ANNUAL INCOME
Under $3,000	$564	34%
$3,000–$5,000	$1,221	31%
$5,000–$7,000	$1,980	33%
$7,000–$10,000	$2,745	32%
$10,000–$15,000	$3,840	31%
$15,000–$25,000	$5,665	28%
$25,000 and over	$14,526	28%

THUS Latest studies indicate that lower-income families tend to bear a heavier tax burden than those with higher incomes—primarily because of rising Social Security levies, State and local sales and property taxes

* Includes Federal and State income taxes; Social Security payroll taxes; sales, property, and all other taxes.

Basic data: U. S. Depts. of Commerce, Labor, Treasury, and Health, Education and Welfare; Federal Housing Administration; Tax Foundation and other private sources

A tax burden that can account for 30% of your income demands consideration. We can redirect some of our spending to reduce taxes and, thereby, increase our *effective* income. Some people, notably accountants and tax lawyers, spend the waking hours of most of their lives giving consideration to the effects, ramifications, nuances, and innuendoes implicit in the direction of income and capital. Unfortunately, only corporations and wealthy individuals can afford to hire such individuals, and, in any case, examination reveals that the equity of the tax system is not so much a function of its nominal progressivity but of *who has control of the 180 billion dollars of income exempted from taxation.*

Much has been said, in Congress and elsewhere, about reform. At this writing, the Tax Reform bill of 1969, hailed as the greatest tax measure ever, amounts to no more than a few movies a year for most of the American population.[2]

To document the injustices of the tax system would require a treatise of incredible length. The chart above stands as *de facto* evidence of an inequitable distribution of exemptions and deductions.

The incredible magnitude of this inequitable burden of taxation is obscured by its very size. It boggles the mind. The incontrovertible fact, however, is that *more than one dollar escapes taxation for every dollar that is taxed.*

Examination reveals that tax preference is given first to capital and then to income. The more you have of either, the safer you are from taxation.

Capital-gains income is taxed at one half the normal rate.

Undistributed corporate income is not taxed. Generally speaking, the income is realized in the form of capital gains when the corporate security is sold. Thus, corporations exist as a means of (i) delaying tax payment and (ii) converting a highly taxable form of income into preferentially taxed capital-gains income.

Depreciation of real estate and other income-producing property is another method for delaying taxes on income and converting the income into capital-gains income, taxed at preferential rates.

These tax-reducing mechanisms are available only to those with capital and/or high incomes. An advantageous choice of investments can entirely vitiate the progressive nature of the income tax and result in a tax burden substantially lower than that carried by most of the population.

Some deductions, such as real-estate taxes and mortgage interest, are preferential. They are unavailable to those who cannot afford a home—primarily the urban poor.

A subtlety easily overlooked is the effect of inflation on taxes. Inflation artifically increases incomes and tax liabilities without increasing purchasing power. For example, suppose a man's income increases by one thousand dollars due to inflation. Even though his employer may have recognized the need to have wages compensate for the decreasing value of the dollar, the Internal Revenue Service will still appear to collect its due. In this manner, the thousand-dollar "raise" becomes subject to, say, a 20% marginal tax, thereby diminishing net purchasing power.[3]

Since the investment media and the taxation system provide a means for the wealthy to escape the negative effects of inflation, the burden of inflationary policy falls on the middle class. Moreover, as we will see demonstrated in later chapters, the burden has long-term as well as short-term effects. We pay the biggest bill when we retire.

The combination of money markets, taxation, and inflationary government policy is the stuff of paranoid scenarios. Ironically, the very people who are least affected and stand most to benefit, protest inflationary policy loudest.

The inquisitive reader will discover that the rationales for tax privilege are endless and that comparisons of one tax to another are so confusing that retiring with the proverbial can of worms would be a simple-minded joy. The rationales (or rationalizations, depending upon your viewpoint) offered for tax privileges all share one common element, however. They are based on *economic pragmatism* rather than *justice and equity*.

Economic pragmatism has two singular virtues: Firstly, it removes discussion from the public domain and makes it subject to the witness of "experts"; rather than making a statement of justice or fact, it is now possible to withdraw behind a smokescreen of esoteric technical knowledge. While it is true that in an age in which God is rumored to be living in Argentina there is a dearth of moral imperatives and that such imperatives, even when given, are suspect, the withdrawal of government into the closets of special knowledge cannot be interpreted as anything but a withdrawal from democratic communication and discourse.

The complexities of national security, we are told, now dictate that democratic process be by-passed. The result has been a policy of Pax Americana, the Bay of Pigs, our extended adventure in Vietnam, and the growing misadventure in Laos and Cambodia. All without Congressional approval.

Similarly, we are told that beating inflation requires some unemployment; the explanation is pat, expert, and facile, but fails to examine just who is hurt or see the real meaning of 5% unemployment. It isn't necessary for President Nixon to shake hands with each unemployed member of the 5%, nor is there much reward for the sacrifice the unemployed will make to save us from inflation.

It would be unfair to public officials not to give credit and recognize the mounting pressure of public office. As our vision of an ordered cosmos recedes before the realities of our disordered human environment, some will grasp at even the smallest straw of potential debate to find a sense of place. It is little wonder, then, that officials increasingly rely on experts, secret knowledge, and technical considerations. Technique is an expedient form of self-defense.

The only problem is that technical factors have a way of displacing considerations of social equity. Problems are no longer perceived directly in terms of changing the world to provide for human happiness, but of adjusting some complicated machine that stands between reality and the Unending Millennium of Bliss.

Conceiving the problem in terms of a machine absolves one from sticky moral questions and reduces everything to a level of mechanical skill, rather like the problem of tuning a carburetor: if the right person turns the right screws in the right direction, the machine, of itself, will lead us to that wonderful Millennium.

In our excitement over the amazing power of the engine, we forget that no one is driving the car.

The second virtue is that this economic pragmatism, this machine view, allows us the perfect escape from confronting our own identity. Given the fascination of the manipulable machine that stands between ourselves and the Millennium, we have discovered that rather than tuning the machine to expedite the arrival of that Millennium, we assume that if the efficient running of the machine will bring us within sight of the Millennium, then perhaps optimally efficient running of the machine will be the Millennium itself, or at least a reasonable substitute. Suddenly we find ourselves dealing with the sort of thing our prehensile grasp was meant for, a problem you can hold in your hand rather than in your soul. If optimal running of the machine defines the new Nirvana, then implicitly the machine, rather than being adjusted to serve our ends, will be adjusting *us*.

Documenting the pre-eminence of economic pragmatism would be a tedious chore. A careful reading of the daily newspaper over a period of time will reveal ample evidence that moral imperatives have a secondary position to economic pragmatism. One example born of the Tax Reform bill should serve to indicate the tone and tenor of the argumentation employed by privilege in the guise of pragmatism.

FIGURE III-D

One small tax for *Washington*
One giant tax for You!!

Dear Fellow Citizen:
    Please read this short message! Your local property taxes will soon have to be drastically increased unless the U. S. Senate rejects proposed legislation which—for the first time in American history—imposes federal taxation on your state and local governments.
    Federal taxation on the interest on municipal bonds will increase the cost of building schools, roads, bridges, water and sewer facilities, playgrounds, hospitals, parks, and all other vital public projects of your state and local governments.
    1. Throughout American history, state and local governments

have issued bonds which were not subject to taxation by the federal government. This principal is solidly founded in the United States Constitution. Now the U. S. House of Representatives has passed a bill which would tax the interest paid on these bonds. If the Senate endorses this bill and it is signed into law by the President, your state and local governments will have to pay much higher rates of interest to make municipal bonds attractive to purchasers.

2. *YOUR* LOCAL TAXES WILL HAVE TO PAY FOR THIS EXTRA COST—ESTIMATED IN THE HUNDREDS OF DOLLARS. HOME OWNERS WILL BE FACED WITH HIGHER REAL ESTATE TAXES AND OTHER CITIZENS WILL PAY HIGHER RENTS. LET'S NOT BE FOOLED BY THE HIGHLY COMPLEX CLAIMS ABOUT "PREFERENCES" AND "ALLOCATIONS." THE PURE AND SIMPLE FACT REMAINS THAT THE HOUSE-PASSED LEGISLATION MEANS EXTRA INTEREST TO THE COMMUNITIES AND EXTRA TAXES TO YOU!

3. The bill passed by the House has another provision. States and cities are told that, if they will accept taxation by the federal government, they will in turn receive a generous subsidy. But—remember—this "bonus" can be adjusted or withdrawn at the will of Congress leaving only you to pay the cost of your new tax. Remember, also, that subsidies can always lead to control!

4. The proposed new taxes would be levied by the federal government as part of a "tax reform" program to insure that the rich pay at least some tax. There is said to be a "taxpayer's revolt" and it is charged that a few wealthy Americans—heavily invested in municipal bonds—are sitting on the beach in Florida clipping tax-exempt coupons and paying no federal income taxes at all. THIS IS PURE PROPAGANDA UNSUPPORTED BY THE FACTS!

IT IS TRUE THAT THERE ARE WEALTHY PEOPLE IN THIS COUNTRY NOT PAYING ANY INCOME TAXES (154 IS THE NUMBER REPORTED BY THE TREASURY). BUT IN THOSE TAX RETURNS THAT WERE PRESENTED TO THE WAYS AND MEANS COMMITTEE BY TREASURY OFFICALS, TAX-FREE MUNICIPAL BOND INTEREST WAS *NOT* INVOLVED.

Furthermore, much of the taxpayers' concern has been caused by the increase in the cost of providing essential local and state services. Now, this legislation will further increase that problem. To tax the interest on municipal bonds is only the first step in a progression leading to: (1) higher municipal bond interest rates; (2) postponement, cancellation, or reduction in scope of vital projects; and (3) higher state and local government taxes (primarily sales and property, both regressive in nature) to supply funds these governments could not afford either to borrow or, if they borrowed, to pay the inevitably higher interest costs.

Imposing a tax on state and municipal bonds is a "reform" that will surely boomerang on the average taxpayer. It is the *local* taxpayer who will foot the bill.

With the heavy burdens facing state and local governments today, the federal government should not enact legislation that will either increase the cost of needed public works or force their abandonment. To defeat this new federal tax, which will ultimately be passed on to you, get in touch with your Senators at once. Tell them that you want your state and local governments free from any form of direct or indirect federal taxation in financing their work.

The advertisement reproduced on page 43 was taken from the Boston *Herald Traveler* and exhorts citizens to protest against the adoption of a tax against interest income on tax-exempt state and municipal bonds.

The first argument for maintaining this tax haven is historical. "Thoughout American history, state and local governments have issued bonds which were not subject to taxation by the federal government." Death and disease are historical facts, as are war, poverty, and strife, but we don't accept them as good because they are historical. Moreover, since the graduated income tax did not exist before 1913, the exemption did not constitute a tax haven in all of American history preceding that date! It has taken fifty-six years for the Congress of the United States to act on a haven of tax privilege it created.

The second argument informs the reader that his taxes will increase by the difference in the interest rates, and exhorts him "not [to] be fooled by the highly complex claims about preferences and allocations." Complexity happens to be a fact of industrial life; the reader is asked to overlook justice and equity in order that he may decrease his tax bill.

The third argument tells the citizen that the provision made by the House for revenue sharing that would compensate for the increased local cost is not to be trusted. We must, in other words, continue to let inequity exist because we cannot trust the Congress of the United States. This argument is not only a deprecation of democratic process, but it is also an appeal to economic animalism. It should be noted, however, that the federal tax reduction obtained in this manner will be greatest for those with the most income, e.g., a man in the 50% tax bracket will have a federal tax reduction of $.50 on the dollar to cover a $1 increase in local taxes, while a man in the 20% bracket will save only $.20. It exhorts us to protect our own interests in the most shortsighted way possible, at the expense of anything.

Perhaps some deprecation of democratic process is justified. If it is, we must certainly inquire as to why, and we must certainly discover that democratic process, if it works at less than perfection, does so because economically powerful special-interest groups exert a disproportionate influence on the workings of government. Those who enjoy tax-exempt income are among this group.

The fourth argument states that privileges existing under the current laws are pure propaganda, by pointing out that no one lives *entirely* on such tax-exempt income. Several years ago, Muriel Dodge, heiress of a considerable fortune, did derive *all* her income from such sources. As a matter of prudence, such devotion to a single mode of investment is eccentric. While few individuals may enjoy total leisure by way of income from municipal bonds, many fortunate individuals obtain after-tax yields superior to those obtained by the general population and, if nothing else, totally vitiate the progressivity of the income tax.

What the advertisement fails to mention is that any increase in taxation that will follow the elimination of the tax haven will be tax-deductible for the home owner, i.e., a source of income previously exempt for a *few* will become a source of tax deductions for *many,* thereby reducing the federal tax bill of the average citizen. This is a federal subsidy that cannot be readily removed.

Most of us don't say the pledge of allegiance to the flag very often once we have left the hallowed halls of the public schools. But I have a vague memory of that pledge, and, in it, we pledge ourselves to a government that attempts to administer "liberty and justice for all." Very few people expect perfection. We all hope for it. But few of us demand that our hopes be justified, let alone fulfilled. Most of us will settle for less if we judge that good *intent* was present when the injustice was perpetrated.

Increasingly, however, we are asked to accept pragmatic justifications as grounds for actions rather than moral ends. Liberty and justice for all can be sacrificed to "economic growth," justice for "national security," liberty for "national unity." Frustrated at finding a simple truth, we accept simple slogans.

Suddenly we find ourselves in a discussion of philosophy rather than walking on the solid foundation of "objective" numbers. We may begin by discussing money, but, in the end, what we do with money and how our system uses money are only the clumsiest of metaphors for the expression of the human spirit. Some refuse a glimpse of the spirit for the reward of grasping a penny; others disdain grasping the penny and forsake the prime tool of human community. The analysis that follows is an attempt to perceive the realities of economic life and bridge the gap between those realities and our aspirations.

How?

4

THE LOGISTIC
IMPERATIVE:
AUTOMOBILES

A philanthropic Spanish king once sold titles to the rich to finance building an insane asylum. When the asylum was built, the king had the following motto inscribed over the gateway: FROM THE VAIN TO THE FOOLISH.

When it comes to buying and operating automobiles, we seem to be both. One of the more ambivalent joys of human existence is that each of us has the ability to impress even our most bizarre psychic needs on the most mundane realities. Some people are just crazy about cars. When I was in high school we used to wait to see one of the town studs drive down the main street of town every Sunday—in his super-cubed, fuel-injected, four-speed synchroed Corvette. We knew he was going to be out on Sunday because that was the day the most people would see him, and he could afford to take the car out only one day a week. At seven miles per premium gallon, it's hard enough for a shoe clerk to keep a Corvette in gas, let alone make the payments.

Super Stud may have been both vain and foolish, but his life did add a poignant note of interest to a small town that would have been intolerably dull if everyone bought from *Consumer Reports*.

The problem with the cost-accounting method of car purchase is that it reduces transportation entirely to a method of getting from point A to point B. Only nominal consideration (other than survival) is given to the manner in which one traverses the distance, and this, to state my own bias, is intolerable. It is intolerable because the driver and his passengers are assigned to a kind of purgatory while they are driving. Life is too precious to admit boredom. If you have to drive, it should not be time contracted out of your life. We will be dead long enough without having to practice at it every commuting day.

My particular bias is toward being able to "do your own thing," provided only that the thing, or appearance of the thing, does not become a *substitute* for the experience or life stance the thing symbolizes. The automobile as Thing has little intrinsic interest; it has interest only in proportion to the polymorphic (or dream) possibilities the Thing presents to our psyches. It is in this inevitable relationship that the fundamental conflict of our material culture appears: if civilization is founded on the renunciation of certain desires, and maturity means the ability to postpone certain gratifications, then industrial society, in providing a constantly expanding stream of materialized dream images, is little more than an extremely involved method for externalizing an internal conflict. The final irony is that the reward for maturity given in the fine print of our social contract is the gratification of basically infantile desires. In even finer print at the bottom of the contract we learn that fine distinctions mean a great deal. Once our dream has been materialized and we are committed to its possession, we discover that possession and experience are mutually exclusive.

Rephrased: you can have your cake, but you can't eat it. The rules of the game require that we die a little with each purchase; slowly, we evacuate our souls. Our dreams become excrement.

The membrane between reality and our dreams is diaphanously thin; to rupture it is to invite insanity. But to strengthen it to impermeability is to stifle the flux of life. Regardless of our feelings, thoughts, and possible misgivings about the Freudian Left and the philosophical stance of Professor Marcuse, there is a certain comfort in knowing that someone, at last, is trying to build a political and social reality for man on some model other than Home Economicus.[1] The better part of humanity has been left out too long.

Since I cannot and should not direct or assume your attitudes, however, I must return to the role of Homo Economicus and the real costs of car ownership. . . .

The lifetime of a car puts it in a kind of bastard area of expenditure. Unlike a house, it has a definite (though extendible) lifetime. Its lifetime is more like that of a dishwasher, hi-fi set, refrigerator, or other household item. Unlike other household items, however, the automobile is relatively liquid and can be sold without fantastic difficulty.

Whether your particular car is a liquid investment, of course, depends on what kind of car it is, what condition it is in, and how many people in your area want your particular kind of car—the same factors that affect the sale of absolutely anything. Regardless of its degree of liquidity, however, the fact of liquidity makes the automobile a form of investment or enforced savings if we finance it.

A general rule of thumb is that an automobile will depreciate about 50% in three years of ownership. The fact that you would own the car without liens in two or three years indicates that you can use the car-financing as a tool for saving if you made a

ILLUSTRATION IV-A

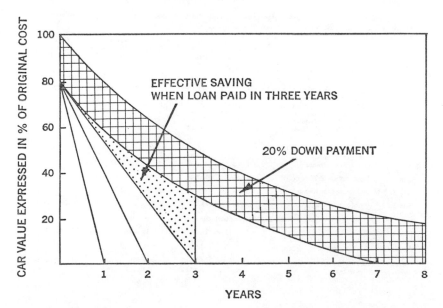

ILLUSTRATION IV-B

COST OF CAR OPERATION
CAR A

CAR A. Medium size 4-door sedan. 8 cylinder engine. Automatic transmission. Power steering. Radio. Cost $3875. Weight 4090 lbs. Used for business. No driver under 25. No accident record or convictions.

		BOSTON, MASS.	PORT-LAND, ME.	MAN-CHESTER, N.H.	RUT-LAND, VT.	PROVI-DENCE, R.I.	HART-FORD, CONN.
ANNUAL FIXED CHARGES							
Item 1.	Insurance:						
	Liability $10,000/20,000 limits	$204.70	*$90.30	$52.30	*$120.20	*$151.10	*$182.40
	Property Damage $5,000 limit	78.50		28.50			
	$1,000 Medical payments	15.00		8.10			
	Uninsured Motorist	2.00		1.00			
	Fire & Theft (Comprehensive)	58.00		16.20			
	Collision $50 deductible	170.00	**109.70	80.80	**108.30	**153.40	**93.10
Item 2.	Taxes:						
	***Local taxes & sales tax if any	130.00	95.00	36.00	23.00	87.00	75.00
	Registration fee	6.00	15.00	25.00	32.00	20.00	10.00
	Operator's license	2.50	2.50	2.50	3.00	4.00	3.00
Item 3.	Depreciation @ 20 per cent	775.00	775.00	775.00	775.00	775.00	775.00
Item 4.	****Maintenance & Repairs	50.00	50.00	50.00	50.00	50.00	50.00
Item 5.	Total annual fixed charges	$1491.70	$1137.50	$1075.40	$1111.50	$1240.50	$1188.50

Cost Per Mile if Spread Over Indicated Annual Mileage (Includes operating cost per mile)

	BOSTON, MASS.	PORT-LAND, ME.	MAN-CHESTER, N.H.	RUT-LAND, VT.	PROVI-DENCE, R.I.	HART-FORD, CONN.
For 5,000 miles annually	33.120¢	26.107¢	24.865¢	25.557¢	28.096¢	27.127¢
For 10,000 miles annually	18.202¢	14.372¢	14.111¢	14.467¢	15.691¢	15.242¢
For 15,000 miles annually	13.231¢	10.940¢	10.526¢	10.763¢	11.556¢	11.280¢
For 20,000 miles annually	10.745¢	9.044¢	8.734¢	8.912¢	9.489¢	9.299¢
For 25,000 miles annually	9.253¢	7.907¢	7.659¢	7.801¢	8.248¢	8.111¢
For 30,000 miles annually	8.258¢	7.148¢	6.991¢	7.060¢	7.421¢	7.318¢

CAR B

CAR B. Small 4-door sedan. 6 cylinder engine. Manual shift. Radio. Cost $2412. Weight 2885 lbs. Used for business. No driver under 25. No accident record or conviction.

		BOSTON, MASS.	PORT-LAND, ME.	MAN-CHESTER, N.H.	RUT-LAND, VT.	PROVI-DENCE, R.I.	HART-FORD, CONN.
ANNUAL FIXED CHARGES							
Item 1.	Insurance:						
	Liability $10,000/20,000 limits	$204.70	*$90.30	$52.30	*$120.20	*$151.10	*$182.40
	Property Damage $5,000 limit	78.50		28.50			
	$1,000 Medical payments	15.00		8.10			
	Uninsured Motorist	2.00		1.00			
	Fire & Theft (Comprehensive)	47.00		14.30			
	Collision $50 deductible	149.00	**93.10	70.30	**91.70	**133.00	**78.90
Item 2.	Taxes:						
	***Local taxes & sales tax if any	79.81	60.01	22.19	14.47	54.12	46.88
	Registration fee	6.00	15.00	20.00	32.00	14.00	10.00
	Operator's license	2.50	2.50	2.50	3.00	4.00	3.00
Item 3.	Depreciation @ 20 per cent	482.40	482.40	482.40	482.40	482.40	482.40
Item 4.	****Maintenance & Repairs	50.00	50.00	50.00	50.00	50.00	50.00
Item 5.	Total annual fixed charges	$1116.91	$793.31	$751.59	$793.77	$888.62	$853.58

Cost Per Mile if Spread Over Indicated Annual Mileage (Includes operating cost per mile)

	BOSTON, MASS.	PORT-LAND, ME.	MAN-CHESTER, N.H.	RUT-LAND, VT.	PROVI-DENCE, R.I.	HART-FORD, CONN.
For 5,000 miles annually	24.766¢	18.347¢	17.513¢	18.346¢	20.200¢	19.553¢
For 10,000 miles annually	13.597¢	10.414¢	9.997¢	10.414¢	11.314¢	11.017¢
For 15,000 miles annually	9.874¢	7.770¢	7.492¢	7.769¢	8.352¢	8.172¢
For 20,000 miles annually	8.013¢	6.448¢	6.239¢	6.447¢	6.871¢	6.749¢
For 25,000 miles annually	6.896¢	5.654¢	5.487¢	5.654¢	5.982¢	5.895¢
For 30,000 miles annually	6.151¢	5.125¢	4.986¢	5.125¢	5.390¢	5.326¢

NEW YORK, N.Y.	NEWARK, N.J.	DENVER, COLO.	CLEVELAND, OHIO	ST. LOUIS, MO.	MIAMI, FLA.	NEW ORLEANS, LA.	CHICAGO, ILL.	SAN FRANCISCO, CALIF.
*$201.60	*$162.50	*$80.30	*$127.30	*$159.10	*$146.30	$93.60 38.00 16.00 6.00 44.00	*$177.70	*$182.40
**225.00	**201.40	**99.30	**108.30	**143.90	**77.90	133.00	**138.70	**153.90
74.00	23.25	70.91	31.00	71.25	23.25	76.75	86.75	79.00
33.00	25.00	7.25	10.00	25.00	27.50	3.00	24.00	8.00
1.00	2.67	.75	.33	.67	1.25	1.25	1.00	.75
775.00	775.00	775.00	775.00	775.00	775.00	775.00	775.00	775.00
50.00	50.00	50.00	50.00	50.00	50.00	50.00	50.00	50.00
$1359.60	$1239.82	$1083.51	$1101.93	$1224.92	$1101.20	$1236.60	$1253.15	$1249.05
30.528¢	28.153¢	25.099¢	26.396¢	27.855¢	25.381¢	27.948¢	28.492¢	28.410¢
16.932¢	15.755¢	14.264¢	14.376¢	15.606¢	14.369¢	15.581¢	15.960¢	15.920¢
12.400¢	11.622¢	10.652¢	10.703¢	11.523¢	10.698¢	11.459¢	11.783¢	11.756¢
10.134¢	9.556¢	8.847¢	8.867¢	9.482¢	8.863¢	9.398¢	9.695¢	9.674¢
8.774¢	8.310¢	7.703¢	7.703¢	8.231¢	7.702¢	8.181¢	8.442¢	8.425¢
7.868¢	7.490¢	7.041¢	7.030¢	7.440¢	7.028¢	7.337¢	7.606¢	7.593¢

*"Package" policy. Usually includes $25,000 bodily injury and property damage insurance, $1,000 medical payments and $20,000 uninsured motorist coverage.
**Combination comprehensive Fire & Theft and $50 deductible Collision insurance.
***Local taxes include excise taxes and permit fees in Maine, Massachusetts, New Hampshire and local property taxes elsewhere. Also included are sales taxes, if any. Taxes are averaged over 5 years.
****This is a contingency figure. The principal maintenance item is computed on a mileage basis. Insurance figures supplied by Liberty Mutual Insurance Company.

NEW YORK, N.Y.	NEWARK, N.J.	DENVER, COLO.	CLEVELAND, OHIO	ST. LOUIS, MO.	MIAMI, FLA.	NEW ORLEANS, LA.	CHICAGO, ILL.	SAN FRANCISCO, CALIF.
*$201.60	*$162.50	*$80.30	*$127.30	*$159.10	*$146.30	$93.60 38.00 16.00 6.00 35.00	*$177.70	*$182.40
**192.60	**172.00	**83.10	**93.10	**122.60	**67.50	116.00	**119.20	**131.10
50.00	14.47	44.13	19.29	44.47	14.47	44.47	54.12	49.00
21.75	15.00	5.00	10.00	20.00	20.00	3.00	18.00	8.00
1.00	2.67	.75	.33	.67	1.25	1.25	1.00	.75
482.40	482.40	482.40	482.40	482.40	482.40	482.40	482.40	482.40
50.00	50.00	50.00	50.00	50.00	50.00	50.00	50.00	50.00
$999.35	$899.04	$745.68	$782.42	$879.24	$781.92	$884.72	$902.42	$903.65
22.454¢	20.462¢	17.453¢	18.187¢	20.066¢	18.119¢	20.066¢	20.587¢	20.612¢
12.461¢	11.471¢	9.996¢	10.363¢	11.273¢	10.300¢	11.219¢	11.563¢	11.576¢
9.129¢	8.474¢	7.510¢	7.755¢	8.343¢	7.694¢	8.270¢	8.555¢	8.563¢
7.464¢	6.976¢	6.267¢	6.451¢	6.877¢	6.391¢	6.796¢	7.051¢	7.057¢
6.464¢	6.077¢	5.522¢	5.669¢	5.998¢	5.609¢	5.911¢	6.149¢	6.154¢
5.798¢	5.478¢	5.025¢	5.147¢	5.412¢	5.087¢	5.321¢	5.547¢	5.551¢

*"Package" policy. Usually includes $25,000 bodily injury and property damage insurance, $1,000 medical payments and $20,000 uninsured motorist coverage.
**Combination comprehensive Fire & Theft and $50 deductible Collision insurance.
***Local taxes include excise taxes and permit fees in Maine, Massachusetts, New Hampshire and local property taxes elsewhere. Also included are sales taxes, if any. Taxes are averaged over 5 years.
****This is a contingency figure. The principal maintenance item is computed on a mileage basis. Insurance figures supplied by Liberty Mutual Insurance Company.

down payment of less than 50%. To accomplish this, the rate of amortization must be greater (faster) than the rate of depreciation.

What we really have is a problem in accounting. If we don't finance the car, the figures given below from the Automobile Legal Association can be used to give us an idea of the out-of-pocket, or cash, expenses. Of the expenses listed below, all are cash expenses other than depreciation. The depreciation is estimated and won't be realized as a cash expense until the car is sold or traded. The fact that we try to estimate the depreciation puts us into a new accounting, the pro forma, in which we recognize that some costs are current and some are related to time. Here's the difference:

TABLE IV-C

CASH ACCOUNT	PRO FORMA
Insurance	
Liability	
Property damage	
Medical payments	Same
Uninsured motorist	
Fire and theft	
Collision	
Taxes	
Local (that year)	Averaged over three to five years
Sales (one year only)	Averaged over three to five years
Operators	
Maintenance and repairs	Averaged as a function of mileage
Operating expenses	Calculated as a function of mileage
(as they occur)	
Finance payments	Depreciation (estimated year by year)

The cash account is what you have to live with, because the cash account is the one that measures expenses *as they occur*. A bank is unlikely to finance your car if they feel it will depreciate faster than the loan balance will decline; if it did, the bank would be granting you a loan on thin or non-existent collateral. This fact would be reflected in the interest rate. Since it is now possible to finance your car for up to five years, some car loans are personal loans in disguise. Good collateral is the best way to rent money at least expense.

Since the finance payments are amortizing a loan faster than the collateral for the loan is depreciating, some of the car payment can be considered Savings invested in an automobile. Like the cash value in a life-insurance policy, however, this savings program cannot be properly banked or otherwise utilized until the car is "cashed in," i.e., sold.

An item seldom considered is the finance cost. Note that the ALA figures, though they assume you have purchased your car for cash, give no value to the lost earning power of the money invested in the car. A three thousand dollar car, when you buy it for cash, is costing you $120 a year (assuming 4%) more in lost interest than the pro-forma figures indicate. Likewise, the cash account indicates no value given to the investment costs of the down payment. As we shall see later in examining housing, such costs should be considered. In this instance, however, there is little you can do about the fact that, inevitably, you could not earn as much with your money invested elsewhere as you will pay for financing; i.e., if you can, buy your car for cash.

While the cash account may be the one you must live and budget by on a day-to-day basis, the pro-forma account is the one for planning ahead, because it gives you a better picture of what owning an automobile actually costs.

It is the differences in accounting that enable many people to deceive themselves about extravagant spending on a car. When you buy the car, the monthly payments seem small in proportion to the newness of the car. As the car ages and becomes less new and thrilling, the payments seem to get larger and larger.

Delusion is the word for believing, either during the purchase of the car or in the constant pinch of the two or three years that follow, that everything will be wonderful when the debt is paid off. It won't be.

The world will not turn rosy with the last payment, because the car will be old, will need repairs, and will have lost much of its original charm. Chances are you will soon be committing yourself to another loan on another car, entering the same payment rat race again.

Insurance may seem expensive; gasoline and repairs may seem expensive. But if you are a normal, ten-to-twenty-thousand-mile-a-year driver, the major cost of owning an automobile is in *de-*

preciation. A four thousand dollar car has twice as much to depreciate as a two thousand dollar car; the sales market may make some odd bumps and peculiarities in the depreciation rates of various cars, but in the end they all wear out. The car that costs more, costs more. Period.

It would appear as though you can't cut corners without castrating your dreams. The appearance is not deceiving—but it is not as painful as it would appear from the perspective of the showroom. So far, we have been figuring all costs in annual increments. Perhaps our perspective on automobiles will change if we start talking about *cost per day.* Looking down the ALA figures in table B, we see that car A will cost us $1700 a year while car B will cost us $1250 a year if we drive 10,000 miles in New York. (Anyone who drove more would be a cab driver or crazy, possibly both.) Is it really worth $4.65 or $3.40 a day to own an automobile? This figure does not allow for garaging, parking, tickets, fines, etc.—not to mention the terror and boredom of driving around the block seventy times.

Some urban families don't own a car. They don't bother to buy one, not because of the expense but because it is just too much bother. Taxis are better. Some urban families take taxis for short trips, rent a car for a weekend to get away, and occasionally lease a car for the summer when they want to leave the city. Depending upon your age and the logistics of your city, the non-ownership method may be a relatively inexpensive way out of the entire hassle.

Obviously, much of the preceding does not apply to the suburban family. The automobile, intended as a convenience, is now a luxury in urban environments and a necessity in suburban environments.

If you are the type who finds it difficult to deal with automobile salesmen when you buy or trade a car, or who dislikes the trials of selling a car through the newspapers and spending the weekend by the telephone, you might look into the costs of leasing a car. In the major cities, the car-leasing business has suffered from immense competition and price cutting. While it is unlikely that you could *save* money by leasing a car, it may cost you little more and save you a good deal of hassling. One driver in particular may save money—the single male driver between the ages of twenty-one and twenty-five. Liability insurance is so expensive for these men that in some areas the cost of insurance *alone* is as much as the lease cost of the car with insurance.

Many drivers carry too little of one kind of insurance and too much of another kind. Most states now require each driver (or car) to be insured for a minimum liability, generally limited to about $10,000 per person, $20,000 per accident. Though such limits may seem like a good deal of money, the amount is minuscule in relation to some of the settlements coming from the courts. A settlement that awards an individual more than $10,000 is no freakish event. It is an everyday occurrence. If you have the misfortune of being involved in an accident, your low-limit liability insurance will only cover the first $10,000 or $20,000 in awards. After that, all the money comes from your pocket and future earnings. Maybe you'll deserve whatever you get (or maybe the jury will feel that way), maybe you won't; but one thing is certain, the expense can ruin *your* life as thoroughly as the injured party's is damaged.

Excess-limits liability insurance is relatively inexpensive in relation to day-to-day court settlements, and the increase in cost is

---

TABLE IV-D
Marginal Liability Costs

LIABILITY LIMIT	SAMPLE RATE	COVERAGE INCREASE	COST INCREASE
$5–10M	$ 88	—	—
10–20M	110	100%	25%
50–100M	145	1000%	64%
100–300M	150	2000+%	73%

---

nominal and probably one of the best buys you can get in insurance.

The same people who carry too little liability (just about anyone driving), often carry too much collision insurance. Insurance, basically, is a means of distributing risk; by pooling the risk of many individuals, each individual is protected against being on the wrong side of probability and suffering a painful loss. If you own a new or valuable car, you probably can't afford to lose three or four thousand dollars. Not many people can. Besides, the financing bank won't let you take the chance.

If you can't afford to lose three thousand dollars, suppose we start with small figures and measure the cost of insuring against that loss. Insurance policies are usually $50- or $100-deductible. Larger-deductible amounts are less orthodox but available.

TABLE IV-E

VALUE	$50-D	$100-D	DIFF.	AS % $50
$3000	$120	$90	$30	60%

When you insure your car, evaluate as honestly as you can *how much you can afford to lose, and weigh that against the cost of the protection;* $50-deductible for automobiles is the human equivalent of insuring yourself against the discomfort of a cold.

On the same track, it would behoove you to check the value of your aging Super Blitz with your insurance agent from time to time. Though you may have bought the machine for three thousand dollars three years ago, and still sense every penny of that sum when you pat the hood, the insurance company may feel differently, even though the cost of protection has dropped very little.

TABLE IV-F
Premium vs. Insured Risk

YR	VALUE	VALUE LESS $100 DEDUCTIBLE	NET VALUE AFTER ALLOWANCE FOR TAX SAVINGS ON CASUALITY LOSS, ASSUMING 20% TAX BRACKET	PREMIUM	PREMIUM AS % NET VALUE
0	3000	2900	2300	90	4.0
1	2400	2300	1800	90	5.0
2	1900	1800	1400	90	6.4
3	1500	1400	1100	90	8.0
4	1200	1100	850	90	10.0
5	950	850	675	90	13.3

Though it seems strange at first, it costs relatively more to insure your car each year. The reason for this is simple. Though the replacement value of the car is constantly diminishing, the cost of replacing *part* of the car is the same as it was three years ago (you should be so lucky). As far as your insurance company is concerned, it is not very long before it is cheaper to write you a check for the Super Blitz than replace its fender. You may not share this feeling with the company, because, after all, the car still runs like a charm and you've gotten to like it. At this point, if not earlier, you should consider the *cost* of the protection. As you can see from the table, after year four you are paying $90 a year to insure something worth $850 to the insurance company. If that seems steep, you should also consider that part of your loss will be underwritten by the Internal Revenue Service in the form of a casualty-loss deduction for everything above one hundred dollars.

Prudence can become a form of extravagance! An interesting and not so obvious sidelight here, however, is the fact that the graduated income tax produces some strange anomalies. In effect, loss deductions against income underwrite, as stated above, our risk of loss. Ironically, however, the same structure that theoretically was designed to put the burden of government on the backs of those who could most afford it, relieves the upper-income groups of risk because it underwrites their losses up to 70% (77% with the full surcharge in effect). If we take the example above and substitute a new car and a 70% tax bracket, we see that the privileged few in that bracket don't need car insurance, because they already have it from Uncle Sam.

Unless you have very generous parents or in-laws, you will probably have to finance your first car and will find that you must finance a few cars after that. If you do, don't just sign any old contract. Truth in Lending has simplified problems that would have taken chapters of prose and pages of equations to illustrate before, but it still hasn't solved the problem of non-readers and deceptive salesmen. A little reading, a little research, can save you several hundred dollars on the total cost of the loan.

The car dealer who offers "bank financing" may be offering just that—but you should not assume that means "bank rates."

Besides, bank rates vary quite a bit. Some banks charge just as much for car loans as they do for personal loans. Why this should be is a mystery, since one loan has collateral and the other hasn't, but chances are against your being able to talk the policy board of the bank out of their blanket rate. The best thing is to use your time on the bus or subway to read the ads. Some of the finance companies only offer to lend you money *now* (!) rather than include tables of monthly payments, because inclusion of the latter requires that they reveal their interest rate, and 18–24% looks pretty steep next to a bank, even a bank with a 6% discount or 11.7% true rate. Some banks go as low as 8.7% (true rate), only slightly more than current mortgage rates.

TABLE IV-G
Table of Rates and Payments
Monthly Payment per $100

INT. RATE	1 YR.	2 YR.	3 YR.
9	8.75	4.57	3.18
10	8.80	4.62	3.23
12	8.89	4.71	3.33
15	9.03	4.85	3.47
18	9.17	5.00	3.62

One thing about discounted loans: since these loans often go to their relatively less-sophisticated customers, information such as the dollar amount of interest you have paid in a given time period is not always directly accessible. Since the interest is tax deductible, you would be wise to ask when and how the interest may be deducted when you sign for the loan.

5

"THERE'S NO PLACE LIKE HOME": THE GREAT AMERICAN HIGH FLYER

According to the 1960 Census figures presented in *This U.S.A.*, some 62% of American families are home owners. The minority that do not own homes is concentrated in the urban poor and lower-middle class. Whether we will remain a nation of home owners is something government policy and trade unionists will decide in the next decade.

As this is written, mortgage rates stand at historically high levels. A rate below 8% is rare and generally requires a down payment that is beyond the means of all but the most prosperous Americans. Skyrocketing land and labor costs have fostered an accelerating shift to apartment building that may very well reverse the long-term trend to home ownership.

TABLE V-A
Owner-occupied Housing

1890	48%
1900	47%
1910	46%
1920	46%
1930	48%
1940	44%
1950	55%
1960	62%

Source: Statistical Abstract of U.S.

Whether or not *you* should own a house is a function of more variables, largely emotional, than any book can deal with in a reasonable number of pages. Like the act of picking petals from a daisy, considering the pros and cons for too long reveals no more than one's fundamental indifference. The analysis that follows makes no attempt to develop an emotional calculus that will give a "yes" or "no" answer to the problem.

Our analysis will be entirely economic. A house, among other things, is an investment. As an investment, it provides a return in 1) tax savings, 2) amortization, 3) appreciation, and 4) services. It also happens to be the largest single investment most Americans make in their lifetime.

Precisely because it is such a large investment, homes are usually mortgaged. At one time the very word mortgage was tainted with malefaction, images of Usury, and perils that would make Pauline hoarse with horror. Now mortgages are an accepted fact of life, as honorable and American as apple pie, if somewhat more difficult to obtain.

Long-term mortgage debt represents a major portion of the nation's consumer debt, something that the most vocal harbingers of economic doom, preachers of puritan penance, and anti-material utilitarians seem to overlook. While we are, as a nation, running slightly amok in the motorized, mink-lined surfboard department of the local store, the longest of all the consumer lines is in transit between the housing development and the local bank.

The time to worry about our economic future is when we notice that the mink-coated surfboard line is longer than the house line.

We can talk about owning a house in any number of ways, because numbers are protean things—not hard, implacable objects.

First we need some guidelines: as any banker will tell you, you can usually afford a home that costs two to two and a half times your annual income. This is because a house usually costs about 12% of its value (more like 15% at current interest rates) to finance and operate per year. Which means, in turn, that we are willing to spend 24–30% of our income for shelter. This is all well and good. You know how much house you can buy (if you are typical), but you have no idea how it will affect your budget or why it might be better than renting. To learn that, we have to divide a number that is a lump sum, very similar to our rent, into all the things that go into keeping up a house. Let's take a concrete example: Suppose you are making $12,000 a year, are married, and have two children. By the above guidelines, you can afford a home costing no more than $30,000, probably a good deal less. A breakdown of the costs for such a home would look something like this:

30M Purchase price @ 1%/M	$300/month total costs
— 6M Down payment	
24M 1st mort. @ 7% f. 25 yrs.	135.00 5 yr. avg. int.
	35.00 5 yr. avg. amort.
	75.00 taxes
	55.00 op. expenses
	$300.00/month

What are you getting, other than a lot of grass to mow and gutters to clean? Is Pride of Ownership enough? For many people, it is. But let us also assume that you want to measure the economic benefits of home ownership.

These benefits come in two *direct* forms, amortization and tax deductions; and one *indirect* form, possible appreciation of original investment. The first two are easy: amortizing at an average rate of $35/month, or $420/year, for the first five years of the mortgage, you are getting an annual simple return of 7% on your investment of $6000. To be sure, the amortization is lower during the first year of the mortgage, but it is still $330, or 5.5%, and both figures are as good as, if not better than, what you could get at a savings bank.

At this point, someone should be asking: "But is paying off your own debt a return on investment???" Yes, it is. Why? Because without committing your down payment to obtain a mortgage, you would not have found a way to *increase your net worth.*

The end goal of all investment is to provide the investor with a means of increasing either his net worth or his purchasing power. If the same down payment were invested in a savings account, where it would return taxable interest, our home buyer would have to get a return of 7% in the first year of his mortgage or

9% over the first five years, because he would be paying taxes on the interest received at a rate of 22%.

The notion of return, of course, is valid only if the buyer can assume that he could not rent the same property for less than it will cost him to buy and operate it, and that the value of the property remains the same or increases. If houses were "used up" like washing machines and cars, we would have to paint an entirely different—and much darker—picture. As it is, land is not getting any cheaper. Even in urban areas, where values have often been depressed, the renewed commitment of the federal government to improving the cities has provided a bottom for the value of urban property.

Building costs are increasing faster than a master carpenter can drive a tenpenny nail; in concert, housing costs are rising so quickly that it seems altogether likely that owning a home may become an upper-middle-class status symbol if something is not done in the near future.[1]

We still haven't totaled the return on investment, because we haven't taken into consideration the tax deductions gained. Again we must make a relative comparison. Our exemplary home buyer has a Doppelgänger, a double who rents but makes the same amount of money and has the same deductions in the form of wife and children. Both, then, have personal tax deductions totaling $2400 (4×$650), leaving a taxable income of $9600. Dopplegänger takes the standard 10% (which we round up to $1000), which puts him in the 22% tax bracket and costs him $1512 in federal taxes. Our home buyer, on the other hand, deducts his interest ($1620) and his real-estate taxes ($900) after he takes off his wife and children, leaving a taxable income of $7080 and a tax bill of $1205, i.e. *the home buyer has just over $300 a year more to spend (or save) than the renter, by virtue of his tax deductions.* The home buyer, indirectly, has increased the return on his investment by $300, or 5%, bringing his total effective return on investment to about 12%!

At that rate, the home buyer recovers his initial investment in just under seven years. He can afford to sell his home and pay a broker's fee and still break even in three years, provided only that he sell his home for what he paid for it.

Buying a home is a rosy thing indeed! Of course, we have not

TABLE V-B

RENT		BUY	
$12,000		$12,000	
− 2,600		− 2,600	
9,400		$ 9,400	
− 1,000		− 2,520	taxes, interest
$ 8,400	taxable	$ 6,880	
$ 1,468	fed. taxes	$ 1,168	fed. taxes

$300 tax saving

mentioned that, very likely, the return on your investment, in true capitalist fashion, will be immediately reinvested in a new patio, painting the shutters, carpeting the living room, replacing the old washing machine, etc. But, regardless of how cynical we are doomed to become about the joys of home ownership, it is something personal, and something we command. In an era in which everything seems out of control, having the luxury of deciding to mow the lawn on Saturday instead of Friday can be construed as the Victory of Free Will and Human Hope—and just enough, when topped off with an underdone barbecued hamburger, to maintain sanity.

In effect, this tax shelter of amortization and tax savings through interest and tax deductions is a form of indirect government subsidy to housing. In the example given, the indirect subsidy amounted to 8% of the operating cost of the house ($300 of $3600).

Ironically, this subsidy is in inverse relation to income. Which means inverse to *need*. Few Americans seem to realize it, but our tax system operates, effectively, to subsidize property. You are taxed in inverse relation to the amount of property you own.

Assuming that the individual will commit a constant two and one half times his annual net income after personal deductions to shelter, whether it to be to support one or more houses, the effective federal housing subsidy for the upper 20% of income earners is almost *twice* that of the lower 20% of income earners. Though this may seem a rather bizarre fact at first, it is another indicator that accounting for the distribution of social benefits is not as simple as some would have us believe.

Economically, we can see that home ownership is a good investment regardless of your income. Even in the low-income groups, the effective return is nearly twice what one would receive in a savings account; moreover, the return is both greater and more certain than one would receive through a similar investment in common stocks.

We find the implications very clouded until the subject is closely examined, but it now seems patently obvious that every economic relationship has its human implications and impact. Lyndon Johnson is out of office . . . and so is his short-lived "Great Society." The election of Richard Nixon to the presidency, followed by the more discernibly conservative election of right-wing mayors in major cities, has been called "white backlash," "the Orange County Bug," and half a dozen other names that evoke images of renewed lynchings, Minutemen, and the resurrection of Horatio Alger. The reason given most often is that the hard-working, tax-paying American middle and lower-middle class has felt neglected. They don't riot and burn buildings. So they resent the poor and government programs. The situation is rather like an athletic child resenting his crippled brother because all the money has gone for a wheel chair when some of it could have gone to tennis lessons. The fact is that all the programs of the "Great Society," the War on Poverty, etc., amount to little when measured against the distributive power of the federal tax system.

As many student radicals point out, it is easy for a liberal in, say, Lexington, Massachusetts, to support increased government programs, because he only has to pay for them rather than live through the turmoil of their enactment. Liberal Lexington parents have nothing to fear in school integration, because METCO, Exodus, and other programs will never provide more than a trickle of tokens to test the dimensions of their possible prejudice. South Boston and a hundred areas like it feel differently, because they *experience* differently.

Not only must the lower-middle class experience the turmoil of change, they must also *pay* for it. The liberals of Lexington and Newton are economically mobile, in full knowledge of the fact that as their property increases in value so will their tax liabilities decrease. The urban middle class, lacking economic mobility, is trapped in a battlefield that distant generals have mapped. Caught between rising urban taxes, diminishing urban services, and the impossible logistics and expense of suburban existence, the lower-middle class can do nothing but stand and fight. And they do. The only trouble is that they fight the wrong people.

Archimedes offered to move the earth if someone provided him with enough pulleys, rope, and a place to stand; there are some people in the money business who are so totally leveraged that one can only believe that they are trying to move both heaven and earth. A home is just about as wild as that. If you had invested in the stock market at any time in the past five years, the best leverage you could have gotten would have been 70% (that is, you would have had to put up seventy dollars cash for every hundred dollars of stock you bought, and paid margin interest on the borrowed thirty dollars). You could have stretched your leverage a bit further by buying bonds, or you could have done some really sophisticated, exotic leveraging by speculating in money or commodities. Ironically, the best opportunity for leveraging, when measured against risk, appears in the purchase of a home. Less than wildly speculative, it even has the approval of the FHA.

If you put 20% down on a house, you are buying the house on 20% margin, a margin figure that hasn't been since before the Great Crash; if you put 10% down, you are buying on 10% margin, which is as good as frozen pork bellies and a lot safer. In the first case, your return on investment will be as indicated in illustration V-c; in the second case, your return on investment is even more attractive.

ILLUSTRATION V-C

Ex.: $30,000 Cost of home, 1965
  — 6,000 (20% down payment) —3,000 (10% down payment)
  24,000 Financed   27,000 Financed
$42,300 Sale price of home, 1970 (6% compound rate of increase)
 30,000 Cost of home
$12,300 Net profit on sale
  2,600 Less 6% commission
  9,700 Net profit on (a) $6,000, (b) $3,000
                262%   423%
Compound growth rate/yr. 21%   34%

The reader should not forget that this return is *in addition* to that received through amortization and tax savings, making the over-all return a very healthy one indeed. Happily for the home buyer, his down payment of 10% or 20% means that he has five or ten times that amount "working" for him, i.e., although he has only put up one fifth or one tenth of the price, he is benefiting from the *total* increase in the price of the house, since he does not share it with the mortgaging bank.

BUT WHAT ABOUT ALL THAT INTEREST????

In what Mr. Galbraith would call the Conventional Wisdom, debt is still a vaguely odorous and sinful thing. The payment of Vile Interest is evidence of the grip monster debt has upon you. Pity your soul! No one talks like that, but the meaning is still there, only the disguise is different. In an irrationally rational age, one speaks in good, hard, irrefutable, irreducible, fallout-proof Numbers.

What they tell you goes something like this (the reader must imagine Henry Fonda or Walter Pidgeon speaking over the sensible American cracker barrel):

DID YOU KNOW THAT THAT DREAM HOUSE MAY COST YOU TWICE (YES, TWICE!) AS MUCH AS YOU REALLY THINK IT COSTS BY THE TIME YOU ARE FINISHED PAYING FOR IT? DO YOU KNOW HOW MUCH INTEREST YOU WILL BE PAYING DURING THE NEXT THIRTY EVER-LOVING, HARD-WORKING YEARS OF YOUR GOD-FEARING LIFE? WELL, SON, TAKE A LOOK AT THESE NUMBERS AND THINK AGAIN ABOUT THAT DREAM HOUSE.

Table V-D
Cost Of $1000

TERM OF DEBT	5%	6%	7%	8% INTEREST RATE
20 yrs.	1580	1770	1860	2020
25 yrs.	1775	1930	2120	2310
30 yrs.	1930	2160	2400	2640

(To dramatize, our cracker-barrel speaker winks at us and asks if we would like to buy our $10,000 house for $21,000. We refuse: we can't afford it and, besides, it isn't worth it. So we retire to our Allstate camper tent and wish we had something else to stuff than our mattresses, because all that money is getting pretty bumpy and uncomfortable.)

Actually, our cracker-barrel speaker will be a little more reasonable than this, because he knows as well as we know that, no matter how much it costs with all the interest, if *everyone* waited until he had the full price of a house we would be a nation of Allstate camp tents surrounding a few hospitals and retirement villages. He tells us:

"IF YOU REALLY MUST TAKE ON THE BURDEN OF A MORTGAGE (flashing image of your daughter being tied to a railroad track as the 5:15 diesel pollutes into view),

FOR GOD'S SAKE, MAN, PAY IT DOWN AS QUICKLY AS YOU CAN."
(flashing picture of grateful smiling children, Boy Scouts, and CARE packages).

The numerical rationale (as obvious as grace) is then offered:

TABLE V-E

GIVEN:
INTEREST RATE I=7.000% FOR 25 YEARS AND PRINCIPAL P=$1000.00
THE MONTHLY PRINCIPAL+INTEREST PAYMENT IS $ 7.07

MO.	INTEREST	PRINCIPAL	BALANCE	CUMULATIVE INTEREST	CUMULATIVE PRINCIPAL
1	5.83	1.24	998.76	5.83	1.24
2	5.83	1.24	997.52	11.66	2.48
3	5.82	1.25	996.27	17.48	3.73
4	5.81	1.26	995.01	23.29	4.99
5	5.80	1.27	993.74	29.09	6.26
6	5.80	1.27	992.47	34.89	7.53
7	5.79	1.28	991.19	40.68	8.81
8	5.78	1.29	989.90	46.46	10.10
9	5.77	1.30	988.60	52.23	11.40
10	5.77	1.30	987.30	58.00	12.70
11	5.76	1.31	985.99	63.76	14.01
12	5.75	1.32	984.67	69.51	15.33
13	5.74	1.33	983.34	75.25	16.66
14	5.74	1.33	982.01	80.99	17.99
15	5.73	1.34	980.67	86.72	19.33
16	5.72	1.35	979.32	92.44	20.68
17	5.71	1.36	977.96	98.15	22.04
18	5.70	1.37	976.59	103.85	23.41
19	5.70	1.37	975.22	109.55	24.78
20	5.69	1.38	973.84	115.24	26.16
21	5.68	1.39	972.45	120.92	27.55
22	5.67	1.40	971.05	126.59	28.95
23	5.66	1.41	969.64	132.25	30.36
24	5.66	1.41	968.23	137.91	31.77
25	5.65	1.42	966.81	143.56	33.19
26	5.64	1.43	965.38	149.20	34.62
27	5.63	1.44	963.94	154.83	36.06
28	5.62	1.45	962.49	160.45	37.51
29	5.61	1.46	961.03	166.06	38.97
30	5.61	1.46	959.57	171.67	40.43
31	5.60	1.47	958.10	177.27	41.90
32	5.59	1.48	956.62	182.86	43.38
33	5.58	1.49	955.13	188.44	44.87
34	5.57	1.50	953.63	194.01	46.37
35	5.56	1.51	952.12	199.57	47.88
36	5.55	1.52	950.60	205.12	49.40

Loyal Family Man is admonished to start Paying Down The Mortgage as soon as he gets his Insurance Program, and Save All That Interest.

There is only one problem with this approach, and the same

problem, or oversight, recurs in most books on the subject. The dollar is regarded as a constant item, a kind of Eternal Verity for the hard-nosed. But it isn't. The dollar, as Grampa will be glad to tell you, just ain't what it used to be. It doesn't buy as much. Like the banana, the dollar has a tendency to decay. The American dollar, having been monkeyed with by two world wars, a depression, Korea, Vietnam, and a rip-roaring cold-war Defense budget, is decreasing in value year by year.

The decrease in the purchasing power of the dollar is called inflation. You've probably heard of it before. . . . Sometimes it creeps, right now it gallops; but it is almost always there, because inflation keeps jobs open, and jobs, to some degree, keep politicians in office.

For reasons too depressing to elaborate, but very much a part of the rational Scheme of Things, senators and congressmen find it much easier to attract the Department of Defense to their home state than General Motors or Sears, Roebuck—though the latter will be more than willing, camp-follower fashion, to move into the area after the Defense Department has arrived.

The generally accepted explanation for inflation is that it is the result of too many dollars trying to buy too little in the way of goods or services. This results when people either spend too much (more than they earn) or when people are paid for producing goods and services that are never consumed by other people in the economic system; i.e., more money is introduced into the system than it is possible to spend within it.

Defense spending, in part, is of this sort, in that bullets, bombs, gas, and shells are removed from the economic system, while the people and corporations paid for producing them are not. One could extrapolate the above reasoning into an argument for civil war and then describe the Black Panthers and Minutemen as nature's response to inflation, but it really doesn't work that way.

At this point, we can groan and reminisce on how big a nickel candy bar used to be, or we can see how it all works. Since 1969 dollars are only worth $.40 in 1940 dollars, we would need $2.50 in 1969 dollars to buy what we could have bought with a 1940 dollar.

But what if we borrowed that dollar? If I borrowed a dollar from my uncle in 1940 and gave him back a dollar in 1969???

TABLE V-F
Purchasing Power of the Dollar, 1940 to Present

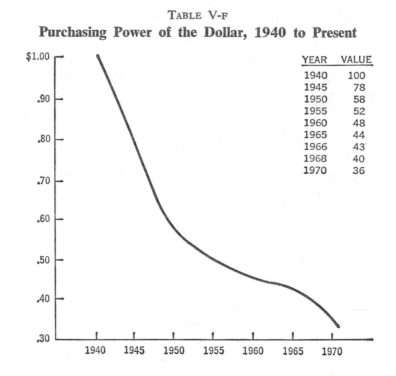

YEAR	VALUE
1940	100
1945	78
1950	58
1955	52
1960	48
1965	44
1966	43
1968	40
1970	36

That's right, Uncle Mendel is the loser he always was! I'm giving him back $.40 rather than a real dollar, because the dollar I am giving back is a 1969 dollar, not the dollar I borrowed.

The only trouble is that most of us don't borrow from Uncle Mendel. We have to go, hat in hand, to the local bank and ask them for the money. The bank wants interest for the use of its money—it wants to make money with its money.

It would appear that unless we have a rich Uncle Mendel we are going to have to pay for the money we borrow and pay enough to cover the cost of inflation to the lender. It would *appear* that way, but it actually isn't so, because interest is tax deductible. Every dollar you pay in interest reduces your tax bill. Since you would have earned the money being taxed anyway, in effect your tax savings decrease the cost of borrowing.

Corporate borrowing is often "free" because of inflation and tax savings. United Mugwump floats some bonds to build a new plant and expand operations. Inflation is running at 3% that year, so the market demands 6% interest on the bonds (3% true interest+3% inflation). The corporation pays $60 a year to bondholders, but that $60 is charged against corporate income, which is taxed at 50%, reducing the company's tax bill by $30. If United Mugwump credited its tax savings against its interest payment, the true *net* cost of borrowing would be reduced to $30. If Mugwump decided to pay off the bonds after one year, it would pay the debt off with dollars that were one year older than the dollars it borrowed and, because of inflation, worth less. The thousand-dollar bond of, say, 1960 is paid off in dollars of 1961, which are worth 3% less than the dollars of 1960. This is what it looks like on a realistic balance sheet:

TABLE V-G

Mugwump bond of '60=$1000 (1960)	6% interest	$60
	less tax savings	30
	net cost	$ 30
	$1000 (1961)=	970 (1960)
− 1000 (1960) returned		$1000
$ 0 net cost of loan		

In essence, Mugwump, by virtue of its tax bracket, has been able to expand its operation and income at no real cost to itself. As we shall soon see, the appeal of debt is a function of one's tax bracket more than anything else. Few individuals enjoy corporate tax brackets. Most of us are stuck in the 19–25% brackets, and this changes our perspective on debt.

The question is *how much* it should change our perspective on debt.

TABLE V-H

Earnest Taxpayer Debt of 1960=	$1000 (1960) 6% int.=	$60
	less tax savings	12 (assumes 20% tax bracket)
		$ 48
	$1000 (1961)	970
$1018 returned		$1018
$ 18 net cost of loan.		

The eighteen dollars seems a rather modest amount when measured against the use of $1000 for a full year.

In practice, we seldom buy something to use for a year, and if we did, it probably wouldn't be worth as much at the end of the year. We *do* buy houses, and what may not be very workable over the short term may be very workable over the lifetime of a mortgage.

It is vitally important to remember that dollars change just as we do—only, hopefully, we are worth more and more while they are worth less and less. Because they do change in value from year to year, the reasoning of the "But what about all that interest?" people is completely false. Not only are they forgetting about the pleasure to be had in the use of something *now,* but they are also being grotesquely inaccurate.

The dollars I borrow to buy a home in 1969 are paid back in dollars of 1970, '71, '72 . . . and '94. All have different present values.

The only way to measure the true cost of a mortgage or any other long-term debt is to (1) change all dollar figures into *constant dollars of the year borrowed* and (2) subtract the tax savings.

The chart above is a graphic summary of data compiled by computer and printed in tabular form in Appendix D. To find out how much, in constant dollars, a mortgage will cost you, find the line that corresponds to your approximate tax bracket, follow it to the current interest rate, and read across to the number in the Total Constant-Dollar Cost column. A man in the 22% tax bracket would discover that for every thousand dollars he borrowed he would return $1153 if the interest rate was 7% and inflation averaged 4%. Contrary to the "all the interest" people, his house will cost him not twice as much as he pays for it but 15% more than he pays for it, *provided* only that the value of the house keeps pace with inflation.

Some people would question whether or not a house will keep pace with inflation, but the overwhelming probability is on the side of the house matching or bettering inflation.[2]

Suppose we follow the example of the man buying the $30M house. We have already seen that he profits through amortization, tax savings, and leverage over short periods of five years, but we

True Net Cost of a Mortgage

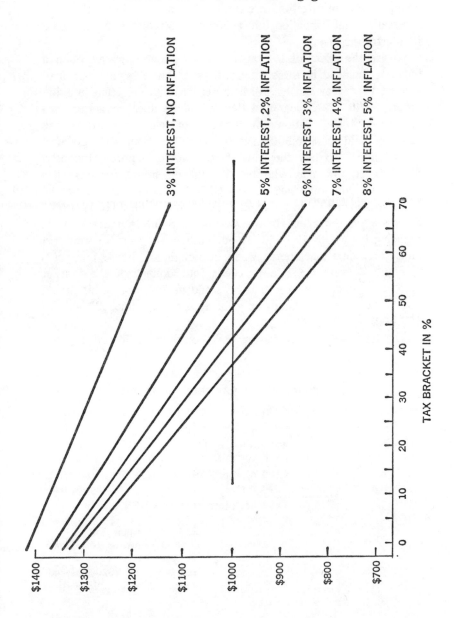

have not made our calculations in constant dollars. Since our tax savings and amortization are realized year by year, it is not necessary to take inflation into account: the return is as indicated in illustration V-c.

To see the effect of leverage, let's see what happens when a house is financed in three different ways: given, again, our man earning 12M/year and his 30M house, let us assume that inflation progresses at 4% a year and that his home does no better than keep pace with inflation. At the end of five years, the house could be sold for $36,300, netting the seller about $34,100 after commissions. To buy the same house would require, obviously, $36,300, so the man who has bought his house for cash has *lost money;* not only has he lost $2200 in commissions, but he has also become liable for capital-gains tax on the $4100 "profit" he made on the sale. He loses another $450 in federal taxes, reducing his net to $33,650. If our cash buyer were to transport himself by time machine to when he bought his house five years ago and convert the sale proceeds into dollars of that earlier period, he would discover that he could no longer buy his dream house, because he would only have present value .82 net=) $27,600!

The leverage men, however, make out very differently:

TABLE V-J
Leveraging in Constant Dollars

```
Sale Price   $36,300
            —  30,000  purchase price
               ──────
                6,300  gross profit
            —   2,200  commissions
               ──────
                4,100  net profit before taxes.
            —     450  taxes
               ──────
             $  3,650  net profit after taxes×PV .82
```

$$=\$3000 \text{ constant dollars}$$
$$=100\% \text{ return or } 10\% \text{ down payment}$$
$$=50\% \text{ return or } 20\% \text{ down payment}$$

Note that each buyer, regardless of how much he put down on the house, nets 3650 inflated dollars more than he put down. Our 20%-down-payment man nets 9650 inflated dollars on the sale: not only could he buy his own house back at its inflated price, something our *cash* buyer cannot afford to do, but he pockets a little under $2400 in change. He could also use the entire sum as a 20% down payment on a $48M house! Our 10% man nets only 6650 inflated dollars but has leveraged his original purchase so that he could buy it back with his profits from the sale and recoup his original down payment! To move from the sublime to the ridiculous, he could also move up to a $66,500 house it if were possible to use the same leveraging.

The reader should bear in mind that there was no *real* appreciation in the value of the house. It did no more than keep pace with inflation, yet the leveraged owners made a profit on their original investment in five years and paid both a full commission on the sale of the house and capital-gains taxes on their paper profit. The cash buyer was worse off than when he started. The reader should also note that no consideration was given to amortization and tax savings over that five-year period.

Leverage is not magic. It works just as effectively to magnify your loss if the house you buy loses value. It is possible that you could buy a house that will decrease in market value either by decreasing in absolute dollars or failing to keep pace with inflation. But the probability is strongly against it.

The fact of the matter is: the Home is the Great American High Flyer. As an investment it lacks the drama of Wombat Computer, Inc., or even such staid, stick-in-the-mud companies as International Business Machines, Zerox, or Polaroid; but investments are for profits, not drama.

Let's compare Home Sweet Home, Inc., with other investments. We will assume that we put down 20%, that the house only keeps pace with 4% inflation,[3] and that we sell it in five years. We amortize about $2100 in five years and net a pretax $4100, giving us a total return, in five years, of $6200 over our original $6000 investment. This amounts to a compound growth rate a bit stronger than 15%. Most investment analysts will agree to call any company that grows faster than 10% a year a "growth" company. Better than 20% is regarded as phenomenal; roller-coaster price charts are built on such earnings. Few growth companies pay much, if anything, in the way of dividends. H.S.H., Inc., pays a 5% dividend in tax savings if you are in the 22% tax bracket, more if you are higher. That's about as good as AT&T, which is not growing a 15% a year. H.S.H. Inc., is the kind of investment analysts, chart services, seers, and Ouija-board manipulators search for constantly—but seldom find.

Another and perhaps more accurate way of looking at housing over the long run is to consider what *proportion* of your expenses are converted into increased savings or increased net worth. As we have already seen, although the gross operating expenses of an example amount to some $3600 a year, the effective cost is only $3300 a year because we have achieved a tax saving. Our disposable income, after payment of taxes and shelter costs, is not reduced by $3600 but by $3300.

Although we are committed to pouring this amount of money into the draining bathtub of our existence, we are pleased to note that the money doesn't drain out quite as fast as we pour it in. Some of it stays behind as amortization. More of it stays behind as appreciation in the value of the house.

FIGURE V-K
Bathtub Flow Chart

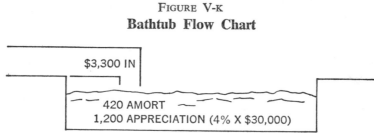

In this instance, private ownership has allowed the owner to convert almost 50% of his unavoidable shelter expenses into *increased net worth*. If the owner is lucky and happens to select an area where the appreciation amounts to 6–8%, the effective savings rate is even larger. Under extraordinary circumstances, such as vacation housing on Cape Cod, ski houses in Aspen, etc., the appreciation rate is such that the house is really a gigantic savings account that you live in or use for vacations.

Given the preceding considerations, it would appear that anyone who doesn't own a house is some kind of nut if he can get the down payment together by any method short of selling his soul.

Still, some people really shouldn't buy houses . . . and some people can't. The people who shouldn't are the people who aren't going to be in one place very long. It would be statistical lunacy to suggest that there is a definite time limit, measurable to the day, on the feasibility of buying a house. It would appear, however, that unless you are planning on staying for at least three years, you would be better off renting than buying.

We are rumored to be a nation of rootless ramblers. As Mr. Wattenberg carefully elaborates in *This U.S.A.*, we aren't so rootless or mobile, on the whole, as our social critics make us out to be. The only trouble is that we all are individuals and not "on the whole"; how often you want to move, need to move, or *have* to move is a function of your age, ambition, education, and vocation. The probability is something each person has to measure for himself. For some, the pleasures of ownership will be enough to make even the risk of a one-year stay bearable. For others, even the prospect of shooting investment goldfish in the proverbial barrel will not be enough of an inducement to buy a home rather than rent.

The final question is "Can you?" There are many people who would like to own a home but cannot, because they live in an urban area where homes and even multifamily dwellings are prohibitively expensive. Property ownership in urban areas is not middle class. The middle class rents, or moves to the suburbs and commutes, leaving the central city to those who can afford it whatever it costs, transients, and those who can't afford it whatever it costs.

The Romans had a thing called condominiums, in which a number of families would contract to build a structure containing several apartments. Each family owned its separate unit but shared the maintenance and operating expenses with the other families in the building. Condominiums are still the rule, rather than the exception, in Europe because they are the only way an individual or family can own its shelter in a highly populated area.

Except for New York and a few other cities, co-operatives are few and far between. Condominiums were practically non-existent a few years ago, but are spreading rapidly. The difference between co-operatives and condominiums is that in a condominium the individual tenant owns his apartment by separate deed and pays separate taxes. He shares no liabilities with his fellow tenants beyond acts of God. The co-operative owner, on the other hand, owns shares in an incorporated building and, as a shareholder, shares the liabilities of the building with all the other tenants. If some of the tenants default on their obligations, as happened in New York during the Depression, the remaining tenants must pick up a portion of the unpaid bills or lose *their* share of the building.

So many co-operative owners defaulted during the thirties that co-operatives were imbued with the smell of bankruptcy; banks became wary, the buildings decayed, and some families were burdened with the maintenance charges of several apartments in addition to their own. The situation grew so bad that apartments on Sutton Place were sometimes *given away* in the early 1940s; in a few instances, canny buyers forced people to *pay them* to take the apartments off their hands.

As suburban sprawl has produced its own problems, co-operatives and condominiums have again become conceptually acceptable. But they are still economically impossible in many areas; and in other areas co-ops are devoted to the low and the high ends of the income scale but neglect the middle, forcing continuation of the suburban exodus and growing tension in the central cities. Hopefully, someday we will have a choice about where we live, and still *own* our home.

In the preceding discussion we neglected imputed income, because it is not germane to the pressing economic problems of middle-class readers. We have discussed housing in terms of leverage financing because this method is the best one for converting current income into capital, and the accumulation of adequate capital for educating one's children and replacing one's earning power is, to this writer, the prime problem facing the American middle class (see chapter 8). Most people *have* to finance their homes.

When we say "imputed" income we are talking about realizing our return on investment entirely in services. If one family has a cash income of ten thousand dollars and rents an apartment, and another family has a cash income of ten thousand dollars and owns a home, mortgage free, we do not consider them to have equal incomes. Although the income that accrues to ownership does not appear on the IRS forms, it surely exists; hence the term imputed.

Since mortgage payments command 17% of gross income in the example used throughout this chapter, necessary *cash* retirement income can be reduced by that amount if the mortgage is paid off. The current housing crisis has long-range implications as well as immediate inconvenience. The discretionary ability to reduce required income at retirement through imputed real-estate income is a major factor in the lives of most Americans. The ability to combine current spending with future investment return is an incredible boon to planning for the future.

With painful irony we note that the tax structure (even reformed!) offers little incentive to builders for the construction of low-cost private housing. Low-income families have the smallest tax incentive to own rather than rent . . . and the smallest opportunity, in any case.

For the elderly who own their own homes, imputed income amounts to a sizable and deserved tax privilege. For the wealthy of any age, home ownership is a tax privilege because it allows a return on investment that isn't taxable. If one assumes that the return on investment a real-estate operator would need would be equal to the prime rate, currently about 6%, a wealthy investor in the 50% bracket receives a taxable equivalent return at 12% on his home investment—exclusive of appreciation!

Whether the wealthy investor owns outright for tax shelter or leverages with debt to obtain the effective federal subsidy is a subtle matter of the relation between the disposition of his income and his capital. To have a choice in the matter is a luxury in itself, but to have to choose between complete tax shelter and federal subsidy is the agonizing equivalent of making a fat boy choose between a sundae and a banana split. Whichever he chooses, he can't help but get fatter.

6

THE WOLF
AT THE DOOR:
INSURANCE

The agent has been in your house for a half hour. He seems friendly enough. In fact, you are beginning to wonder just when he is going to get down to business and sell you some life insurance.

"Suppose you died *yesterday?*" he asks out of the blue.

"What?!"

"Suppose you died yesterday? What would happen?"

Very likely, the phrase "God forbid" has been interjected somewhere in the dialogue. It softens the harsh effect of the question and lets you know that the agent wants you to live.

The "yesterday" bit takes you by surprise. Death is always tomorrow. On a few occasions, such as awaiting take-off in a jetliner or counting the sheeted bodies along the median strip of the highway, death moves into today. But we never consider it "yesterday"! The agent, we find, has taken the high ground by surprise. We are at his mercy.

You cannot be replaced; your earning power *can* be replaced. Replacing your earning power is what life insurance is all about. When all the emotional baggage is finally put to rest, we must face an investment problem involving the provision of assigned sums of money at certain rates of return over different periods of time. If you and your family were machines, we could arrive at an insurance figure in one step. But children, wives, and time make a difference. We aren't machines.

This chapter is divided into three parts to deal with three separate but interlocking problems: 1) how much insurance? 2) what kind of insurance? and finally, 3) how is it sold?

1. How Much and What Kind?

Our first problem is how much insurance you should have. This amount will determine the outside limits of expense and help us select among different types of policies. The most rigorous and careful method for calculating your needs is available in *The Consumers Union Report on Life Insurance*.[1] Their method divides your wife's life into periods relating to the Social Security payments your wife and family would receive and then uses present-value figures to shrink the necessary total to the most efficient package, assuring proper coverage at minimum expense.

The calculations, as we shall see, are somewhat involved, but they take maximum advantage of Social Security and recognize it as more than an inconvenient payroll deduction. At best, most of us think of our Social Security payments as a small pension fund whose benefits are incredibily far removed from our present needs. A look at the monthly payments table below, however, indicates that our Social Security is a substantial part of our life-insurance protection needs.

The value of Social Security in terms of life insurance is somewhat more dramatic if we calculate the amount of money required to provide such an income. Let's assume that you have two children, ages four and six. You expect to send both of them to college. If you were to die, Social Security payments of $126 per month, or $1512 a year, will be made to your family or your child until he or she reaches the age of twenty-one. Using present-value tables (see Appendix A) and assuming that you would receive a net return of 4% on your money, Social Security benefits are worth $18,700 to your four-year-old and $17,100 to your six-year-old, or a total of $35,800! When you consider that your wife will receive about $120 per month or $1440 per year until the youngest child reaches eighteen, and that this sum is worth about $15,100 in insurance, Social Security can be perceived as a blessing worth $50,000! The size of the blessing, of course, depends upon the ages of your children, your wife, and your past earnings.

TABLE VI-A[2]
Income vs. Benefits

Examples of Monthly Cash Payments

AVERAGE YEARLY EARNINGS AFTER 1950[2]	$899 OR LESS	$1800	$3000	$4200	$5400	$6600	$7800
Retired worker—65 or older Disabled worker—under 65	55.00	88.40	115.00	140.40	165.00	189.90	218.00
Wife 65 or older	27.50	44.20	57.50	70.20	82.50	95.00	105.00
Retired worker at 62	44.00	70.80	92.00	112.40	132.00	152.00	174.40
Wife at 62, no child	20.70	33.20	43.20	52.70	61.90	71.30	78.80
Widow at 62 or older	55.00	73.00	94.90	115.90	136.20	156.70	179.90
Widow at 60, no child	47.70	63.30	82.30	100.50	118.10	135.90	156.00
Disabled widow at 50, no child	33.40	44.30	57.60	70.30	82.70	95.10	109.20
Wife under 65 and one child	27.50	44.20	87.40	140.40	165.00	190.00	214.00
Widow under 62 and one child	82.50	132.60	172.60	210.60	247.60	285.00	327.00
Widow under 62 and two children	82.50	132.60	202.40	280.80	354.40	395.60	434.40
One child of retired or disabled worker	27.50	44.20	57.50	70.20	82.50	95.00	109.00
One surviving child	55.00	66.30	86.30	105.30	123.80	142.50	163.50
Maximum family payment	82.50	132.60	202.40	280.80	354.40	395.60	434.40

[2]Generally, average earnings are figured over the period from 1950 until the worker reaches retirement age, becomes disabled, or dies. Up to 5 years of low earnings can be excluded. The maximum earnings creditable for social security are $3,600 for 1951-1954; $4,200 for 1955-1958; $4,800 for 1959-1965; and $6,600 for 1966-1967. The maximum creditable in 1968 and after is $7,800, but average earnings cannot reach this amount until later. Because of this, the benefits shown in the last two columns on the right generally will not be payable until later. When a person is entitled to more than one benefit, the amount actually payable is limited to the larger of the benefits.

SOURCE: *Your Social Security*, U.S. Government Printing Office.

Between the time of your death and her own death, your wife would live through three distinctly different periods, each of which is keyed to the Social Security benefits. In the first period, your wife is involved in raising the family you started. During this time she will receive Social Security checks in amounts that vary with the number and educational status of your children. Since this period would commence with your death, it would be advisable to have the income-producing money fairly conservatively invested so your family would not be caught short in an unfortunate dip in security prices, etc.

The second period—the so-called "shadow period," as agents fondly call it—commences when your parental responsibilities are at an end. So are the payments from Social Security. From the time your youngest child reaches the age of twenty-one until your wife reaches sixty-two, no further benefits will be forthcoming from Social Security. Since this period may be as far away as twenty years, we discount the money needed fairly aggressively. We can also carefully weigh the likelihood that your wife will get a job. Many women do. If you are fortunate enough to have a wife who is well trained, you might consider making only nominal provisions for this period.

One thing the insurance agents never mention is the possibility that your wife might remarry. If you are the possessive type, the thought might be painful. If you are a reasonable human being, there is nothing wrong or repulsive about a realistic consideration of such a possibility.

The third period begins when your wife reaches sixty-two and is eligible for her first Social Security retirement-benefit check. Like the benefits that preceded it, this sum is variable. To find out exactly how much insurance you need, see Appendix A. It will suffice for the moment, however, to realize that once this calculation is done, most readers will discover that they are grotesquely underinsured and that the cost of adequate insurance would press the most ample of incomes. This fact must be borne in mind while we consider what most agents try to sell.

Many agents, particularly those with the least experience, try to sell "family plans"; family plans are insurance packages that include ordinary-life, decreasing-term for the income earner, and small term policies for the wife and children. They are seductive in that although they seem to cover all your insurance needs, *the real dimensions and priorities of your needs are seldom, if ever, measured.*

Salesmen can be very persuasive. They can also be very persistent. If you love your wife, the salesman has that much more on his side. As any good salesmen will tell you, the first thing a salesman must do is get his customer to say "yes." It can be a yes to anything:

"Is the sky blue?"

(Can I come over?) . . .

"Do you eat spaghetti often?"

(Do you agree that your family needs at least this much protection?) . . .

"Isn't it nice when the day begins with a sunrise?"
(Would you sign here, please?)

Suddenly you discover you have bought a life-insurance policy. You don't know much about it or if it is enough, but, it is, after all, "really free." If you protest afterward that the amount isn't enough to protect your family or that you don't like the return offered on your savings within the ordinary life policy, the agent will (a) promise to sell you more when you can afford to protect your family properly, and (b) challenge you.

He rolls his eyes, winks at you, and says, "Sure . . . invest your money; sure, insurance isn't the most profitable way to invest . . . but can you look me straight in the face and tell me you can save the amount of money you say you are going to save—and then invest it?"

If you are even vaguely human, his comment will touch an anxious bone or nerve ending. It *is* difficult to save. Some people can never do it. Because he knows you aren't sure whether or not you can, the salesman offers to let the insurance company be your Big Brother and watch over your piggy bank.

The fact that you are even considering life insurance is evidence that you are an adult and not a child. You don't need a big brother, particularly not a big brother who has a curious resemblance to Fagin.

2. The Industry Probability Built

That finely printed document that is your insurance policy may seem like the beginning and the end of the entire business when you lock it in your safe-deposit box, but it is the equivalent of a snowflake on the cap of an iceberg. Although the most dedicated purveyors of Life Insurance will shout that it is an incredible social Blessing inspired by nothing less than Divine Intervention, the real business of life insurance is Money. *Your* money.

The sale of policies and the payment of death benefits are all the customer ever gets to see. The important business of the industry takes place in the time between those two events. The company makes its profits (the end of all industry) by getting a better investment return on your policy dollars than it guarantees you for the contractual period of your policy.

As any investment analyst will be glad to tell you, there is no real way of knowing how much an insurance company is worth, because the bookkeeping is so complicated and the variables are so unlike those of other businesses. But rest assured. Your Company is scrambling just as hard to invest your policy dollars as its salesmen are scrambling to pull them from your mortal paw.

All told, the industry has to get rid of some $150 million a *day*. Yes, a day! As one investment matures, another is found. Some investments are good for thirty days, others thirty years. Although the investments are constantly changing, the total amounts to almost 200 billion dollars. The return the industry gets on these investments less what it guarantees you is what provides the impetus to work hard and expand.

One of the ironies of our relationship with the company is that while the contract we have with the company to deliver x dollars at our death (the crux of all life insurance) may mitigate the economic pain of a premature death, the company has control of immense assets. These assets, which we have entrusted to unseen investment officers, may be used to change the face of America (through mortgages, loans, bonds, etc.—debts and investments of all shapes and sizes) in a way that will make *our lifetime* unpleasant, or at least cross the grain of our philosophical predispositions.

In short, are you sure you want someone doing something you don't like with your money? To some readers, this question may seem absurd. Life insurance is necessary to protect Our Family and we cannot be concerned with the moral implications of our investment. This view is noble and necessary in a 1930s philosophical framework: life is hard; its hardness makes passing the moral buck forgivable when necessary for such reasons as Preservation of Real-Estate Values and Protection of The Family.

But times change. Passing the moral buck is no longer a pragmatic possibility. The world is too small; what we thought was passing the buck turns out to be a game of socioecological musical chairs, with all of humanity left chairless.

Just as Harvard students demanded that a "moral audit" be

performed on the Harvard endowment so that Harvard students would not gain scholarships on profits from the sale of napalm, each of us must recognize the ubiquitous power of money and examine whether the money we entrust to the hands of others is committed to the investments that make a more-, or a less-, acceptable world.

Actually, the dilemma above exists only in one type of life insurance, the so-called ordinary life policy. It is this policy, however, that is the heart of the industry. Without it, insurance would be reduced to making an acceptable profit over probability rather than attempting to make profits by way of superior investment skill.

The table below, or tables very much like it, is the root of all life insurance. The table tells me how many people die in a given year. The number does me, a singular mortal, very little good, except to tell me that at thirty I can expect to live another 41.25[3] years and that the chances are almost five hundred to one against my dying this year. The odds are comforting, but they do little to protect my family in the unlikely event that I am among the 2.13 people per thousand at thirty years of age to die in 1970. It is, however, an immensely helpful number to an immortal institution.

Suppose you and nine other men in your neighborhood are the same age and worry about dying without providing for your families. You decide to form a protection pool, pledging that each member of the group will put up whatever is necessary to provide the family of the dead group member with $1000. Each of you agrees to put up an amount of money corresponding to the odds against his death, which will be kept in the group protection pool until someone dies.

At twenty-seven years of age, each man would have to put up $1.99, because that number corresponds to the death rate. The protection pool would have $19.90 (10×$1.99) for death benefits. Since a death in the first year would cost the pool $1000, you can be sure that each member of the pool would be very conscious of the others' health! If, by some statistical quirk of fate, one member of the group died (odds against such an event are 50 to 1), the individual members of the pool would

TABLE VI-b

Mortality Table (CSO 1958)*

Commissioners Standard Ordinary

AGE	NUMBER LIVING	NUMBER DYING	DEATH RATE PER 1,000	EXPECTANCY, YEARS	AGE	NUMBER LIVING	NUMBER DYING	DEATH RATE PER 1,000	EXPECTANCY, YEARS
0	10,000,000	70,800	7.08	68.30	50	8,762,306	72,902	8.32	23.63
1	9,929,200	17,475	1.76	67.78	51	8,689,404	79,160	9.11	22.82
2	9,911,725	15,066	1.52	66.90	52	8,610,244	85,757	9.96	22.03
3	9,896,659	14,449	1.46	66.00	53	8,524,486	92,832	10.89	21.25
4	9,882,210	13,835	1.40	65.10	54	8,431,654	100,337	11.90	20.47
5	9,868,375	13,322	1.35	64.19	55	8,331,317	108,307	13.00	19.71
6	9,855,053	12,812	1.30	63.27	56	8,223,010	116,849	14.21	18.97
7	9,842,241	12,401	1.26	62.35	57	8,106,161	125,970	15.54	18.23
8	9,829,840	12,091	1.23	61.43	58	7,980,191	135,663	17.00	17.51
9	9,817,749	11,879	1.21	60.51	59	7,844,528	145,830	18.59	16.81
10	9,805,870	11,865	1.21	59.58	60	7,698,698	156,592	20.34	16.12
11	9,794,005	12,047	1.23	58.65	61	7,542,106	167,736	22.24	15.44
12	9,781,958	12,325	1.26	57.72	62	7,374,370	179,271	24.31	14.78
13	9,769,633	12,896	1.32	56.80	63	7,195,099	191,174	26.57	14.14
14	9,756,737	13,562	1.39	55.87	64	7,003,925	203,394	29.04	13.51
15	9,743,175	14,225	1.46	54.95	65	6,800,531	215,917	31.75	12.90
16	9,728,950	14,983	1.54	54.03	66	6,584,614	228,749	34.74	12.31
17	9,713,967	15,737	1.62	53.11	67	6,355,865	241,777	38.04	11.73
18	9,698,230	16,390	1.69	52.19	68	6,114,088	254,835	41.68	11.17
19	9,681,840	16,846	1.74	51.28	69	5,859,253	267,241	45.61	10.64
20	9,664,994	17,300	1.79	50.37	70	5,592,012	278,426	49.79	10.12
21	9,647,694	17,655	1.83	49.46	71	5,313,586	287,731	54.15	9.63
22	9,630,039	17,912	1.86	48.55	72	5,025,855	294,766	58.65	9.15
23	9,612,127	18,167	1.89	47.64	73	4,731,089	299,289	63.26	8.69
24	9,593,960	18,324	1.91	46.73	74	4,431,800	301,894	68.12	8.24
25	9,575,636	18,481	1.93	45.82	75	4,129,906	303,011	73.37	7.81
26	9,557,155	18,732	1.96	44.90	76	3,826,895	303,014	79.18	7.39
27	9,538,423	18,981	1.99	43.99	77	3,523,881	301,997	85.70	6.98
28	9,519,442	19,324	2.03	43.08	78	3,221,884	299,829	93.06	6.59
29	9,500,118	19,760	2.08	42.16	79	2,922,055	295,683	101.19	6.21
30	9,480,358	20,193	2.13*	41.25	80	2,626,372	288,848	109.98	5.85
31	9,460,165	20,718	2.19	40.34	81	2,337,524	278,983	119.35	5.51
32	9,439,447	21,239	2.25	39.43	82	2,058,541	265,902	129.17	5.19
33	9,418,208	21,850	2.32	38.51	83	1,792,639	249,858	139.38	4.89
34	9,396,358	22,551	2.40	37.60	84	1,542,781	231,433	150.01	4.60
35	9,373,807	23,528	2.51	36.69	85	1,311,348	211,311	161.14	4.32
36	9,350,279	24,685	2.64	35.78	86	1,100,037	190,108	172.82	4.06
37	9,325,594	26,112	2.80	34.88	87	909,929	168,455	185.13	3.80
38	9,299,482	27,991	3.01	33.97	88	741,474	146,997	198.25	3.55
39	9,271,491	30,132	3.25	33.07	89	594,477	126,303	212.46	3.31
40	9,241,359	32,622	3.53	32.18	90	468,174	106,809	228.14	3.06
41	9,208,737	35,362	3.84	31.29	91	361,365	88,813	245.77	2.82
42	9,173,375	38,253	4.17	30.41	92	272,552	72,480	265.93	2.58
43	9,135,122	41,382	4.53	29.54	93	200,072	57,881	289.30	2.33
44	9,093,740	44,741	4.92	28.67	94	142,191	45,026	316.66	2.07
45	9,048,999	48,412	5.35	27.81	95	97,165	34,128	351.24	1.80
46	9,000,587	52,473	5.83	26.95	96	63,037	25,250	400.56	1.51
47	8,948,114	56,910	6.36	26.11	97	37,787	18,456	488.42	1.18
48	8,891,204	61,794	6.95	25.27	98	19,331	12,916	688.15	.83
49	8,829,410	67,104	7.60	24.45	99	6,415	6,415	1,000.00	.50

Note: For female lives ages 15 and over use age in Table 3 years younger than true age.

* Flitcraft, Incorporated, New York.

become liable for $1000—$19.90, divided by 9, or just under $109!

Such an event would probably bring a quick end to the local protection pool. Although you would know that the odds were on your side, the burden of potential expense would be too large to justify the protection received. If the group manages to get along for five years without a death, its pooled resources would have grown to $104.20 and the liability of each group member would have diminished to just under $100. An improvement, but still an uncomfortable amount to risk. At the end of fifteen years, the group would have accumulated $419.70 (this assumes the money is kept in a cookie jar or piggie bank, rather than being invested), reducing the survivors' risks to just under $65.

As the reader has probably suspected, a quicker way to make the risk more acceptable is to increase the pool. If the protection pool had been started with one thousand people instead of ten, the pooled money would have amounted to $1999, leaving us only with the problem of fractional people: 1.99 people don't die, one does or two do. If one person dies, there is a retained surplus in the fund. If two people die, the fund is short $1.00 or 1/10 of a cent per member.

Although the rate at which people die is constant, the risk the pool takes in having to dip into its collective pockets decreases as the number of members in the pool increases. *A very large pool is called an insurance company.*

The larger the pool of people insured by the company, the more the death rate of those in the pool approximates the rates in the mortality table. Although the company has the same liability per person with two people as it has with a hundred thousand, its actual *risk* is diminished, because its insured "sample" approximates the behavior of the general population more closely as the sample expands. The company's rates reflect the general population experience. Ultimately, the insurance company functions as a kind of conduit or distributing agency.

In its capacity as a pool and distributing agency, insurance is a fantastic blessing. Not only does it keep widows and orphans off the cold streets of hard life, but it also serves to reduce the anxiety any concerned husband will feel for his wife and children. The blessing becomes a mixed one when the method by which it is delivered is considered; it becomes mixed to an anger-provoking degree when one considers some of the myths perpetrated to enroll customers.

A life insurance company once advertised, "The man who dies without life insurance doesn't die, he ABSCONDS." While it is rather difficult to agree that not having life insurance is a crime, it certainly is inconsiderate and rather thoughtless not to make some attempt to protect one's family.

What we have neglected is the fact that the mortality table is only the raw material for the final product, the policy. Looking back to the table, you will see that while the death rate is rather low at twenty-seven, it has a depressing way of increasing, year after year. At forty, your chances of dying are 3.53 per thousand; at fifty, they are 8.32 per thousand, at sixty, 20.34 per thousand —and the rate keeps going up. It reaches 1000 at age ninety-nine.

It is only logical that if the death rate increases with age, the insurance rate must increase in proportion until the cost becomes prohibitive. If we are buying nothing but life insurance, we must face the mathematical necessity of either paying more money for the same amount of protection or paying the same amount of money for less protection. The first option is sold as "term insurance" and generally comes in five-year packages. A few companies sell a twenty-year policy, or "term to 65," or "term to expectancy."

To sell you term insurance, the company looks at the mortality table to see what the probability of your death is over a given period, averages the amount with some nudging to the higher side, adds a little to have in reserve against something running amok in its sample, and, finally, adds the costs of selling the product, administration, bookkeeping, overhead, etc.

The real cost of the product is not always entirely obvious, because there are two kinds of insurance companies—mutual and stock. If you were buying term insurance from a stock company, they would quote you one rate. Period. If you were buying from a mutual company, they would quote you a rate and then tell you that you could expect a "dividend" at the end of each year, which would lower the net cost of the insurance. "Mutual" means that the policy owner becomes a stockholder (effectively) with the purchase of a policy and is entitled to his share, prorated to his policy, of surplus the company experiences. "Dividends"* are not guaranteed . . . but they come through pretty well.

The term insurance of the stock company will be quoted at a price between the gross and the net-after-dividends price of the mutual company.

TABLE VI-C

Typical Rates per Thousand Dollars of Coverage

Sample:

5-YR. R.C. TERM	AGE 25	AGE 30	AGE 35
Mutual	$5.80	$6.38	$7.43
Stock	5.46	5.67	5.97

This pricing is almost always true, regardless of policy type. Both types of company invest your policy payment shortly after it is received, the only real difference being that the mutual company shares its mortality risk with policyholders while the stock company assumes the risk that its policyholder-mortality experience may differ from the mortality table.

Arguing the merits of either type of company is an endless task. At first sight, mutual companies would seem preferable, but it is altogether possible that the stock companies have better investment departments because the stockholders demand it. Moreover, management is more subject to recall in a stock company, because the lines of control are more clearly defined. Finally, the stock company must compete with the mutual company; any sizable difference in the ultimate net cost of insurance should eventually result in decreased sales for the stock company.

* Not to be confused with stock dividends, mutual dividends are the return of surplus reserves.

The cost of the mutual company's insurance is *understated* because the "dividend" money is out of your hands for a period during which it can be invested.

There are two problems with term insurance. If we buy a five-year policy, our health may deteriorate in the following five years, making us uninsurable[4]; and as we age, the premium increases. Eventually it increases faster than our ability to pay, even though we still need insurance protection.

Our other option from the mortality table was to pay the same premium for decreasing coverage. This type of policy is generally known as home owners', or mortgage, insurance because it is written over twenty-, twenty-five-, and occasionally thirty-year periods. Although this type of coverage is excellent, life is more uncertain than the amortization table of a mortgage. You could, for instance, find yourself an "autumn parent" just as your oldest child graduates from college. Chances are against such events, but the number of women who have a "surprise" child at thirty-nine is disconcertingly large. The child may be a joy, but it remains that the family has acquired another long-term responsibility just when responsibility was expected to diminish. And you might have become uninsurable in the interim.

If you don't think of these things, you may be certain that the agent who tries to sell you some insurance *will*. That's because he wants to sell you another kind of policy, which he will call "permanent," otherwise known as straight or ordinary, life.

The mortality table cannot be changed. The package we buy it in can. What we want is a single policy that provides constant coverage at a constant premium. We can accomplish this by making life insurance a form of investment!

Voilà! Hurrah! Straight life, then, is a kind of Doomsday machine among insurance policies. It does everything and ends everything: it is the answer to All Possible Rainy Days!

In effect, the company charges you more (than is necessary to insure your life) so that it won't have to charge you more later. The excess is credited to your account and invested at a given rate of return. If you die soon, the company pays off the face value of your policy (from other members of the pool) less your savings, which it returns to your family. As the years go by, your excess increases. As your savings increase, the *liability* of the com-

pany decreases, i.e., your constant-premium dollars are buying
less and less protection. The straight, or ordinary, life policy
is really a variation on the decreasing-term policy.

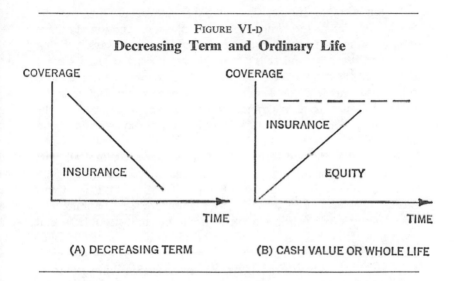

FIGURE VI-D
Decreasing Term and Ordinary Life

(A) DECREASING TERM   (B) CASH VALUE OR WHOLE LIFE

Note that until the investment aspect of the policy was introduced, the essential and total business of the company was largely
dependent on the success of its gamble with its section of the
population pool. With the addition of money to invest for the
long term, each company has a means for competing with other
companies in some way that requires skill—investments.

The qualities that make ordinary life ideal for an insurance
company, however, by no means make it ideal for you as a consumer. In the first place, ordinary life costs so much more than
renewable term or decreasing term that you probably won't be
able to afford the coverage you need with ordinary life insurance.
This leaves you with a decision to make: either you can work to
pay an extravagant amount of insurance premiums, or you can
have a reasonable premium and be underinsured.

Both options are unacceptable. If you point this out to the
agent, he may introduce another policy—often called "modified

ten"—in which the premium is low for ten years, the rationale being that you will be earning more money later. The rationale is correct, but if you extrapolate it to its obvious extreme, you will drop ordinary life altogether and buy term, because it gives you the *most protection per dollar.*

If you were to suggest this notion to the agent, however, he would shudder at the "impermanence" of such a notion. Perhaps it is a paranoid fantasy on my part, but I have always felt that the agent regards (and sells) term insurance as the Used Car of the insurance world. Yes, he will sell it to you . . . but with reluctance. He lets you know that it is against his Better Judgment. Because term insurance is not labeled "permanent," he seems to present it as though it had a thirty-day warranty and might fall apart at any time.

Such verbal or non-verbal suggestions, however, are all part of the incredible psychodrama of the insurance triangle: agent, husband, and wife using a symbol of life and death (and immortality! Never forget that!) to manipulate or communicate. The interaction is worth a book in itself; the only trouble is that the agent, if he has any experience at all, is like a scratch golfer matched against the Thursday morning mother's group—he can't help but win. Whether he plays on love, responsibility, fear of death, fear of life, or greed, he can maneuver the mumbo jumbo of the insurance man's tarot deck to grab you where it hurts.

As much as it requires technical knowledge, the situation requires self-knowledge. Some men who cannot express their affection have loaded themselves down with a burden of life insurance that surely must drive them to an early death; ultimately their love is expressed not through their life but through their death, in the purgatorial existence of the well-provided-for young widow commuting between New York and Florida. Other men who feel a quiet resentment or vague hostility that they cannot express otherwise, may balk at the purchase of life insurance and thus punish their wives in their death as they never had the courage to while they were alive.

Every couple must evaluate what the marriage contract means for them. For some it will mean a responsibility, whether dead or alive, to support the family. For others it will mean much less. The first commitment is the one the agent seeks. It is a Good

One. And it is certainly Responsible. It also reduces much of the Uncertainty of Existence. But what does it say about life, living, risk, and love? To my knowledge, the marriage vows did not mention insurance. They mentioned love, honor, and respect and made me feel that the relationship I was gladly entering was a tool not for ending the uncertainty and chanciness of life but for improving it. I think my wife shares this feeling . . . and I know that she shares my feeling that *life* is a matter of risk, death a certainty.

You know that you are a real grownup and not just a big boy who wears a tie all the time, when you talk about buying life insurance and then go out and buy it. My wife and I talked about it and decided that our life was together; life insurance was necessary, but its cost should not interfere with our savings, investments, and (hopefully) present needs.

No, you can't have everything. But you can sure try, and have a lot of fun trying. While you are trying, you can think about priorities: if you can't have everything, what comes first?

At this point, we can begin to meld Numerical Reality with People Reality. The salesman will tell you that while your insurance policy is protecting your family in the event of your death, it is also building "living values" in case you live. In fact, these "living values" are exactly what make your policy "permanent"; over the years, the surplus premium money builds until the company is more savings institution than insurance company. (see previous chart). In some instances, the cash value of the policy may approach or even exceed the face value of the policy! In this event, the company is entirely a savings medium. It is no longer insuring your life, because it is holding money you paid in.

The next thing the salesman is likely to say (probably while he is showing you a table of values similar to the one above) is that since the probability is that you will live to age sixty-five (more than seven in ten do), you (you lucky fellow!) will probably be taking the cash value built up in the account to live on in retirement. "My God", the amazed man says, "you get more back than you put in! . . . you were insured all that time and it cost you NOTHING! . . . What a bargain!"

What he doesn't tell you is that the excess over what you paid in in premiums is all taxable as ordinary interest income. Pre-

TABLE VI-E

Cash Values vs. Time for a Typical
$10,000 Non-Participating Policy

YEARS POLICY IS IN FORCE	AGE WHEN POLICY IS TAKEN OUT		
	25	30	35
1	—	—	—
2	—	30	80
3	50	160	230
4	140	290	390
5	240	430	550
10	740	1150	1400
15	1320	1940	2300
20	1980	2790	3250
AT AGE 60	5080	4580	4210
65	5880	5470	5170

sumably you will be in a lower tax bracket, because your income will be lower. Your tax deductions will also be lower, however, since you will probably have paid off your home mortgage
and kicked the last of your children from the family nest. If you
owned a large policy you might suddenly find your retirement
married to the rate of return offered by the insurance company;
rather than walk into the tax liability, you might choose a longer-
term pay-out option or an annuity. While this would diminish
your taxes, you would avoid the tax at the expense of accepting
a lower-than-market return on your money.

It would be unfair to suggest that the salesman is being dishonest
when he declares that when all is said and done and you are
happily retired in DelMar Valhalla, your life insurance will have
cost you nothing. But *alternative uses for the money must be considered as well as the time difference between the time the policy
was purchased and your retirement.* If the insurance did, indeed,
cost you "nothing," your premium dollars must at least maintain
their purchasing power. Moreover, to the degree that your policy
was an investment medium as well as an insurance policy, we

must compare alternative programs of insurance and investment. As we shall soon see, ordinary life just does not make the grade.

To examine our options out of this protection/retirement bind, we need to determine what return on our investment the company is giving us.

The average policy will accumulate a little less than six hundred in cash value by age sixty-five for every thousand dollars of coverage starting at age twenty-five. It will accumulate a little more than five hundred dollars in cash value for every thousand dollars in coverage starting at age thirty. If the premiums for these policies were invested, they would have to obtain a net rate of return of *less than 1%* to accumulate to such a small amount. As compensation for this low rate of return on your money, the insurance company guarantees to complete your savings program.

If you took the alternative of buying protection only (term insurance) and investing the difference, you would accumulate the usual cash value by obtaining a net return of about 3% on the saved difference.

Viewed in the most realistic terms, cash-value life insurance is purchased at the cost of investing your premium dollars more profitably elsewhere. The return offered by the insurance company, moreover, is so low (when measured against inflation) that the notion of retiring on the accumulated cash value is untenable. In essence, *the true cost of ordinary life insurance is the possibility of adequate funds for retirement;* and that, to this writer, is an exorbitant and inhuman cost. Life before death!

Crossing from the purely economic to the human, nothing comes more dear in this life than certainty. The guarantee of the insurance contract, while it gives us a certain, definite amount of money, comes at the expense of investment freedom.

While it may be healthy to insure your life and protect your family against your possible untimely death, it is not healthy to cling to complete certainty and avoid *all* risk. The salesman, again, may start playing psychic games with you; to have completely resolved one's feeling about death is an exceptional achievement . . . the achievement of a lifetime, if you will. Most of us put death out of mind and live from day to day. We resent the ants—but know we cannot be complete grasshoppers. The salesman can play on guilt for our latent grasshopper and on our secret desire to avoid death altogether by buying a life-insurance policy. (Surely, if lighting a cigarette is guaranteed to bring a train or bus, then buying an insurance policy will shoo away death.)

Since we can't put all our eggs into one policy basket, let's see how we will do, using the same amount of money some other way.

The cost difference between typical ordinary life and five-year renewable term is shown graphically below:

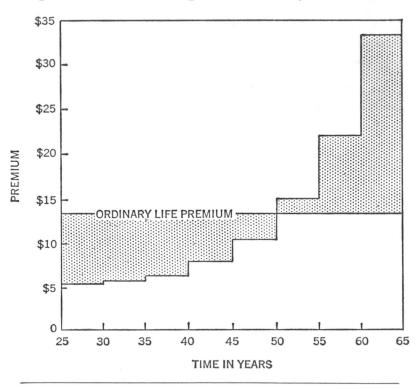

FIGURE VI-F

Step Rates for Term Compared to Ordinary Life Premium

The shaded area indicates the surplus dollars available for more-profitable modes of investment than life insurance. This money must be invested so that the man insured can reduce his insurance every five years, thereby maintaining his margin of money free to invest. If he cannot do this, he will face the necessity of *increasing* his insurance/investment portion at the crossover point.

The shaded area is deceptively narrow because our need for insurance coverage will decrease as our invested surplus increases. It is here that the joys of compound growth rates become evident. At 3%, a dollar will grow to only $2.42 in thirty years: but at 9%, a dollar will grow to $13.26 in the same time. *Obviously, the faster our growth rate, the more rapidly we can do exactly what the insurance company does, insure less and invest more, because our need for protection will be constantly diminishing.*

The table below indicates how such a program would go, assuming a rate of return one might expect from common stock, and

TABLE VI-G

Comparison of Three Insurance Programs

Annual Cost=$135.

	8% RETURN		6% RETURN		
AGE PERIOD	PRIN. AT END OF PERIOD	INS.	PRIN. AT END OF PERIOD	INS.	CASH VALUE ORDINARY LIFE POLICY
25–30	$485	$9,515	$460	$9,540	$320
30–35	1,195	8,805	1,180	8,820	930
35–40	2,255	7,745	2,020	7,980	1,610
40–45	3,755	6,245	3,120	6,880	2,360
45–50	5,925	4,075	4,540	5,460	——
50–55	9,185	815	6,400	3,600	——
55–60	14,200	——	8,920	1,080	4,860
60–65	21,700	——	12,460	——	5,700
Final principal	$21,700		$12,460		$5,700

compares it to the cash value of an ordinary life policy. The calculations were made assuming that the total of coverage and principal must always be at least $10,000 and that the face value of the term insurance is decreased as the principal mounts.

Since even the most conservative mutual fund will produce a net return of 6% over the forty-year period, the dramatic difference in accumulated principal or cash value indicates that it is difficult to make a logical case for ordinary life policies.

The compounding effect is such that the earlier you start, the better. There is something else to consider, also: the younger you are, the more you can afford the increased risk of equity investments. Since return is related to risk, the young man who conscientiously plans is well positioned to prepare for his retirement and protect his family at the same time. As he grows older, he can shift to more-conservative forms of investment. The ability to change his form of investment is not something the ordinary life insurance buyer has. He saves. He's married to the financial tables of the industry.

If the insurance industry suffers a substantial conflict of interest in the construction of its product, the situation is aggravated by the manner in which the product is marketed.

Our rituals of maturity are harder to spot than those of less-developed areas. We have no lion hunts, no marking ceremonies, no hunting rituals. In America, one comes of age in stages. We are awarded a driver's license, the right to drink, and (for half of us) Draft Status. We receive our first credit card as we graduate from college and, very likely, our first visit from an insurance salesman. He appears again when we marry, follows the arrival of all our children, and pops up sometime during our thirties to sell us an annuity or a pension plan. When he comes, he tempts us to record life's verities in larger and larger amounts of life insurance, assuring us each time that our Loss will be immeasurably more painful than it would have been the year before.

There was a time when the insurance salesman arrived with a miniature casket under his arm and a bouquet of roses, implying with little subtlety that *his* policy was all that separated your a) darling, b) beloved, c) devoted, Wife, or a) beautiful, b) charming, c) lovely, Daughter, from Life on the Street. This approach has lost its credibility with the post-Depression generation of middle-class Americans who buy the bulk of all life insurance. The salesman you meet now is an entirely different breed of cat. His panting becomes evident only when you are about to sign the contract. He specializes in the soft sell, lets you know that he also has a wife and 2½ children (he may even pull out some pictures), and will very likely ask you to tell him about yourself so that he can appraise your needs. He leads you to believe, through a series of subtle references and slightly hard-nosed comments, that underneath that soft, hibachi-guarding, family-loving exterior there is a superhuman evaluator, a Mensch with Saichel, if you will.

In reality, he has probably worked for the company for less than a year, isn't even sure of his way around the policy book yet, and is scared to death because he has just run out of relatives and the rent is due. He is going to sell you whatever he can, as fast as he can, and deposit the check before you change your mind.

*   *   *

So where are you now? You have a starving man in your house and he's wedged his feet under the cocktail table. How did he get there? What is he trying to do?

SCENARIO: *The Short, Unhappy Life of an Insurance Salesman*

SCENE I: John Jobless, boy loser, on the park bench. John has one suit, dandruff, and impetigo. He manages to conceal his halitosis only by cornering the market in Sen-Sen and, consequently, has a totally and permanently blackened tongue. He reads the paper and spots a small ad for a "sales, go-getter," in "the financial field," a "man who needs to clear $1200 a month", etc., and follows the telephone line to the office, where, before he knows it, he has become a representative for Family Lovers Assurance. Jobless represents Family Lovers, but he is *not* employed by them. He is on his own, working on commission. He sits at a desk and makes lists of relatives, down to, and including, cousins four times removed. He visits them all. A few help him. He sells a few policies. Banks a few dollars. And now he has run out of relatives, is getting hungry, and *you*, you jerk, have been dumb enough to send in your birth date after being sucked in with an offer of a free car-washing kit through the mail!

SCENE II: Jobless is sitting at the agency with a stack of car-washing kits piled on one end of the desk, a yellow pad covered with doodles in front of him, and a sheet of names and numbers next to the telephone on his right. He calls you (if your wife answers, he will ask for you by your first name), tells you who he is, and offers to bring the car-wash kit "by" so he can tell you about a new insurance program that will save you money. Numbly (he always calls just as you are sitting down to dinner, a time when you will say yes to anything), you agree and before you know it, he is in your house with his feet wedged under the cocktail table.

Chances are, he will offer you the same policy regardless of what you tell him about yourself and regardless of what your income is. The policy will be the same whether you make eight, ten, twelve, or eighteen thousand dollars a year, regardless of whether or not you own a home with mortgage, etc. It will be the same policy because it is the only one he knows how to sell and is about all he knows about insurance.

Although the industry has not been making a gaudy display of the figures, the life expectancy of the life-insurance salesman makes the butterfly look like a specialist at longevity. Chances are just about nine out of ten that your agent has been working with Family Lovers for less than a year, and fairly high that he has been with them for less than six months.[5]

The industry that sells itself as a secure, changeless, supra-Death institution sells its product with insecure, ever-changing, and short-lived salesmen. The irony would be a source of humor were it not for the fact that most people are incredibly mismatched with their insurance. They own insurance, forget about the needs of their families, dismiss possible death from their minds, and subject their families to gruesome risks, because all they own is a $10,000 whole-life policy with a rider insuring the life of each child for an additional $1000. They really need at least $50,000 of protection if they are to have any at all.

The agency system (as the contract/commission sales arrangement is called) is the cause of this incredible mechanism of conflict of interest and propagation of misinformation.

So where are we? Before we can even buy insurance we have to find out *who* we will be buying it from! Your insurance needs will change as your life changes; under the agency system the probability is immensely against your seeing the same agent twice.

What you don't need is someone whose mission in life is to sell you one policy and move on. You need someone who knows he can sell you a lot of different insurance provided he services your needs. He is called a general agent. He can sell you policies from different companies, pick and choose, and fight for you when necessary, He is not married to one company, one policy, or one kind of insurance. He can insure your house, your car(s), your furnishings, your boat, and even your life. If he is an active agent, chances are he can help you get a good mortgage for your house.

Essentially, you are putting all your insurance eggs in one basket. The concentration makes it a worth-while basket for an agent to watch. The business will be worth while for him and will entitle you to ask him questions as they occur to you. But the best thing is that a good agent will be able to answer all your questions intelligently. Because he *knows* he is going to get your business, he will be less tempted to sell you something that you don't need or that is not entirely appropriate to your situation.

There is only one problem: finding him. I can't tell you where. Good agents aren't listed in the Yellow Pages under GOOD AGENTS and no one company has cornered the market on either good or bad agents. Ask your friends, ask your boss: word of mouth is still the most reliable reference system.

One more word about the agency system. The eight or nine out of ten who fail at selling insurance, fail not because they have inadequate knowledge of the product they are selling, but because they are poor salesmen. The ones who survive are good salesmen. This excellence, however, is no guarantee that their superior sales ability has engendered an understanding of the product, or concern for appropriate fit of the product to the customer.

The ones who survive have to be sharp; if you are lucky, he will be good *and* sharp. Unfortunately, what may appear as *good* to us is only *sharp* for the agent. Most of us are rank amateurs at the game of buying life insurance and want to stay that way.

It requires no great sensitivity to realize that I have an ax to grind when it comes to insurance. If some of my comments seem unkind in relation to the insurance agents you know, consider yourself blessed. I have a good agent and am grateful for his help in preparing sections of this chapter. But I am also aware that the good agent is the exception that proves the rule.

What I find most aggravating is the fact that an industry that has a valuable product—a product that is, indeed, a social blessing when properly used—should sell their product in such an inept way. Insurance is only properly used when it is properly sold, and the agency system is such that few salesmen are in business long enough to know their product. Those who do know their product still must live with an intrinsic conflict of interest that is a severe test of integrity. Too many of them play the psychodrama of the sale, hoping you will forget that the real business of life insurance takes place not in your living room but in the investment department of the company.

In researching this chapter, I spent a lot of time with insurance agents. I have a small collection of car-wash kits, leather notebooks, telephone pads, wallets, etc., brought as "gifts" in the eager hands of young agents. Most of the agents I met were pleasant. Most were well-meaning. But you can mean well and do harm because you are too inept, too dumb, or too brainwashed.

These sad souls should not represent a danger to anyone curious enough to read this book.

In general:
- Try to get one agent to handle all your needs.
- If he doesn't now what you are talking about when you mention present value or discounted value, he doesn't know his business.
- Don't buy from someone who urges you to switch companies; be wary of those who want you to switch policies.
- Remember that you are transacting economic business, not seeking emotional catharsis.
- If you don't like the way he looks or the way he talks, or if you

don't feel comfortable with him, don't do business with him. There are plenty of other agents.

If the actuarial tables prove out, you will be doing business with this man for thirty or forty years, perhaps longer. . . . Don't sign anything right away; think about it.

Not very long ago, insurance was a sacred cow. To comment critically on the industry was tantamount to un-Americanism, sacrilege, and pederasty, all rolled into one. While many Americans still wax sentimental—warm and mushy—about the Benefits, the critics of the industry are becoming more vociferous each year.

So far as the investment value of life insurance goes, the cat is out of the bag. Although the facts have yet to receive the necessary impetus to make them the Spiro T. Agnew of the investment world, more and more people are considering forms of investment outside their insurance policies.

The insurance industry, you can be sure, is worried about this. If people are no longer content to save their money inside their insurance policies, they won't sell as much insurance. As a result, many companies are forming mutual funds to be sold along with the policies to keep competitive in the "Informed Market."

The problem, of course, is that the same shmoos who don't know enough about life insurance to sell it properly are going to be trying to sell you some mutual funds while they are at it. The prospects are grim indeed.

7

WILSON'S KOOL-AID

I'd like to tell you a story. Ultimately, the story has an investment moral with footnotes and corollaries, but, for the moment, all of us who suffered investment trauma in Schlock Electronics last year can at least feel comforted by the fact that many presumably smart people made equally fantastic mistakes.

Our story is called "They All Laughed When Mr. Wilson Sat Down with His Copying Machine."

Everyone laughed because the price of his machine seemed like a lot of money for something that made what secretaries were supposed to do automatically with carbon paper. Not only that, but the machine was too large to fit on a desk. People would be trekking all over the office to get copies. The copier would be little more than an expensive variation on the water cooler.

All the experts, with their charts, tables, slide rules, and demand projections, told poor Mr. Wilson to take his machine home. They were going to stick with those $500 desk-top copying machines. That's where the Money was, they said.

Poor Mr. Wilson had to go home with his admired but rejected machine and wonder if the Smart People were smarter than he was. He worried about it. So did everyone else in the company. And all the stockholders, too.

Finally, someone asked, "Hey, wait a minute! When you had your Kool-Aid stand, did you make your customers buy *the stand* before they could get any Kool-Aid?

Of course you didn't!

You sold it to them by the glass!

"Sell it by the glass!!"

The Xerox Corporation has been selling its Kool-Aid by the glass ever since. Sales recently passed the billion-dollar mark, and the company is among the hundred largest industrial firms in the country. Mr. Wilson is happy with his stand.

You can also bet that all the Smart People at IBM who passed up an opportunity to buy Haloid Corp., as Xerox was formerly named, have been a little chagrined ever since.

There are, as promised, two morals to this story: The first is that everyone, absolutely everyone, can make investment mistakes. If the first moral has to do with clarity of vision, the second has to do with the field. A company may have a fantastic technical and scientific staff (as many small companies do) but lack a competent and knowledgeable marketing staff. The reverse can also happen. The result is always the same: without the capacity to deliver its product to the marketplace and put the profit from its sale on the books, a company cannot make money. Unless you are incredibly nimble it also means that you as an investor, cannot make money on such companies.

The success that has come to Xerox is the result of both the technical and the marketing skills of the company employees and management. The company has a product that creates and expands its own markets.[1] When a user leases the Zerox 914 copier and pays five cents a copy, the usage increases day by day until a larger machine with a larger lease fee—but lower *per copy* fee—is economically justified. Just as General Motors has built its success on having a wide variety of models (all placed in strategically close price brackets) and the car buyers' urge to "trade up" so that the company not only sells more cars but "more car, per car," Xerox has another kind of upgrading built into the marketing of its product.

Even Xerox can make mistakes, however. At one time, Xerox could have acquired Digital Equipment, just as IBM could have acquired Xerox. It is possible that IBM was too busy making computers and Xerox was too busy xeroxing when Opportunity came their way. I doubt, in any case, that the respective managements felt they already had a good thing and should let someone else have a chance. It just doesn't work that way. Strange as it may sound, it is possible that the managements of both companies were becoming less flexible with Success.

Xerox and IBM may have lost opportunities and they may

be worth less than they *could* be (you won't see too many stockholders' lawsuits on that issue), but they have not *lost* actual money—which is what the private investor often does.

Ironically, many have lost money precisely because of Xerox and IBM: in the hopes of finding *another,* many investors throw their surplus dollars at the hottest thing moving.

The equity markets offer more ways for the novice to lose money fast than the sleaziest of boardwalk game stalls. And they are usually the ones offering the hottest thing moving. Although it may grate against the Puritan conscience of many, it is possible, though not probable, that even the most inexperienced of investors can make some money by being in the right thing at the right time, regardless of its temperature: on occasion, justice, real or poetic, does not obtain in the investment world. This reality is the source of ulcers for many investment managers and great spiritual pain to the novice.

. Profits in investments do not always lie on a firm foundation of Value. While manipulation is frowned upon by the SEC, promotions take place with daily monotony. Even the most conservative of investment managers may, on occasion, take a short and pleasurable "ride," just for diversion from thinking about what is Real, Solid, and Wonderful.

Before we go on to attempt some examination of just how to find value or learn what constitutes it, let's take an instructive side trip through the statistical forest.

We know from chapter 6 that our investment in life insurance gives us a return of about 3% on our investment. This return, the lowest in the spectrum, is sweetened by a promise to complete our savings program if we happen to be among the unfortunate few who will be on the wrong side of the actuarial tables.

At this writing, the money market has soared skyward, creating investment returns on savings that are the highest in decades. The man with money to save will receive a return, usually currently taxable,[2] of 4–6½%.

Though lacking the sweetening of life insurance, the return of insured savings accounts is safe enough, and quantitatively large enough, to make us consider shifting our savings dollars away from insurance companies and into banks.[3]

If we are willing to gamble on the direction of the money

market, we can put our savings dollars into corporate or municipal bonds. The latter enjoy the advantage of being tax-free, and both have the limited excitement of fluctuating in value as a function of the over-all cost of money. Most older bonds have taken a considerable beating of late, decreasing in value as the cost of money has increased. The investor who bought bonds in 1950 is a very sorry fellow.

Finally, we have equity investments: common stocks, convertible bonds and debentures, real estate, land, etc.—all are investment media in which we have converted our dollars into the enterprise itself (rather than putting our dollars at the disposal of enterprise for a fee) and accepted the risk that others may differ with us in estimating the value of the enterprise.

Return on equity investments comes from three sources: 1) dividends on the stock or interest on the convertible bond before it is converted into stock, 2) recognition in the marketplace that the enterprise is earning more money than it did before, and 3) re-evaluation by the marketplace of the *potential* for the enterprise to continue increasing its earnings. The first item, dividends, is in the here and now. The second two considerations can very well be in the never-never, as well as expensive, because they are so luxuriously intangible. Because they are subject to speculation, the second two items involve immensely more risk than the first. They also offer the advantage of preferential tax treatment and represent a form of income that may be realized at the investor's convenience.

If you were going to buy a stock for dividends alone, you would, for the most part, be defeating the purpose of your investment, because you could get a similar or higher return from a fixed dollar investment in savings bonds. In fact, if the return here and now competes with fixed dollar investment returns, the investor would do well to wonder if the larger return has not been purchased at the expense of future growth.

Since some risk is involved, one can fairly safely assume that investors want compensation for that risk. According to a study done by the Chicago Graduate School of Business, the average return on investment in common stocks was 9.8% in any given time period between 1926 and 1965.

TABLE VII-A

Cash-to-Portfolio, Tax Exempt

TO	1/26	12/26	12/27	12/28	12/29	12/30	12/31	12/32	12/33	12/34	12/35	12/36	12/37	12/38	12/39	12/40	12/41	12/42	12/43	12/44
12/26	-1.6																			
12/27	15.3	30.0																		
12/28	23.9	37.7	45.5																	
12/29	7.8	9.6	0.1	-30.0																
12/30	-2.3	-3.5	-13.0	-31.7	-37.2															
12/31	-11.1	-13.5	-21.7	-36.3	-40.8	-47.8														
12/32	-11.0	-12.7	-19.0	-30.3	-32.1	-31.0	-11.1													
12/33	-2.7	-3.2	-7.7	-15.6	-11.8	-1.3	36.9	108.4												
12/34	-1.2	-1.6	-5.2	-11.3	-7.0	2.4	28.2	55.0	13.8											
12/35	2.2	2.1	-0.8	-5.7	-0.5	9.3	32.9	53.5	31.2	50.4										
12/36	6.6	5.5	3.1	-0.4	5.3	15.3	37.5	54.5	40.9	56.8	63.9									
12/37	0.5	0.1	-2.3	-6.2	-2.8	3.3	16.1	23.1	8.2	6.6	-10.9	-46.0								
12/38	2.8	2.5	0.4	-2.9	0.9	7.0	18.7	25.1	12.9	12.4	1.1	-16.2	30.7							
12/39	2.6	2.3	0.3	-2.6	0.9	6.0	15.7	20.5	10.1	9.0	0.4	-11.2	12.9	-3.3						
12/40	1.9	1.6	-0.2	-3.0	0.2	4.7	13.0	16.9	7.9	6.4	-1.1	-9.8	6.3	-5.0	-9.9					
12/41	1.2	0.9	-0.8	-3.3	-0.5	3.5	10.8	13.8	5.8	4.2	-1.9	-9.2	2.6	-5.5	-9.0	-10.2				
12/42	2.0	1.9	0.4	-1.9	0.9	4.8	11.6	14.3	7.2	6.0	0.9	-4.9	6.1	0.6	1.1	7.6	31.1			
12/43	3.5	3.6	2.2	0.2	3.1	7.2	13.8	16.5	10.2	9.7	5.5	0.9	12.3	9.4	12.1	22.2	47.1	56.7		
12/44	4.6	4.7.	3.5	1.7	4.7	8.7	15.2	17.9	12.3	12.0	8.4	4.6	15.7	13.7	17.1	26.8	45.6	49.3	38.1	
12/45	6.3	6.5	5.5	3.9	7.0	11.3	17.6	20.4	15.4	15.5	12.4	9.3	20.3	19.4	23.7	33.6	51.4	55.4	50.1	5
12/46	5.5	5.7	4.7	3.2	6.0	9.9	15.6	18.0	13.3	13.1	10.2	7.2	16.3	15.0	17.8	24.2	34.8	34.5	26.0	2
12/47	5.3	5.6	4.6	3.1	5.8	9.3	14.6	16.8	12.4	12.1	9.4	6.7	14.7	13.6	15.5	20.3	27.5	26.3	18.9	1
12/48	5.1	5.2	4.2	2.8	5.2	8.5	13.5	15.5	11.3	11.0	8.4	5.8	12.7	11.7	13.3	17.0	22.5	20.8	14.2	
12/49	5.7	5.8	4.9	3.6	6.0	9.1	13.8	15.7	11.7	11.5	9.1	6.8	13.3	12.3	13.9	17.3	22.2	20.8	15.2	1
12/50	6.5	6.7	5.9	4.6	7.0	10.2	14.9	16.7	12.9	12.8	10.6	8.5	14.8	14.1	15.6	19.0	23.5	22.4	17.9	
12/51	6.9	7.1	6.4	5.1	7.5	10.6	15.1	16.7	13.1	13.1	11.0	9.0	14.8	14.1	15.6	18.6	22.6	21.6	17.7	1
12/52	7.0	7.2	6.5	5.3	7.6	10.5	14.8	16.4	13.0	13.0	11.0	9.0	14.5	13.8	15.1	17.9	21.5	20.4	16.8	1
12/53	6.6	6.8	6.1	5.0	7.1	9.8	13.9	15.3	12.2	12.1	10.2	8.3	13.3	12.5	13.7	16.1	19.3	18.1	14.3	1
12/54	6.1	8.2	7.6	6.4	8.7	11.4	15.5	17.0	14.0	14.1	12.2	10.5	15.5	14.8	16.2	18.7	21.9	21.0	18.2	1
12/55	8.4	8.6	8.0	6.9	9.2	11.9	15.9	17.4	14.5	14.6	12.7	11.1	15.9	15.2	16.6	18.8	21.8	21.1	18.6	1
12/56	8.5	8.7	8.1	7.0	9.2	11.8	15.7	17.1	14.4	14.4	12.6	11.1	15.6	15.1	16.2	18.2	20.8	20.2	17.9	1
12/57	7.8	7.9	7.3	6.3	8.3	10.7	14.3	15.5	12.9	12.9	11.2	9.7	13.9	13.2	14.2	15.9	18.3	17.5	15.1	1
12/58	8.8	9.0	8.4	7.5	9.5	11.9	15.5	16.7	14.3	14.4	12.7	11.3	15.5	15.0	16.0	17.8	20.2	19.4	17.3	1
12/59	8.9	9.1	8.5	7.6	9.7	12.1	15.6	16.8	14.4	14.5	12.8	11.5	15.6	15.0	16.0	17.6	19.9	19.1	17.1	1
12/60	8.8	9.0	8.3	7.5	9.4	11.6	14.9-	16.1	13.9	13.9	12.3	11.1	14.8	14.2	15.1	16.6	18.7	17.9	15.9	1
12/61	9.3	9.5	8.9	8.1	9.9	12.2	15.4	16.6	14.4	14.5	13.0	11.8	15.4	15.0	15.8	17.3	19.3	18.5	16.5	1
12/62	8.6	8.8	8.2	7.3	9.1	11.2	14.3	15.3	13.2	13.3	11.8	10.7	14.0	13.5	14.3	15.6	17.3	16.5	14.6	1
12/63	8.9	9.1	8.5	7.7	9.5	11.6	14.6	15.6	13.5	13.6	12.2	11.0	14.3	13.8	14.6	15.8	17.4	16.7	14.9	1
12/64	9.1	9.3	8.8	7.9	9.6	11.6	14.5	15.6	13.6	13.7	12.4	11.3	14.4	14.0	14.7	15.8	17.4	16.7	15.0	1
12/65	9.3	9.5	9.0	8.2	10.0	12.0	14.9	15.9	13.9	14.0	12.6	11.6	14.6	14.2	14.9	16.0	17.5	16.9	15.4	1

A quick perusal of the table indicates that this return was not a humdrum, year-in, year-out event. People do not leap from twenty-story windows because they are bored with their dividend checks.

The return is geared very strongly to the anticipated fortunes of the country, rather than the regularity of the dividend. A somewhat slower look at the numbers indicates that as the period of investment increases, the variation from the average rate of

Rates of Return on Investment in Common Stocks Listed on
The New York Stock Exchange With Reinvestment of Dividends
(Per Cent Per Annum Compounded Annually)
Cash-to-Portfolio, Tax Exempt

	FROM 12/46	12/47	12/48	12/49	FROM 12/50	12/51	12/52	12/53	12/54	FROM 12/55	12/56	12/57	12/58	12/59	FROM 12/60	12/61	12/62	12/63	12/64
.9																			
.4	−0.5																		
.5	−1.0	−2.9																	
.9	5.4	8.2	19.3																
8	12.4	16.6	27.0	35.8															
.4	13.3	16.4	23.1	25.2	14.9														
.4	12.9	15.2	19.7	19.8	12.4	8.9													
.9	10.5	12.1	15.0	13.7	7.5	3.5	−3.1												
.5	15.5	17.7	21.3	21.6	17.9	18.5	22.8	54.8											
.4	16.2	18.2	21.4	21.7	18.5	19.1	22.2	37.2	19.0										
.3	15.6	17.2	19.8	20.0	17.0	16.9	18.6	26.7	13.3	6.5									
.5	12.3	13.5	15.3	14.8	12.0	11.1	11.1	14.5	3.4	−3.7	−12.9								
.2	15.2	16.7	18.7	18.6	16.5	16.5	17.5	21.9	14.5	13.0	17.4	57.9							
.3	15.3	16.6	18.6	18.6	16.6	16.6	17.6	21.2	15.0	14.0	17.6	36.0	14.4						
.2	14.0	15.2	16.8	16.5	14.9	14.8	15.3	17.8	12.4	11.2	13.1	21.9	6.4	−1.9					
.2	14.9	16.0	17.5	17.3	16.0	16.0	16.6	19.0	14.6	13.9	16.1	23.7	13.6	12.9	27.6				
.3	12.8	13.7	14.9	14.5	13.1	12.8	13.0	14.7	10.5	9.4	10.4	15.1	6.3	3.8	5.9	−13.3			
.8	13.2	14.0	15.2	14.9	13.5	13.3	13.5	15.0	11.3	10.4	11.5	15.7	8.7	7.4	10.4	2.0	17.7		
.1	13.4	14.2	15.3	15.0	13.7	13.5	13.8	15.3	11.9	11.2	12.3	16.2	10.4	9.7	12.8	7.6	18.5	16.3	
.5	14.1	14.9	15.9	15.8	14.5	14.3	14.7	16.2	13.1	12.5	13.6	17.7	12.7	12.4	15.9	12.9	22.6	23.4	28.3

return decreases; moreover, the probability of having a positive over-all return increases immensely. As one moves the dates for the return intervals beyond the depression years, the probability of achieving an *impressive* average return increases.

You and I, however, can go broke in *any year,* regardless of how good it is. The solidarity and regularity of the numerical tables aside, we must remember that these figures are AVERAGE returns on more than one thousand stocks in a given time period. Every year has its special losing disaster. You could be the one to pick the loser five years running. Unlike the afternoon quiz shows, the loser's prize isn't just as good as the winner's.

If the average total return from more than one thousand stocks is 9.8% over any given time period, it should be obvious that just as increasing the *duration* increases the probability of meeting the average, increasing the *number* of stocks held also increases the probability of such an event. Whether we want to or not is another issue, which we will deal with shortly; right now we are going to take a look at the difference between the various rates of return.

FIGURE VII-b

(REPEATED IN TABULAR FORM IN APPENDIX A).

Growth of $1 at Various Compound Interest Rates

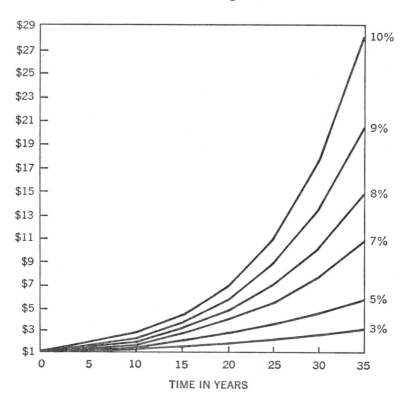

TIME IN YEARS

The difference, small as it at first seems, is impressive. The dollar that grows (triples!) to $3.26 over forty years at 3% becomes $45.25 over the same period at 10%. The difference will buy a lot of hamburger.

Few people have already saved all the money they intend to invest. Most likely, you can anticipate being able to save $X a year, in which case, illustration VII-c is more pertinent.

TABLE VII-c

(REPEATED IN TABULAR FORM IN APPENDIX A).

Cumulative Value of $1 Saved per Year at Various Interest Rates

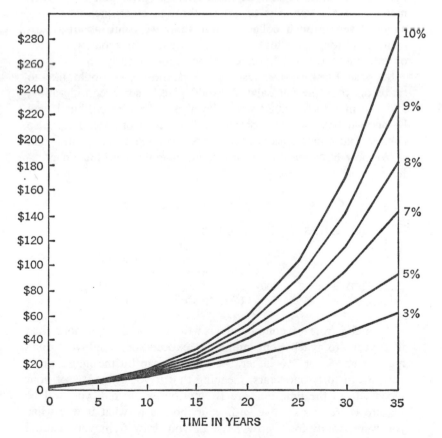

TIME IN YEARS

Here we find that $1 saved every year at 10% becomes $442 in forty years, while it becomes only $75 at 3%; at 7% or 8% (after-tax net rate) our savings will still mount to $200 or $259 respectively. Such are the joys of compound interest: what makes Norman O. Brown reach for his Kaopectate and Marx ulcerous with rage may yet provide us with Golden Years that truly are. The return is average, but the results are such that we all aspire to rampant mediocrity. Closer analysis reveals dimmer prospects.

The growth of numbers in *absolute* terms may seem impressive, but we have yet to measure our return against the certainty of our human needs. Again, we must examine priorities. If we save money, we are saving it to get us through emergencies and put our children through college. After that, we think about retirement. And long after that, we start to daydream about *what kind* of retirement we will have. Or about retiring early.

Suppose I asked you, just for kicks, how you would like to retire on your present salary? You'd give it some consideration, and you might say yes. It would be nice to have more, but it will be enough because the mortgage will be paid off, etc. Let's also assume that you can save 5% of your income to meet this goal.

We now have the dimensions of an essentially arithmetic problem:

Illustration VII-d

$$(G)^n = 1/wS \qquad \text{where} \quad \begin{aligned} &S = \text{savings rate} \\ &G = \text{growth rate} \\ &n = \text{number years to age 65} \\ &w = \text{withdrawal rate} \end{aligned}$$

$$(G)^n = 280, 340, 400 \qquad \text{or} \qquad = 7, 6, 5\% \text{ respectively}$$

(*See Appendix B*)

At a 5% rate of compound growth, it would take more than fifty years to reach your minimum expectation. And you don't make it at 6% or 7% either. At 8% you can hit the magic number 280 in forty-one years, meaning that if you save 5% of your income from the time you are twenty-four years old, you will be able to retire at sixty-five with your income at what it was when you were twenty-four, provided that you draw from your capital at a rate of 7%. (As a point of reference, the withdrawal rate above is just a trifle under the rate of the typical annuity at age sixty-five).

We have a number of options at this point. The first is to start rationalizing our disappointment. All those wonderful numbers and charts of just a few pages ago have turned from roses to rage. The number of men who can start a savings program at age twenty-four and keep to it regularly is rather small. Many far-more-established families make only the most sporadic efforts at savings or investments.

Our only choice is to try to grouse the facts away. O.K., you say, but 1) you didn't make any allowance for the fact that a man will be saving more as he gets older and has more income! Very true. But it is also true that as he earns more, his expectations will increase in proportion.

2) You didn't count Social Security! Also true. But I didn't count the effects of inflation, either. Let's play our average investment scenario against a backdrop of inflation: You earn $10,000 a year. You're twenty-four. And you save $500 a year. In the course of forty-one years you are fortunate enough to average an 8% net compound rate on investment, and now, at sixty-five, plan to retire on a 7% draw from your investments, which will provide you with $10,000 a year. If we assume an average 2% rate of inflation, however, the *buying power* of your future income is reduced to $4440 . . . and your Social Security benefits. The sum offers enough to consider retirement without breaking into a cold sweat if one forgets that the slack taken up by Social Security becomes proportionately less as your income increases above the Social Security maximums.[4]

Obviously, cash-value insurance is a hopelessly inadequate vehicle to meet retirement needs. Other forms of savings are almost as inadequate. Even with an average return in common stocks, retirement allows precious little in the way of extras. Caligula would not be jealous.

How we feel or act depends very much on our expectations. All we *know* is that plugging numbers and rates together indicates that a man without substantial property to start, cannot expect, under normal circumstances of investment and saving, to retire with more property and capital than necessary to take him through the remaining years of his life with an occasional splurge on an artificial kidney connection.

Viewed in terms of the past, such expectations are an immense improvement. But, then, life was "brutish, nasty, and short" in the past. Now it is long, dreary, and alienative. Essentially, the middle and upper-middle class has obtained a precariously tenured economic position by way of compounding prudent savings with moderate-risk investments. The reward for practicing all-American virtues is the need to continue practicing them. Dessert never follows the spinach diet.

If we are to avoid this kind of programmatic stalemate we must take one, or more, of three options: 1) save and invest more of our current income, 2) seek further capital or retirement benefits through our employer, or 3) attempt to achieve a better-than-average return on our investments. There is, of course, a fourth option, which is to re-evaluate our needs and expectations. For better or worse, this option requires a large degree of removal from the mainstream of American life.

Traditionally, Americans save about 6% of their income. The figure varies from year to year, largely as a function of public optimism about employment, expenses, etc. The blank percentage is an empty number, however, since some Americans save more than others. Some don't save at all, but are in chronic debt; others, much higher in the income spectrum, not only save more but reinvest the income from their savings. Obviously, the more money you make and have, the greater the chance you will be able to set more aside for the future. All you have to do is endure and prevail over consumer temptation—a struggle that would make Ulysses long for the tortures of the sirens' call.

The second option has some interesting possibilities and a growing number of advocates. There are secretaries at University Computing (a fast-growing computer utility) who drive Cadillacs to work, a fringe benefit from the stock options they were given when the company was young, poor, and very hungry. With almost monotonous regularity, you can find articles in *Redbook* and *McCall's* written by the wives of young engineers and physicists who have trouble adjusting to having half-million-dollar stock options in a high-flying electronics firm.

Profit-sharing plans are more run of the mill and less dramatic, but they are a powerful incentive for staying with some companies. According to an article in *The Wall Street Journal*, many profit-sharing young bankers can expect to retire as millionaires. You can buy a lot of gold watches with a million dollars.

The trouble with such fringe benefits is moral rather than economic. Economically, profit-sharing and pension plans are hard to fault. Morally, they leave something to be desired. They are hard to leave. The longer you stay with a particular company, the harder it is to give up the return of a profit-sharing plan. The dilemma tends to quiet the voice of corporate dissent.

Company pension plans, often as not, become a weapon to still rebellious thoughts. It's anatomically impossible to bite the hand that feeds you when it is wrapped tightly around your economic throat.

Our final option within the given value system is to seek a higher-than-average return on our equity investments.

Easier said than done. In fact, we have yet to examine how we are going to get an *average* return. Here we learn to our great dismay that the average investor is setting his sights high when he aspires to mediocrity.

As stated earlier, the average stock may return 9.8% from year to year, but the average is composed of thousands of stocks, a number of which will compete with your heart as they sink into the netherworld of investment losers.

Even if you ignored the American Exchange or the over-the-counter market, the stocks on the Big Board are enough to drive even the least-fastidious investor to nibbling at the rinds of his fingernails. Some of the larger and more placid enterprises emit dividends with the regularity of a longshoreman's belch, moving in price only in response to cataclysmic events:

UNIVERSAL MUGWUMP down ½ as California disappears.

Others, smaller and born to the age, fluctuate like the thumping heart of a speed freak. Selling at an earnings multiple* of approximately 350 times last year's *loss,* the investment is a paper lion in a match factory.

* The ratio of market price to per-share earnings.

In between are all the most common of common stocks, the stocks that might be considered the investment equivalent of Mr. Nixon's "Forgotten Americans"; they pay their bills, raise their corporate products, and smart under their increasing tax burden. Neither varicose giant nor fey product of the technological moment, they grow quietly and wait with the meek to inherit the earth.

Reading the financial section of the daily paper may give us some idea of the size and current temperament of the stock market, but it is only a small help in making investment decisions. Although the day-to-day world may give us some ideas about what products are good and what products are bad, it gives us no idea of how important a particular product is to a company, whether the new product changes the prospects of the company, how a prime-rate change will affect the profit margins of the company, etc. Since we have decided beforehand to be careful and astute, we visit the local brokerage house.

At the brokerage house, we discover an entirely different and fascinating world. Rows of desks face a Cinerama screen of changing numbers and unchanging letters. Telephones ring constantly, numbers flash on electronic displays in response to call letters, and high above it all a magnified tape parades the trading prices of stocks. In the lobby, rows of research books await our perusal, as do copies of in-house research reports on various companies with titles such as:

"SHOULD YOU BUILD YOUR INVESTMENTS IN STEEL: Current Prospects for the Industry."

Pages of numbers and statistics follow with conclusions such as "Buy on Weakness," "Sell on Strength," "Hold," "Attractive at 55," etc. Though generally written in the ponderous style known as Investment Consideration, the great majority of these reports have little real content beyond their introductory value, and constitute an adult transformation of a game known as Simon Says.

"Buy United Mugwump at 55 and
Get Out of Jail Free!"

Two other writing styles to be found in these reports are:

Due Indecision: "Provided the market has fully discounted the mounting losses at United Mugwump, the stock merits the close scrutiny of intermediate-term buyers."

Due Indecision Preferred: "United Mugwump, though currently overpriced, is the strongest of all the mugwump manufacturers. Their strength is all the more amazing for the acknowledged fact that mugwumping is a declining industry."

Actually, reading of any sort is next to impossible in the typical brokerage office. The Angst of the watchers and ozone from the solenoids behind the screen combine to give the customer (and the broker!) a sense that SOMETHING IS REALLY HAPPENING. IF THERE EVER WAS A TIME TO BUY, IT IS NOW. NOW. BUY NOW. SELL. BUY. NOW! One of the reasons for this overpowering sensation is that it grates against our Puritan expectations to see a room filled with people doing nothing.

Most of the time, very little of any real consequence is actually happening. The quickening of the pulse is not the excitement of capital gain, but the joy of the marketplace. This sense of the marketplace so eerily created through electronics is a joy to some —but it is not at all conducive to sound decisions.

Unless you have a friend who will recommend one, you will meet your broker entirely by chance. In the typical house, street customers are sent to brokers in rotation.

Brokers, by necessity, must be all things to all men until they can command enough business to select their customers. When they command enough business to select their customers, you don't meet them by walking in off the street. Unless you happen to have a Rich Uncle, you probably won't even see The Man With Enough Customers. This leaves us with the Politicians. Some are good, some are bad. Most are indifferent. A broker gives the illusion, rather than the reality, of contact with the investment world.

I do not mean to suggest that the brokerage business is full of hucksters and criminals; nor do I wish to induce paranoia in the reader. It behooves us, however, to examine what our best interests are and how capable the people who serve us are of following them.

Brokers make their living by selling stocks. And buying stocks. Their income is in proportion to the volume of business they do —"production," as it is called. In some houses, their income will be a straight percentage, in others there is a salary and a variable bonus; whatever the arrangement, the ultimate measure of a broker's earning power is the volume of business he does for the brokerage house.

Some brokers deliberately "churn" accounts. Others fastidiously maintain that they advise their customers objectively. I'm sure many *try* to be objective. But the investor should always bear in mind the impetus of the marketplace; the position of the broker is necessarily short-term. For the most part, so is *his vision*. Without a noticeable bend in his integrity, a broker will opt for change more often than stasis. Change is his business. Unfortunately for the investor, change in the marketplace is not synonomous with growth in investments. Better investment decisions are made at Lake Cumquat than at the brokerage office.

Another humiliating item we should be aware of is the volume of business a broker must do to make a living. To make $10,000 a year, a broker must do about $2,860,000 a year in volume[5]; even assuming that all transactions are part of a round trip (buy and sell), a broker must handle $1,430,000 a year. How much money he has to have in all his accounts then becomes a function of account turnover. Whatever the turnover rate, the small and regular investor is not very strategically placed to receive much attention. Moreover, if he is earning only $10,000 a year, your broker is pretty far back in line himself when it comes to talking with the house analysts, etc. The hoped-for intelligent exchange between customer and broker is most often a case of the blind leading the blind, burdened by conflict of interest.

If the prospects of the average investor walking in off the street are depressing, we must remember that it is a two-way street. Brokers seldom get credit for being right, but they always get the blame for being wrong. Some novice investors expect incredible deeds from their brokers, as though a $3000 account has the right and power to usurp the lifeblood and talent of the best minds on Wall Street—let alone the average broker.

Generally speaking, the smaller the account, the more-irrational the expectations of the investor and the more demands he will make. Brokers know this. They also know that there is only so much time per trading day and that they cannot afford to spend a half hour on the phone with Mr. Greed, explaining why his five shares of International Merkin haven't doubled in the last week.

Even so, the broker's life probably would be tolerable if the transactions with his customers were only about money, how much, and when. But they are not. All too often, the broker finds himself thrust into the role of a vital but undefined character in his customer's life psychodrama. These psychodramas, or games, range from the relatively petty ("You-just-want-me-for-the-commissions, If-only-I-hadn't-listened-to-you, Why-did-you-lie-to-me? If-it-weren't-for-you-I-could-make-a-bundle" to Job-like allegories that test the customer's true relation to God. This particular game, like all games, comes only in All or None. None, of course, is the more important, because most games are played to be lost.

MY GOD, MY GOD, WHY HAST THOU FORSAKEN ME? is an extremely popular game which may account for the decline of formal religion as well as the growth of "People's Capitalism." In this game the broker is Chief Witness to the abandonment and spiritual travail of the investor. Seeking a sign from God, fifty shares of International Merkin are purchased. The ensuing price collapse of IM is a sign to the investor that he was, indeed, born under a distant dwarf star and is doomed to a life of hard work and pain. The reader may create other scenarios at will for such games as "It-was-too-good-to-be-true," "I-had-it-coming," "It-always-happens-to-me," "If-you-liked-it-so-much-why-didn't-you-buy-any-you-son-of-a-bitch," etc.

The broker's chief defense against accumulating a lot of people who should be seeing a psychiatrist is to offer them a mutual fund. With hundreds of mutual funds to choose from, it is a rather difficult task to select a fund suited to the needs of the customer —as difficult as buying a stock—but *the best fund for the customer's needs is invariably the one described in the prospectus on top of the pile in the upper lefthand drawer of the broker's desk.*

All things considered, many brokers will opt for a larger one-time commission than all the headaches of numerous small accounts. The management of the brokerage house probably agrees with them, if not for the sake of employee mental health, at least for the sake of profit margins, and encourages brokers to switch small customers into mutual funds. A few houses have an unwritten rule not to accept transactions with a commission under $25; instead, they push the customer to mutual-fund investments.

To the outside observer, such tendencies may seem like killing the goose that lays the golden eggs, because there is only one transaction (and therefore one commission) per customer, but this is not at all the case. In exchange for a strong sales effort (i.e., having the prospectus in the upper left-hand drawer of every broker's desk), the mutual fund will direct *its* commission business on transactions to the brokerage house. So very little is lost by herding small customers into mutual funds.

The funds will get our attention shortly. At the moment, however, let's assume that you have money to invest, you have found a reliable broker, and you are interested in making some good, profitable investments. If you could, in theory, get a gross return of 9.8% on your investments by blindfolding yourself and sticking pins in the financial page, it should be obvious that you are hoping to get a *larger* return on your investments than the average, because you are going to be more diligent than the average pin sticker.

The next problem is whether the diligence is worth it and what degree of diligence and skill is required to increase the probability of doing better.

Let's assume for the moment that you are thirty years old and have saved $5000. (!) You want to invest it. Let's assume also that you want to do twice as well as the average pin sticker and achieve a compound growth rate of 20%, which will increase your first-year growth by $500 over the average. What every investor must ask himself is how much of the additional increment is capital growth and *how much is a different form of earnings?*

The reader may think this a peculiar question, but it has a great deal of relevance to the life stance and attitude of the investor. For some unfathomable reason, people who regard their time as intensely valuable (doctors, lawyers, etc.) when they work for other people or perform services, often discount the value of their time to zero when they are working for their capital. When you are thinking about investments, you are in a working partnership with your capital.

Few investors stop to ask themselves what this partnership is really netting them when, if considered in rational terms, their investing activities actually amount to little more than a part-time job "on the side."* To follow our hypothetical case a bit further, let's assume that you read the New York *Times* financial section every day (except Saturday) and *Fortune* every month. On the average, this might take three hours a week, or 150 hours a year. It will also cost you about $75 for the newspaper and subscription. On a balance sheet, our results will look like this.

$500 additional profit increment over random return
— 75 materials cost
$425 net before labor
÷ 150 =$2.83/hour

In other words, when weighed against the increased value of your investments, your time has a market value of less than three dollars an hour. If you make $6000 a year, this would be the equivalent of overtime without the benefit of time and a half. If you make $12,000 a year, you are selling your services to your capital at half their market value for your full-time profession.

At this point it might be well to point out that the hypothetical case is brightly painted, because the extra increment of return is *highly uncertain*. A novice investor is expecting to double his return merely by reading the New York *Times* and *Fortune!* Maintaining the time requirements already mentioned, the graph below indicates how much capital is required to justify your labor for the 10% annual increment.

Since any investment counselor would be delighted to virtual ecstasy to maintain a compound growth rate of 20% in the funds he manages, and since the probability is against a young man

* Do you know any lawyers who practice dentistry as a hobby?

TABLE VII-E

Capital Required to Justify 150-Hour-Per-Year Time Input Assuming You Can Double Normal Return "in Your Spare Time at Home."

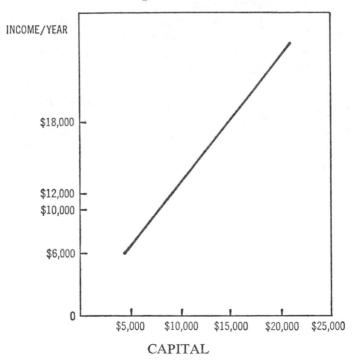

CAPITAL

having accumulated the amount of money available for investment that would be required even to meet our given hypothetical case, it goes without saying that on a purely economic basis, it does not pay for most people to manage their investments. If you are a graduate of the Harvard Business School or the Wharton School of Business and Finance and happen to have $250,000 or more idling in your checking account, it might be worth while to become a full-time capitalist. Under most other circumstances it is economically unsound to manage your own investments.

One might argue, however, that the initial underpaid period is a necessary training—a kind of informal apprenticeship. One might also argue that the stock market is fascinating and that it really isn't work. Or, it could also be argued that the comparison of investment time to labor time is invidious, because the implicit assumption is that one is available for work twenty-four hours a day at the same profession.

Each of these arguments has some validity and deserves attention. Few people who have had any involvement with the stock market and investments would say that it is a bore or an activity totally lacking in rewards, fascination, or challenge. But one must also ask, as he is taking the reins of his investment future in his hands, whether it is prudent to make a hobby of the economic security and future of his family.

Again, while it is true that no man can be working at one job twenty-four hours a day, it might be well worth while to consider why investments, rather than original employment, are chosen for additional work. Perhaps the willingness to put time into investments over one's career occupation suggests a need to reconsider one's choice of profession?

A visit to any brokerage office will reveal the small hordes of vaguely desiccated men who sit at the back of the board rooms watching the tape. Even the most casual of observers cannot help but suspect that the tape is the emotional cathartic of their existence. While the board room has the saving grace of keeping dirty old men off the streets who might otherwise be haunting the playground of the local grammar school with their Rolls Royces and pockets full of lollipops, it is also a reflection of a life bare of human alternatives. Shuffleboard has more genuine possibilities for human contact and drama, even if it lacks the glamour of the ticker tape. After all, what does it really mean when IBM gains ten points?

*   *   *

Let's suppose, though, that you are one of those strong and tough-skinned souls who can invest his capital with only one concern, having more money at the end of the year than at the beginning. The *Times* and *Fortune,* though excellent and informative reading, still amount to little more than a tale of the Stork in relation to the true facts of investments.

Just as a parent might tell the tale of the Stork to save himself from embarrassment at the hands of a precocious child, some embarrassed companies tell obscured half-truths when they report their earnings.

Standing between every would-be investor and the company he wishes to judge is a Kafkan apparatus, operated by gimlet-eyed accountants, known as the Annual Report. So highly polished that the smallest glimmer of truth would be blinding, so circuitous in its routes and reasoning that it would baffle the CIA, and so irrelevant in its content, is this rose-colored machine of deception that it is virtually useless unless studied for endless hours.

Worse, even when studied for endless hours, final perception of the company's true earnings is accessible only to someone with some expertise in the company's business. Without considering the difficulties involved in accounting for acquisitions, mergers, etc., let's examine the problems involved in a single-product company.

Depreciation charges can materially affect a company's earning power in the present. Since the depreciation is an estimate of how quickly the capital investment is being "used up," the estimator's motives bear some examination. He may want to give the appearance of profitability to an unprofitable company.

Computer-leasing companies, for instance, originated in a different estimation for the life of the third-generation computers. Computer manufacturers, with heavy investments in development and manufacturing costs, had constantly found themselves long on leases and short on cash. Pressed between ongoing research and manufacturing costs, the computer manufacturers leased their computers based on four-to-seven-year depreciation terms.

The leasing companies, however, are assuming that the computers will have a lifetime of about ten years, a position that gives them immense leverage and selling power in the current market while waiting to see whose estimation of a computer's lifetime will be most realistic.

Essentially the computer leasers are betting against technological developments that will render their computers uneconomical in the marketplace. As different analysts sway to the zephyrs of reason, the price of the leasing-company stock plummets or skyrockets.

This example is a rather well-publicized one. Somewhat more-esoteric problems arise when one considers the problems of "interfacing" the machines with their programs. Some companies may write programming costs off as they occur (i.e., they are expenses), while others may capitalize the development cost and depreciate the programs over a number of years. The difference in charges against current income can make the difference between making and losing money on the earnings statement. The company that expenses such costs is stating its earnings conservatively; in fact, if the program is good for more than a year, it may be penalizing current earnings for the sake of future earnings. On the other hand, another company may capitalize its programs over an unreasonably long period of time and thus paint a rosy picture of current earnings at the expense of future earnings.

The distant shareholder, in the fashion of the true capitalist, is predisposed to penalizing current earnings (rewards) for the sake of more-glorious future earnings. Raised within the Judaeo-Christian traditions, we all *know* that tomorrow's rewards are better than today's. While the corporate entrepreneur may share this article of faith with the distant shareholder, the tactics of further capitalization require a different and somewhat hypocritical stance: at the direction of management, the accountants must make the earnings appear as favorable as possible within the legitimate vagaries of accounting practices. In this manner, a dreary statement of net loss is transformed into an inspired account of innovative profits. The company report has a tendency to degenerate into a public-relations device.

The spectrum of juggled numbers neatly columned in shiny annual reports is little more than a response to the problem of keeping existing shareholders happy while attracting new ones at the same time. In the ideal corporate world, capital is raised through retention of earnings and debt financing, but this ideal is in conflict with the intimate relationship of technology to capital concentration. Increasingly, competitive necessity requires more equity capital. And that requires the full use of accounting vagaries.

When the corporate entrepreneur opts for the less conservative of the accounting practices, he is essentially taking a pragmatic stand: "the end justifies the means." Unfortunately, the investment end does not always justify the means. Today's account of innovative profits may very well be cited tomorrow as the root cause of bankruptcy.

Since these reports represent the corporate solution to the problem of satisfying existing stockholders while attracting new ones, we can make a few intuitive guesses about whose reports say what. A large company with a wide distribution of distant shareholders must, of necessity, give greater weight to existing shareholders even if this comes at the expense of capital expansion. Conversely, the more-intimately involved shareholders of a smaller enterprise will be more likely to approve "way out" accounting practices on pragmatic grounds. The company is the same, no matter which way you add up the numbers that describe it; this being the case, company reports are seen increasingly as a marketing device and, as such, have numbers that are added according to the rule of Least Resistance, Greatest Need.

To elaborate on the rather glib statements above would require a text on accounting and corporate relations. For the most part, however, the accounting of the company is a matter of indifference, provided it is consistent (an IRS requirement) and reasonably sane. The vast majority of business enterprises are that— consistent and reasonably sane.

While sophistication may provide some calculus of investment value for the economist, the marketplace has a depressing tendency to ignore this sublime calculation.

Sophistication may be an asset of debatable value, but it is entirely clear that the investor must at least have lost enough innocence to acknowledge the fact that a Proper Accounting and Approval by Peat, Marwick, Mitchell & Co. says more about the arithmetic skills of Peat, Marwick, and Mitchell than it does about the prospects and profits of Transylvanian Night Flights, Inc.

A few blatant examples:

The company had a product that was going to Revolutionize Absolutely Everything. In short, it was the Xerox of the Moment, and the Earnings Report hinted at the same. A closer look, however, revealed that *all profits* had come from the sale of limited production rights for the product. The product itself had been produced at a loss! Moreover, the company that had bought the partial production rights was owned by the son-in-law of Revolutionary Product, Inc. Since the President of RP owned 20% of the company, and since the stock was selling at forty times earnings, every dollar put into earnings by the sale of rights was worth forty times that when reflected in the price of the stock, even considering the dilution caused by his 20% ownership, an 800% profit is still a handsome return on investment!

The stocks of franchising companies have had considerable play in the past two years. Some have become so extravagantly priced in relation to earnings, that serious attention has been focused on an otherwise rather drab gathering of food marketeers. Not only are some of their fundamental accounting practices highly dubious, but so are the activities of a few founding fathers.

The following indicates the nature of the bad smell.

High annual growth rates can be had by either rapid increases in the earnings of operating franchises or rapid increases in the number of franchises sold. Some franchises, sorely tempted by the glorious heights promised for the price of their stock, are tempted to increase franchise sales irresponsibly. Performance Systems, formerly Minnie Pearl's Chicken Systems(!) had sold some 1200 franchise outlets by 1968 but had only 120 operating. Of those sold, a good number were sold to companies established by individuals close to the company who purchased the franchise wholesale with 30% cash and a note for the balance. Since then, many of the operating franchises have closed, and earnings that were taken on the basis of notes have entirely disappeared— along with the price of the stock.

Even the name is a little dubious: Performance Systems obviously has more dramatic appeal than Minnie Pearl's Chicken Systems. (How about Capt'n Queeg's Quahog and Chowder Stands or Old Black Joe's Collard-Green Distributer Systems?) And that's why the company name was changed.[6]

Performance Systems, however, has no corner on the Dubious Practices market. Dangerously misleading earnings reports in the franchise group can usually be attributed to two specific areas: the manner in which the company treats the initial franchise fees, and the handling of the lease covering the equipment used in the franchise outlet.

Some franchise companies sell direct, single-location franchises.

Agreements are signed and money passes hands only after a proper location has been found for the franchise. Since the building and operation of the franchise is expected to follow shortly after the franchise fee is taken into earnings by the parent company, the fee itself can be viewed as the beginning of a "continuing earnings stream." The only problem here is that the parent company may overestimate its market, overselling franchises to the eventual detriment of the profits of all the preceding franchises, thus decreasing the wonderful flow of coins into the company coffers. At this writing, the American hunger for donuts, hamburgers, heros, and hot dogs seems bottomless. Regardless of the seeming unfathomable depth of this market, it does have a measurable bottom, and some of the many who are attempting to make their fortunes in filling the American stomach will inevitably (and ironically) starve.

Even if one takes the sociologically depressing view that the spread of franchising is following in the wake and economic necessity of the declining sole proprietorship, the increased volume of the franchise operations still implies that as their growth accelerates the rush of individuals to the protective net of national advertising and expertise, the ultimate number will be smaller than the present.[7]

If the future of the more conservative franchise operations is fraught with dangers and pitfalls, then what of those involved in dubious practices? Some of the franchise companies sell the franchises wholesale by geographical area. A cosmetic franchise buyer once told me that he had bought the entire state of Connecticut for four cents a person! The franchise fee is taken immediately into earnings, but, unlike their more conservative rivals, there is no guarantee that further earnings will develop within a year. In fact, there is no guarantee that the franchise operations will ever be established!

The second major area of dubious practice is the manner in which the lease or note covering the equipment used in the franchise outlet is incorporated into earnings. A specialty sandwich shop franchiser recently made some interesting changes in their accounting methods that will have a dramatic effect on earnings.

In the past, the company took $30,000 into income for the sale of each franchise. Although the apparent fees have actually been reduced, the company will now take $100,000 into earnings for each franchise sold!

How?

Simple.

Previously, the company's $30,000 per franchise was received in the following amounts: $10,000 down payment, $10,000 initial franchise fee, and a security deposit covering the leased equipment in the amount of $10,000. Since the change in accounting, the initial franchise fee has been increased to $25,000, while the down payment and security deposit have been eliminated. As a result, the *immediate cash cost* of a franchise has decreased by $5000—a decrease that should increase their potential market.

This decrease, however, was achieved at the cost of a fifteen-year contract under which the equipment for the operation is leased to the franchisee at the cost of $250 per week. The company is taking the *entire amount* receivable under this contract into earnings *immediately!* The contract, whose gross value is $195,000, nets the company $75,000 after deducting $45,000 for purchase of the equipment and $75,000 for the company's expense in financing the equipment over that period.

One wave of the accountant's magic pencil has increased the *per-franchise earnings* of the company by 230%!

The only problem, of course, is that the reality of that $100,000 is contingent upon both the equipment and the franchise operating for fifteen years, an unlikely proposition at best. Moreover, the lease cost of the equipment is such that it may well put a strain on the profitability of the franchise: it certainly puts a strain on the paternalism and raison d'être for franchise operations. Since our franchise buyer could pay off his $45,000 equipment loan in less than four years on an 8% bank loan and save himself almost $140,000 in lease fees, *the decreased risk of a franchise over a sole proprietorship is being paid for very dearly.* Since an awareness of such facts is bound to spread, it may well sour the prospects of good and bad franchise operations alike . . . and the price of their stocks as well.

At this point, the reader is probably reconsidering the virtues of life insurance or wondering which mattress should be devoted to savings. My purpose, however, has not been to dissuade readers from investing in common stocks, but to illustrate, with a few extreme examples, the dangers and pitfalls of investing without a thorough understanding of both the specific security and the type of business the company performs.

Strangely, people who ponder and compare for months before they buy a new car or look for years before they buy a new house will often invest their money with the casualness of Gatsby. Perhaps this casualness is an expression of exaggerated relief, having at last found an expenditure that will not involve us in further expenditures. This is the only real difference in the two expenses—one commits us to variable further expenses while the other offers the possibility of returning us some (variable) income.

It is astounding to see how cavalier and casual otherwise oppressively prudent people can become. Investments seem to be a kind of nervous outlet for a spontaneity many are afraid to express in more-mundane circumstances. Somewhat more ominously, since investments are future-oriented by definition, the casualness of many may indicate how thoroughly most people discount the future.

On the other hand, if the explanation is relief, then it is also some indication of how thoroughly consumerized we are. Since we are constantly involved in the exchange of our labor for goods that will sustain our labor or mitigate the discomforts of life, anticipating the further exchange of labor for services as a result of the first exchange, the process of investment seems almost wantonly profligate. When one considers that our employment security itself is related by national economic policy to full production and consumption, then the process of investment becomes almost titillatingly sinful and irresponsible.

The barriers to profitable investment—educational, psychological, and economic—are such that we would be wise to consider "letting George do it" and concentrating our time and talents on our professions and families. Propaganda of the mutual-fund industry notwithstanding, investment in mutual funds is probably the best solution to the problem of investment yet devised.

The best solution to the problem is to hire an investment counselor. Since most such accounts have a minimum asset value of $100,000 and have increasingly required at least $250,000, the number of people who can avail themselves of such services is necessarily extremely small—less than 2% of the population has net assets of $100,000 (houses, furniture, clothing, jewelry, insurance, etc.), let alone that amount in negotiable securities. The mutual fund is the middle-class access route to investment counsel. The ability to buy investment talent in increments as small as fifty dollars comes at the cost of a sales charge (load) for most funds, and direct personal contact with the talent you have hired. This latter cost may seem nominal at first but it has ramifications (dealt with in chapter 9) that are less than pleasing.

Picking a mutual fund is as difficult as picking a stock these days. Although the Upper Left-Hand Drawer Fund is probably the one you will get, funds come in all shapes and sizes: closed-end funds, with a fixed number of shares whose value depends upon the estimation of the market and may be above (premium) or below (discount) the net asset value of the fund's investments; open-end funds, with an expanding number of shares sold at net asset value, sometimes growing in assets to billions of dollars; and load, low-load, or no-load funds, the former being sold by aggressive sales forces motivated by commissions, the latter being sold as a by-product of a pre-existing investment counsel, or brokerage, business.

If the terms above classify funds by the way their shares are sold, we must still classify them in terms of investment philosophy and goals. With more than twelve hundred registered investment companies purporting to have virtually every goal other than fostering the transmigration of souls, the meanings and distinctions become finely delineated indeed. The spectrum from capital preservation and income to maximum capital gains is, in theory, measured by increasing risk. In terms of formal titles, the spectrum would run as follows: bond/preferred income, balanced (these run another spectrum), growth, and speculative.

No particular type of fund has proved itself best in all investment climates, and conclusions as to which type of investment philosophy is best tend to depend on which side of the Depression you were born on. Since risk is a function of market climate as much as anything else, any limited investment pattern, no matter how "conservative," can result in a loss of purchasing power.

The advent in recent years of young and radical investment tigers who decried the conventional wisdom of Balance and Preservation and declared that performance was the best measure of investment success, has shaken the investment community. Depression survivors now gleefully point out that the Performance People got their comeuppance in the whipsaw and declining markets of '68, '69, and '70. The final story is yet to be told.

From a pragmatic point of view, the debate has little relevance to the problem at hand because it is a statistically verifiable fact that, on the average, investment results bore little relation to investment intentions. Over the long run, most funds, regardless of their name, specialty, or object, produce results that are astoundingly similar. Likewise, there is *no statistical evidence* to suggest that *load* funds perform any better than *no-load* funds: they have more money because they are more aggressively marketed.

Worse, there is some indication that professional management isn't worth all that much. While some funds can, and do, rack up outstanding gains from time to time, few are capable of sustaining large gains over substantial periods of time. Michael Jensen, an economist, concludes his study of mutual fund performance with the following comment:

> The evidence on mutual fund performance discussed above indicates not only that these 115 mutual funds were *on average* not able to predict security prices well enough to outperform a buy-the-market-and-hold policy, but also that there is very little evidence that any *individual* fund was able to do significantly better than that which we expected from mere random chance. It is also important to note that these conclusions hold *even* when we measure the fund returns gross or management expenses (that is, assume their bookkeeping, research, and other expenses except brokerage commissions were obtained free). Thus on average the funds apparently were not quite successful enough in their trading activities to recoup even their brokerage expenses.
>
> It is also important to remember that we have not considered in this paper the question of diversification. Evidence reported elsewhere indicates the funds on average have done an excellent job of minimizing the "insurable" risk borne by their shareholders.

Thus the results reported here should not be construed as indicating the mutual funds are not providing a socially desirable service to investors; that question has not been addressed here. The evidence does indicate, however, a pressing need on the part of the funds themselves to evaluate much more closely both the cost and the benefits of their research and trading activities in order to provide investors with maximum possible returns for the level of risk undertaken.[8]

Now that we have surveyed the given statistical facts, we can make some final weighing of the pros and cons—and alternatives —of mutual fund investments. We know that barring unusual misfortune or luck in selection we can count on a long-range pre-tax return of about 9% compounded. We also know that a combination of growth orientation, the $100 dividend exclusion, and favorable treatment of capital gains, will diminish the effects of taxation on our rate of return until we are well into our investment program. Moreover, we know that it is National Policy to maintain employment by maintaining production and that this policy will have the long-range effect of increasing industrial production and corporate capital bases (hence stock prices) while decreasing the value of the dollar. In measuring the risks of capital investment against the virtual certainty of inflation, we find the risk justified by the increased return. In any case, as indicated before, the return is necessitated by our retirement needs.

In addition to being the only mode of investment discussed so far that meets our long-range requirements and the problems posed by reality, mutual funds offer liquidity, the possibility of investing in convenient increments, and the built-in advantages of dollar cost averaging.

Mutual funds, because they can be purchased on a monthly or a quarterly basis in amounts that fit the surplus income of the investor, are an ideal vehicle for dollar cost averaging. By investing a constant number of dollars in stocks that vacillate in price, the investor is buying more shares when prices are down and fewer when prices are up. The net effect is to lower the average purchase price on the stock, thus diminishing net losses in down markets and exaggerating the gains in upward markets.

TABLE VII-F
Dollar Cost Averaging

As the accompanying chart and table reveal, the practice of dollar cost averaging does not remove the possibility of loss when the market is below the average cost, but it clearly demonstrates that the successful prosecution of the method will lessen the amount of loss in declining markets and increase the opportunities for greater profit in rising markets. It further establishes that, (1) the average dollar cost will be below the average price of market fluctuations; (2) the fluctuations in in the average dollar cost will be narrow in comparison with actual market fluctuations and that (3) by lowering the average dollar cost the investment income yield will be increased. It is the mathematical means by which the risk of market fluctuations may be turned into a definite investment advantage and removes the hazards of guessing markets by recognizing that "time, not timing" is the secret of investment success.

Instead of buying 120 shares with $1200 as an investment, $100 is invested 12 times at reasonably regular periods of time with the following results:

(1) At point (3) the market has declined 50%, but a loss of only 29% is sustained.

(2) At point (4) the market is down 60% but the loss has been confined to only 32.5%.

(3) At point (7) the market has recovered to the original starting point, but instead of just being even, a profit of 57% could be realized.

(4) At point (12) the market is off 20% and an original investment of $1200 in 120 shares would indicate a loss of $240, but the systematic purchases would have resulted in an accumulation of 200 shares with a profit of $400.

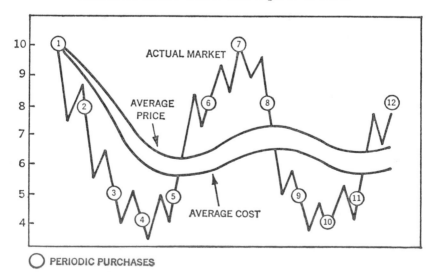

DOLLAR AVERAGE COST

INVEST-MENT	TOTAL INVESTED	MARKET PRICE	SHARES BOUGHT	TOTAL SHARES	AVERAGE PRICE	AVERAGE COST	MARKET VALUE	PROFIT (LOSS)
1.	$100	$ 100	$10	10.0	10.	$10.00	$10.00	$ 100.00	$ —
2.	$100	200	8	12.5	22.5	9.00	8.89	180.00	(20.00)
3.	$100	300	5	20.0	42.5	7.67	7.06	212.50	(87.50)
4.	$100	400	4	25.0	67.5	6.75	5.93	270.00	(130.00)
5.	$100	500	5	20.0	87.5	6.40	5.71	437.50	(67.50)
6.	$100	600	8	12.5	100.0	6.67	6.00	800.00	200.00
7.	$100	700	10	10.0	110.0	7.14	6.36	1,100.00	400.00
8.	$100	800	8	12.5	122.5	7.25	6.53	980.00	180.00
9.	$100	900	5	20.0	142.5	7.00	6.32	712.50	(187.50)
10.	$100	1,000	4	25.0	167.5	6.70	5.97	670.00	(330.00)
11.	$100	1,100	5	20.0	187.5	6.55	5.87	937.50	(167.50)
12.	$100	1,200	8	12.5	200.0	6.67	6.00	1,600.00	400.00

At (3) market off 50%, loss limited to 29%; at (4) market down 60%, loss 32.3%; at (7) market again even, profit 57%; at (12) market off 20%, profit is 33-1-3%. Single purchase of $1200 at $10 would result in 120 shares with loss of $240, but 12 periodic purchases acquire 200 shares with profit of $400.

What most people don't like about mutual funds is the commission. Mutual fund salesmen like to pooh-pooh this cost by saying that "in the long run" the cost is nominal. Since the 8.5% commission is actually 9.3%, the cost is hardly insubstantial and must be justified by what it buys. If the fee brought any certainty of a greater return than that offered by the no-load funds, it would be justified. *But there is no statistical evidence to support this notion:* the average no-load fund is as good as the average load fund.

How much the commission can cost you in terms of your investment future is indicated by the following figures:

TABLE VII-G

AGE AT BEG. OF PROGRAM			COMMISSIONS INVESTED AT 9%
25	353	} $1/yr. commission becomes	$35,300
30	225		$22,500
35	142		$14,200

(Figures assume a compound growth rate of 9% on the commissions of $100/year generated by an investment program continued to age 65.)

Obviously, the salesman who argues in favor of the load fund is arguing for the sake of his stomach rather than your future. No matter which number you pick, commissions amount to the start of a significant investment program in themselves and should not be written off lightly.[9]

One mutual fund liability the salesman in unlikely to mention is the fact that net asset value, the price at which you purchase your shares, is usually *higher* than net cash value. In some funds, *unrealized capital gains* may constitute as much as 30–40% of portfolio value. Eventually these gains will be realized and passed on to you as a shareholder in the form of a taxable capital gain. This pre-existing capital gain, however, will be a gain for tax purposes only, subjecting you to a tax liability in proportion to your tax bracket. In the 20% tax bracket, an unrealized capital gain of 30% makes you liable for taxes costing 3% of your initial investment.

The best way to avoid or minimize this unnecessary cost is to make your purchases *ex-dividend,* or shortly after the annual report.

Ironically, just as mutual funds are becoming a securities market of their own, some *stocks* differ little, in reality, from mutual funds—at least in several crucial respects.[10]

Although this notion of the large and diversified industrial company approaching the mutual fund as a means of safe investment has possibilities, it involves the investor in somewhat more research and understanding than he might otherwise need. With a reluctance that will be explained later, I conclude that mutual funds are the best investment for most people because they offer *security* as well as the return of common stocks.

The reader who opts for his own investment program must gird himself and learn. If you are willing to become involved in selecting and managing your investments, you must also be willing to consider investment forms other than common stocks.

Many people are attracted to real estate because it is so much more direct and palpable, an investment represented by stone and mortar rather than a slim piece of engraved paper stored in the recesses of a safe-deposit box. As an investment, real estate not only has all the upward potential of the stock market, but it also has the virtue of being relatively recession-proof—people will give up their deodorants and TV sets before they give up their apartments.

The real investment virtues of real estate are leverage and tax shelter. A third virtue, not easily had in buying shares of Corporation X, is control.

Leverage and tax shelter may be obtained by buying shares of syndicate trusts or limited partnerships. In ventures of this sort, the investor enjoys all the tax advantages of real-property ownership, but is not burdened (or privileged) with the problems of property management.

Direct control is hard to find. In a society in which it is an almost hopelessly aggravating task to determine who is responsible for what service and then communicate with him, management control, whatever the liabilities, offers the investor the unique experience of being in direct control of a palpable and real piece of property. The thought of finding such power so directly concentrated in one's hands almost boggles the mind!

Unfortunately, involvement in such control is manifested more often in removing forgotten socks from vacated closets than in the esoteric manipulations of finance, at least for the small investor. This conflict of being and image is seldom resolved until one experiences "being" in the form of midnight telephone calls in reference to an unfixed leaky faucet in 2-D.

Real property usually sells at a multiple of earnings running anywhere from one to eight, the multiple being a gauge of investment safety and quality. The owner of the multiple-one or -two building is easily distinguished in a crowd because he wears a black cape and a mustache. He also carries a hammer and a box of tenpenny nails so that he might nail shut the door of any recalcitrant tenant—after he has thrown the tenants' belongings on the street. This investor, of course, is playing a game of identity with his investments; just as the stock investor can play "my god, my god, why hast thou forsaken me?" the slumlord (as he is known at the local NAACP headquarters) is usually playing a game called "I'm really a good guy . . . but what can I do???" There are many ways to seek the Soul of Man. Looking through his anus is not among the best.

Reasonable risk investments usually start at five times earnings, i.e., the building returns 20% of its purchase cost per year before operating expenses, taxes, insurance, and maintenance. Since these expenses and a return on investment of 8½% would total only 13% in a good building (*Better Homes and Gardens* figure) and should not, in any case, amount to more than 15%, it is reasonable to assume that the owner's investment produces a cash return on investment unless there is something very weird about the financing or operating expenses of the property.

Cash return on investment, however, is becoming rare as multiples rise and investors realize the appreciation potential of real property. Most urban property has been bid up in price to 6–7½ times earnings, and costs so much to operate that it will not produce a cash return on investment unless the investor minimizes his use of investment leverage, i.e., though a building may produce some cash earnings with a 40% down payment, it will produce no cash earnings with 20%.

This change has occurred in the past ten years and is attributed by many real-estate agents to the demand of professional men—doctors, lawyers, etc.—for tax-sheltered investments. Less risky than pooled oil-drilling ventures, ranches, or citrus-farming combines, investments in real property offer a cash flow on investment by way of tax savings in a manner very similar to that on one's own house.

If, for instance, a piece of property is purchased for $100,000 and mortgaged for $80,000, the owner would amortize about 8% of the building's value in five years. Since his original investment is only $20,000, his $8000 amortization amounts to an 8% annual return on investment. This is his return if the building takes in only enough money to pay all the bills.

For tax purposes, however, the owner can depreciate the building between $10,000 and almost $18,000, giving him a *loss,* for tax purposes, of $2000–$10,000, which would provide him with a tax savings of $1000–$5000, assuming the investor is in the 50% tax bracket. Add to this return the leveraging effect of just keeping up with inflation, and the return on real property becomes very attractive.

Some observant readers who are looking for some kind of poetic justice to keep investors from making money coming and going will note that since the investor hopes to sell the building for as much as (or more than) he originally paid for it at some future date, he will have to pay taxes on all the depreciation he took during the intervening years.

True. But only if he sells the building. The tax can be postponed indefinitely—forever, if he wills it to his wife or children.[11] At worst, the investor has involved the Internal Revenue Service in a kind of investment arbitrage in which he has exchanged highly taxable earned income (say 50%) for capital-gains income taxable at a maximum of 25% . . . and he has enjoyed the profits from investing his tax savings over all the years between purchase and sale.

As people have become more tax-sophisticated, such mechanisms are increasingly used to mitigate the effects of the graduated income tax. At the present writing, the graduated income tax is a standing insult to the gullibility of the taxpaying public.[12]

The use of depreciation—on virtually anything—and limited partnerships[13] has increased to such a volume that the Union Bank and Trust offers a service to executives whereby it analyzes suitable partnerships and loans a good portion of the investment to the executive. The investor then amortizes his loan by writing a check for his tax savings to the loan department of the bank. Tax savings seldom amortize the complete investment, but in the highest tax brackets they are good for 60–80% of the investment!

While there are relatively few people in the 50% tax bracket, there *are* enough to virtually pre-empt certain investment media. The expectations of return in these media are considerably higher than the mutual funds and stocks to which most of this chapter was devoted.

So far, we have restricted ourselves to examining the pragmatic aspects of investment reality and our financial position, present and future. Not far beyond the crystal reality of the numbers, we have seen implications and glimpsed possibilities that need summary and exploration.

Only one conclusion is obvious: the forces against the accumulation of capital—inflation, taxation, return on investment, and conflicts of interest in the marketplace—are such that only the smallest minority of Americans will enjoy anything but the most meager retirements. And even this can be won only by fighting a dogged battle against the pressures of our own society.

8

I'M ALL RIGHT, JACK! . . .

"Saving one's way to capital ownership was never easy, but it used to be done just often enough to perpetuate the illusion that it could be done by anyone sufficiently toilsome and parsimonious."

—LOUIS KELSO

In the chapters preceding, we have discussed the commonly accessible varieties of economic experience. For the most part, these experiences present themselves to us *problematically* rather than *ethically*. Our final task is the summation of our numerous economic problems and an examination of how this total circumstance affects the quality of our life.

Unless we are blessed with an independent income, most of us have three major lifetime economic projects: 1) protecting our family against economic loss in the event of our death, 2) providing an education for our children (see Appendix C), and 3) replacing our earning power when we can no longer work.

No simple formula will provide answers for all people. Accurate solutions to the problem would require the constant calculation of an expert and a well-programmed computer.

In the summary that follows, we are going to attempt, in broad outline, a determination of our economic imperatives, based on a realistic appraisal of investment returns.

In the age range of 25–35, when we would need maximum protection and would most likely be least capable of affording it, even the least-expensive renewable or decreasing-term insurance costs .3–.6% per thousand dollars of protection. If we consider, further, that our coverage, as a general rule, will need to be ten to twelve times our annual income, we then realize that our minimum adequate insurance bill will absorb 3–7% of our annual income. Since ordinary (cash valve) life insurance costs about three or four times as much as term, it is obvious that such insurance, to afford adequate protection, would require impoverishment in the present, as well as pre-empting investment funds for

TABLE VIII-A

Social Security Benefits and Contributions vs. Income

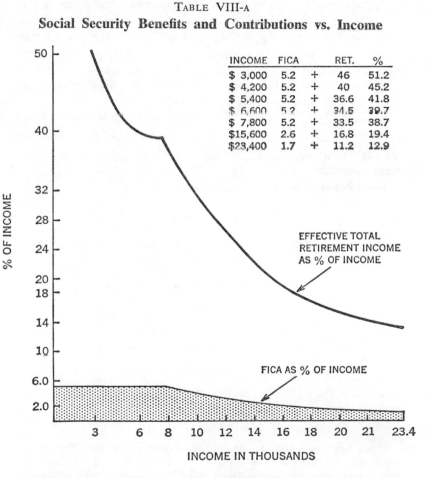

INCOME	FICA		RET.	%
$ 3,000	5.2	+	46	51.2
$ 4,200	5.2	+	40	45.2
$ 5,400	5.2	+	36.6	41.8
$ 6,600	5.2	+	34.5	39.7
$ 7,800	5.2	+	33.5	38.7
$15,600	2.6	+	16.8	19.4
$23,400	1.7	+	11.2	12.9

% OF INCOME

EFFECTIVE TOTAL
RETIREMENT INCOME
AS % OF INCOME

FICA AS % OF INCOME

INCOME IN THOUSANDS

(It should be noted here that the Social Securities benefits and limits are undergoing rapid changes.)

the future. Regardless of conservative arguments against investment risk, most people will agree that a positive risk is better than a negative certainty.

Before we can determine our retirement needs, we must examine what current expenses will diminish or disappear. Social Security deductions absorb some of our current income and promise to replace a portion of our income when we retire. Since our incomes will change from year to year over our lifetime, there is no final calculus for the relation of Social Security to our income. We can only approximate it. As our income rises above the limit of Social Security maximum, the proportion of our income it will eventually replace also decreases. The net effect of these two factors is illustrated above in Table VIII-A.

When we take our insurance and investment costs into consideration and assume that our mortgage will be paid off and our children educated, the income that must be replaced at retirement diminishes considerably.

But does it diminish enough? Example:

TABLE VIII-B

100	less	4.5*	S.S. payments, current
		26.0	S.S. payments, retirement
		7.2	Education fund, two children
		10.00	Insurance and investments
		15.0	Mortgage payments
		62.7	Total income not requiring
+++++++			replacement
		37.3	Income that must be replaced at retirement.

In the example above, we have assumed that the family income is $10,000, as in the insurance case in Appendix B. Insurance costs will absorb slightly more than $560 of the $1000 allowed for insurance and investments, leaving only $440 for

* This figure will undergo considerable change in the next five to ten years due to programmed changes in FICA income limits and an increased payment rate. We must also consider that 17.2% of income for insurance, investments, and an education fund is a substantial savings rate, one that few families can sustain. Fifty percent income replacement is a more reasonable figure.

retirement savings or about 12%/year of the income we eventually hope to replace.

Using our growth equation from the preceding chapter and adding a factor for inflation we discover:

Table VIII-c

$$G^N = 1/s^1/_W \times 1/(1-i)^n$$

N=40 at age 25	G=1/12/100×7/100 div 1/.45=264= 8%
35 at age 30	G= =240=9+%
30 at age 35	G= =214=11%

Since the compound rate of return required is *net after taxes*, it is obvious that retirement plans must begin quite early. It is also obvious that common-stock investments, although they offer the highest possible return generally available, are only *marginal solutions* in meeting the requirements of our general economic problem.

How each of us will fare in the achievement of these projects depends not only on the rate of return we achieve on our investments—which we can determine and relate to investment media—but to highly individual variables such as the age at which we complete our education, marry, begin our family, and join the working population. Accumulating the equity for the down payment on a house may absorb all surplus income for years, delaying education and retirement investments. The married graduate student/parent assumes a number of simultaneous economic burdens that will result in considerable strain in the present. This must be weighed against an earlier future decrease in economic responsibilities to children.

As economic projects are completed, more income is freed for investment or consumption. Savings that were pre-empted by the educational requirements of our children can be directed to retirement, once the children have been put through school. The same applies to liquidating our mortgage debt. Regardless of the fact that we cannot invest one dollar for every dollar released, because of the diminished tax shelter, our investment program can be substantially enhanced once these projects are completed.

This period of relative freedom and high investment, however, may be brief to the point of non-existence. Assuming that your last child is born when you reach the age of thirty, the investable income that child absorbs will not be released until you reach age fifty-one or older. Likewise, assuming that you do not move after age thirty, an extremely unlikely assumption, you will not be free of mortgage debt until age fifty-five or sixty.

The compounding effect is such that even though the amount of money you may be able to put aside will increase tremendously for this ideal fifteen- or ten-year period, it will not add substantially to your capital fund or more than nominally reduce the rate-of-return requirement.

The prospect of increasing earnings must also be taken into account. Those few capable of meeting their defined goals from current income, will find that all increases in earnings provide additional money for savings, thus reducing the apparent pressure for a high rate of return. Readers who jump to increasing future earnings as the solution to their problems must first make a serious and realistic appraisal of their earnings prospects.

A few fortunate souls can look forward to the experience of being able to finance their children's educations from current earnings rather than savings. The *Fortune* study cited in chapter 1 indicates that some of the over-$25,000-per-year families find this possible. The ability to do this indicates a surplus income of some proportion, and regardless of how its growth potential is reduced by the foreshortened compounding period, families with rapidly increasing incomes will be less pressed to meet their expectations than other families.

The important factor is the *rate* of increase. Few of us are inclined to notice our profligate use of electric power, the increased number of miles we drive, the better cuts of meat we eat, etc. *Much of our material improvement remains invisible against the backdrop of a constantly rising standard.* If income increases only with the cost of living and productivity, our increased capacity to save will not significantly alter our investment requirements, because our standard and expectations will be rising with the national standard. In fact, our lower savings rate in previous years will act as a retardant by way of weighting the compounding effect toward the lower savings rates of previous years. In any case, we have given no consideration to Parkinson's Law that "expenditures rise to meet income." . . .

Now that we are enlightened and can perceive the necessary trees in the forest of our probabilistic universe, rational self-interest dictates that we save the amounts prescribed in the manner prescribed. The problem is graphically summarized below:

The graph shows a family of curves relating age, savings as a percent of income, and rate of return on those savings. If you are, for instance, thirty years old and save 10% of your income, you must have a net compounded return on those savings of 6.4%, assuming that inflation averages 2% over the investment period and that you intend to replace 50% of your current purchasing power with investment income from an annuity at retirement.

Even assuming that most readers will have incomes above the national median of about $9000 it is highly probable that only that minority of readers blessed with generous parents, early recognition of the virtues of birth control, and Spartan self-discipline, will discover they are currently meeting their investment requirements.

Disturbed readers should bear in mind, as they try to rationalize past failures and gird for future savings, that the goals considered are not extravagant. If anything, these projects are modest and entirely within the realm of our social responsibilities as parents and citizens. Assuming successful completion of our projects, we would leave no vast material surplus in our estates: indeed, as constituted, we would produce life time material surplus consisting of no more than a paid-for house and our personal possessions. . . .

Looking beyond our own personal tree, to the dimensions of the forest, we find that most Americans cannot meet these minimum expectations, because they cannot invest. Although none of the many studies on saving agree on the precise rate at which most families save, evidence suggests that fewer than one family in five manages to save more than 10% of its income. If we further consider that fewer than one family in five owns common stocks and that most Americans save their money at *pre-tax* interest rates between five and six percent, it is clear that eighty out of every one hundred Americans cannot replace their incomes at retirement. Returning to Table VIII-D, the darkened area indicates how far away from achieving these goals most Americans are.[1]

TABLE VIII-D

Family of Curves Representing Savings Rates and Returns Required to Replace 50% of Income at Retirement, Assuming Different Starting Ages in a 2% Inflation Environment and an Annuity Withdrawal Rate of 8%

AGE AT BEGINNING OF PROGRAM

		25	30	35	40
	3	17.8	20.0	23.8	27.8
NET	4	14.3	16.6	20.0	25.0
RETURN	5	11.0	13.5	16.6	21.8
ON	6	8.8	10.8	13.9	18.5
INVESTMENT	7	6.8	8.8	11.6	16.1
	8	5.2	7.0	9.6	13.5
	9	3.9	5.6	8.1	11.9

SAVINGS REQUIRED AS % OF INCOME

PROBABLE MAXIMUM FIXED DOLLAR INVESTMENT RETURN

AGE 40

AGE 35

AGE 30

AGE 25

SAVINGS RATE

80% OF ALL AMERICAN FAMILIES

NET RETURN ON INVESTMENT

Some factors have immense effects. For instance, although those with incomes below $7800 a year have relatively more of their income covered by Social Security, they are least capable of saving and investing to make up the difference or educate their children. To make matters worse, such incomes are rather hard-pressed to find purchasable housing. In 1968 almost 60% of the population had incomes below $9000. Twenty-thousand-dollar houses are rather hard to find these days. Using the usual rule of thumb, only one family in five can afford the average new house.

Those whose incomes are more-protected by Social Security may be unable to acquire housing within their income range, thus increasing the income they will need to replace at retirement. Rather than amortizing a mortgage and realizing the paid-up investment return in the form of services upon retirement, these people, constantly growing in numbers, are facing a future of endless rent payments. For the six Americans in ten who currently earn less that $9000 a year, the growing housing crisis has costs far greater than inconvenience in the present. It may mean impoverishment in the future.

Just as there are variables that make for an even gloomier picture, there are factors that work to diminish the gloom. Company pensions and profit-sharing plans reduce the number of people who must supplement Social Security with their own direct investments. Likewise, government and institutional pension plans also mitigate the gloom.[2] Finally, state-supported schools and scholarships from all sources reduce the financial burdens of those families without the means to educate their children.

Mitigate, however, does not mean eliminate. By whatever statistical standard you hold to the economic realities, the majority of Americans—dishwashers, automobiles, and electric carving knives notwithstanding—must be considered poor, because they are incapable of completing minimal economic life projects. Not only are the odds against getting rich, they are also against completing one's life in reasonably middle-class circumstances. Given a variety of savings rates, inflationary government policy, and the spectrum of investment media, it is virtually impossible for all but a few Americans to prepare adequately for the future.

Reading the augury on a national scale, we have purchased the appearance of wealth by displacing poverty in time. To be old is to be poor. Period. Tomorrow is the day of reckoning.

Decades ago we bought the Consumer Society idea. We bought and overbought. Now we are grotesquely overextended.

One inevitable but fairly obtuse interpretation of the preceding chapters is that most Americans should entirely reverse their saving habits: rather than buy whole life and keep savings accounts, we should buy common stocks and term insurance. The conclusion is inevitable because it is a mathematical necessity; it is obtuse because it is a problematic response that allows an ethical void to continue. Changing one's mode of investment, aside from the cataclysmic economic effects it would have on the economy if *everyone* did it, could do little more than improve our relative competitive position with other Americans and our prospects for a reasonable retirement. It would do nothing to change our essential relationship—or our society—for the better.

*   *   *

"I'M ALL RIGHT, JACK!"

Hardly.

At this point, we must part ways with some of our fellows. Some will be leaving us now, in hot pursuit of more savings, higher returns, and, in general, the means to escape the statistical sink most of us find ourselves in.

Good luck to them. But we are left with a rather enormous problem.

What if everyone did it?

In good times, we compete with our socioeconomic peers for economic mobility; in bad times, we compete with *everyone* for survival. Regardless of the economic environment, equity and ethical behavior are, perforce, abandoned to a narrowly concealed economic animalism. The shape of life is technologically transformed, but the substance remains the same.

The classic hero is a man capable of sustaining ethical behavior under trying conditions, circumstances to which ordinary men would succumb. In the past, before technology revolutionized the interdependence of our social relations, the failure of any individual to live up to the ethical ideal was an occurrence that only lent brilliance to the beauty of those who did; today, these constant failures are not the setting for jewels but the seeds of destruction. The ethical failures of government, business, and individuals not only diminish the quality of life; they threaten its very existence.

Why? . . . A Larger Perspective

9

A NECESSARY
DIGRESSION
ON EXPECTATIONS,
VALUES, AND
THE TECHNOLOGICAL
ENVIRONMENT

The previous chapter is something of an embarrassment. Our neat examination of money has suddenly turned on us, becoming a Medusa of loose ends, requiring analysis and appraisal before we can continue.

Not only must we ask ourselves whether or not we are our brother's keepers but . . . who is our brother? . . . and do *we* have a keeper?

We can start by identifying our expectations.

The struggle to insure, educate, and provide for retirement while financing the present is the nexus of middle-class experience. These projects are the practical manifestations of values millions of Americans would identify as the cornerstones of a Good, Responsible, and Productive Life.

These values, no matter how widely held, are by no means universal. For the wealthy, retirement has been provided for by pre-existing capital, the funds for education are being earned by that capital, and insurance is not so much a problem of providing a source of income as it is one of offsetting the burden of estate taxes. Life has a different perspective; the wealthy allocate capital, while the middle class allocates energy. The means are entirely different, but the ends are identical.

There is a community of ultimate (. . . if not immediate)

interests. As good, upstanding, and diligent members of the middle class, we *know* we shall eventually be rewarded.

Not so, however, with the poor, or those whose identifications lie with the lower-middle class. Life insurance is a luxury for a man whose earnings are limited; whose job may be automated in a matter of years. Very often, education is the same kind of luxury, even when its necessity is realized. Providing for a distant retirement, to the man whose job future may be measured in months or at best a few years, is academic.

In the past, the technological environment was such that different sets of expectations could coexist; in fact, this diversity of expectations made optimum economic development possible at the historically negligible cost of social exploitation. A lack of potatoes in Ireland produced an abundance of railroads in America. Impoverishment for a class, still relatively better than starvation, led to a growing capital pool which was used to increase the productive capacity of the nation and, ultimately, better the life-style and consumption standards of future generations.

The technological environment, however, has changed, forcing an accelerating convergence of expectations. Those who opt to fend for themselves and ignore the larger implications of their economic surroundings are only postponing the inevitable. We shall all bear witness. And part of the cost.

As research continues, a growing proportion of our *human* productive capital—the total mix of talent available—will be irrelevant to the technological environment. Human capital that can be *utilized* will become increasingly scarce, altering the traditional power relationship between knowledge and capital. The factory worker with an uncertain productive future is raising children that may have no productive future at all.

No amount of discussion would produce agreement on what the ultimate goal of our social-welfare institutions is; direct observation offers one minimum standard largely devoid of philosophical implications: *No American shall starve in a publicly distasteful manner.* Given this standard, the future technological environment dictates that free food and/or free education must be provided at public expense.

Charity is the benefit the majority bestows on the unfortunate minority. As Americans, we prize our independence, our ability "to stand on our own feet"; we delight at the material bounty that allows us to give to others less fortunate than ourselves. We cherish our charity not only as an opportunity to manifest our compassion but as a means to prove our rectitude and the value of our central beliefs. The giving that is more difficult in times of scarcity is all the more valuable for the knowledge that there is no guarantee we would receive if the shoe were on the other foot. Our capacity to give with minimum sacrifice is the closing argument for the veracity of this "Best of All Possible Worlds."

Charity, however, is very much a question of proportion. In a society of ten human beings where one is blind, the survival of the single blind man proves the goodness of the group. The blind man is an unfortunate witness to God's unfathomable ways. In a society where nine human beings are blind and *one* has vision, the survival of the nine is no longer a matter of charity; it is a gift from the one and only true living god—the man with eyes!

At the moment, our society resembles that of ten human beings one of whom is blind. Our values reflect this basic proportionality and are propagated and enforced by our social and political institutions.

The problem is that the technological environment is causing a basic change in that proportionality. Worse, both we as individuals and our institutions have been reluctant to accept the implications of the changed environment. Perhaps the difficulty is that we cannot alter our values without damaging our egos, which are so bound to outmoded value structures. Whatever the cause, the practical effects are only beginning to be felt.

The game we play, Musical Chairs of Achievement, is the only game in town. We see our adversaries in the game and laugh in flight, even knowing that one of our number will be unable to obtain a chair. Our group solidarity is increased by the certain knowledge of scarcity, and the chance that governs its distribution and our fate.

The game, however, develops a sinister aspect when chance

is removed while scarcity is maintained. Suddenly we find ourselves assigned to seats as we begin the game; the game progresses not by competitions for a decreasing number of seats but by perception of an increasing musical tempo and the removal of a chair—with assigned occupant—at regular intervals.

Where scarcity is allocated by chance, society's compensation is called Charity; when it is allocated by design rather than chance and still called Charity, immense Power accrues to those few who are masters of the design. Power of this sort is the basic ingredient for paranoid technocracies whose ends are wholly unrelated to our human need for social organization.

Even if we adopt a more hopeful view of the inevitable future, it must be admitted that a value system that labels as cripples those human beings incapable of productive employment when they are, at the same time, the product of generations of inquiry, toil, and innovation, bears intense re-examination.

Where scarcity is the norm, production becomes an existential and moral imperative. Whether one is an American Paul Bunyan or a Russian Stakhanovite, the hero is the Producer. The man who is unemployable now or will become unemployable in the next decade is cast aside not because he is incapable of producing, but because his talents are inappropriate (or inadequate) to the methods of production. Although many people see some unemployment as a necessary cost of rationalized and efficient production because they believe in the primacy of production, few have altered their value system to accommodate this operational imperative. As a consequence, although the circumstances of unemployment are perceived rationally, the moral judgments associated with unemployment tend to be irrational.

Even though we know a man has been, say, laid off because of decreased consumer demand, we still secretly believe that he is a bum.

A man whose employment is limited only by his intellectual and emotional endurance is powerfully disposed to view unemployment with a lack of sympathy.[1] At best, the overworked white-collar or professional will tend to view unemployment in terms of charity. "There, but for the Grace of God . . . ," we chant to ourselves, burying ourselves in a kind of schizophrenia.

On the one hand we recognize the imperatives of the system for rational and efficient operation, while on the other we suppress the human origins of the system. We applaud the productive capacity of the system and our intelligence in creating it, yet view the freedom from work enforced on those whose usefulness does not meet the fine requirements of the machine as reprehensible and irresponsible.

The technological environment is the final determinant of our social environment, hence the efficacy of all our acts. In a world in which the game is Musical Chairs of Achievement ruled by chance, the primacy of our approach to economic projects illustrated in the first chapter is clear. All we can do is attempt to understand the environmental variables as they affect us individually and then seek paths that will maximize our performance within the caprice and constraint of those variables. We measure our performance by the sum value of our assets.

We find ourselves, however, in a world where the Musical Chairs of Achievement are ruled by design. This requires a complete change in operating perspective. A game ruled by chance offers latitude in calculating the net benefits that accrue to players of the game. Indeed, because the game is ruled by chance, responsibility for the sum and distribution of benefits is impossible to allocate.

Not so in the game ruled by design, for the design requires a calculus of benefits where those benefits accrue to individuals, to individuals as members of groups, and to groups as part of the whole.

As the production system approaches its boundaries of efficiency, and technology collapses time and space, the tolerance limits for this calculus of benefits diminish. Selective impoverishment is no longer an economic possibility, because it is too visible and too intolerable to those who must suffer it. We are, indeed, our brothers' keepers.

Failure to cope with this increased responsibility and discomforting relatedness can lead only to a paranoid technocracy—for only such an organizing mechanism could maintain the illusion of chance.

Intellectually we are all Keynesians; but for a few articulate though somewhat encrusted conservatives such as William F. Buckley, Jr., virtually all of us believe that the marketplace works to less than total perfection and that our political institutions exist not only to provide those services that are necessarily public but also to monitor, regulate, and, in general, nurse the machinery of business in order to provide an orderly (but not controlled) environment.

Our hearts, however, are politically positioned to the right of our minds. Though the "Invisible Hand" of Adam Smith has again and again proven itself to be palsied, spastic, or epileptic in action, our emotional insistence on the marketplace as the final arbiter of Value is a clear indication of our ambivalence toward existential freedom.

The marketplace is the Ouija board of the businessman; our business culture has made an altar of the marketplace, upon which the businessman places his product as a sacrifice. Disappearance of the product from the altar is a sign of God's favor; if it remains and must be swept aside to make room for the products of other supplicants, it is a sign of disfavor. What often parades as pragmatism in the face of an uncertain world, is in reality faith seeking substantiation.

God rules the universe of chance. Discussion of whether we perceive his rule as one of genuine chance or an unfathomable design we experience as chance, is the substance of disputations between believers and non-believers. Incorporation of design into the stated ends of human activity threatens both parties to this disputation and confronts us with absolute responsibility for our fate.

Our project, however, is not the psychoanalytic interpretation of history, but some determination of our relation to the world as evidenced by our economic transactions. The preceding paragraphs, then, must stand not as the final comment on the meaning of history, but as an indicator of the root causes of the current crisis of our social and political institutions. In a more specifically economic application, our cultural heritage predisposes us against Planning. While we pride ourselves on our increasing understanding of the probabilistic universe of science, we still experience our humanity in a determinist universe. Such pleasures of childhood, though bittersweet, are difficult to sacrifice.

*   *   *

Following the implications of chapter 8 to their logical conclusions will allow us to interpret our position more quantitively and less philosophically.

In chapters 1–7 we gained an understanding of commonly available economic and investment experiences and learned how to utilize them to our best advantage. We also learned the limits of what we could expect under ordinary circumstances. In chapter 8 we put all this together in an attempt to unify our investment requirements in terms of future plans, and discovered that we weren't saving enough money. Some were saving enough money but weren't saving it at the right rate of return. It comes to the same thing in the end.

We also learned that *most* Americans weren't saving enough money, regardless of their expectations. Very likely we could argue about the degree to which present investment will fail to meet the requirements of our future technological environment, because we could argue about expectations and the rate at which those expectations will converge, but we must certainly agree that in the light of future demands, we are saving less than we should.

Savings may be increased to appropriate levels either publicly or privately. Either way would result in decreased consumption, because people would defer present purchases for the sake of increased saving. In the standard economic scenario, decreased consumption would result in decreased income, the amount to be determined as a multiple of the increased savings. In the economic environment of the nineteen seventies, such an increase in savings might diminish the capital shortage, thereby minimizing the decreased-income effect. Since the long-term effect of the increased savings would be to guarantee the consumption standards of individuals, the deprivations of the short term must be weighed against the increased long-term consumption and income. Unfortunately, the measuring scale is a political one. Such scales favor the short term.

We must also, however, consider the *mechanism* by which savings would be increased. We could rely on individuals to save more, once they have been educated to the need for greater savings. There is, of course, no guarantee that all people would save adequately, and many would argue against any such guarantee because of the negative effects security is purported to have on the human character.

Some attention, in all likelihood, *should* be given to the effect of our social organization on our character, but the conservatives' argument intrinsically negates the function of our institutions. What, if anything, do our political and social institutions exist for but to implement programs deemed necessary for the general social good?

On a more practical level, perhaps we should consider the consequences of allowing such matters to remain in private hands. If we once agree that individuals must save more to maintain themselves and perpetuate the economy, how will industries dependent upon consumer purchases react? If tax dollars are appropriated to educate people to the necessity of greater savings, then industries dependent upon such expenditures will surely increase their appropriations, urging people to spend and consume rather than save. The battle for our collective economic futures will be fought in the already overtaxed public mind.

It isn't overly cynical to imagine the Congress, in mediating an "intelligent compromise" between the public and the interests of our corporations, passing a bill that would require all Consumer Products to be branded with the following label:

CAUTION: PURCHASE OF THIS PRODUCT MAY BE DETRIMENTAL TO YOUR FUTURE PLANS.

Such a gesture, embodying the current concept of the political Mandate, would, of course, be wantonly empty.

Worse, we must also consider that our problem involves not only the amount of money people save, but the rate of return they obtain.

Since it has been demonstrated that the generally conceded rate of savings would require the high compound rate of return generally available only in common stocks and real-estate investments, we must, of necessity, envision a long-term flow of funds from fixed dollar investments to equities. Though this flow would ultimately reach some kind of equilibrium, the ramifications of this flow are enormous. Savings and loan associations, mutual banks, credit unions, and commercial banks would suffer an immense drain of funds. Life-insurance companies would experience an immense increase in demand for policy loans. To some degree, this has been the experience of these institutions in the past three years—inflationary expectations and tight money have caused a shift of savings dollars from these institutions to investments such as corporate bonds, etc., all in search of a return that will compensate for inflation.

In the unlikely event that the government was successful in urging people to save more money, we could expect permanent alteration of our money markets, the debt/equity structure of corporations, etc. Housing, one of our most pressing social needs, would be crippled. If financing were available at all, it would come at such a price that individually owned houses would indeed become, as envisioned in chapter 5, an upper-middle-class status symbol.

Another factor we have neglected in considering increased private savings, is that individuals can be coerced not only by external mechanisms such as advertising but by an even subtler coercion in the form of a consumption standard that attends a given job. The consumption standard of an office clerk is not dictated by his job but *limited* by it; as an employee, he is constantly forced to measure his wants against his capacity to satisfy them. In some occupations, however, the job itself dictates the standard of consumption. Where income is ample to fulfill the standard, the coercion is manifested through control of what is consumed; where income is inadequate to meet the consumption standard, the worker is forced on a treadmill of increasing debt. Though the story is most likely apocryphal, it has been rumored that General Motors grooms its executives by placing them in jobs in which the consumption standard associated with the job is far beyond the income attached to the job; the man's future is then determined by how well he handles his debt/equity ratio, negative cash flow, and the inevitable stress of being in such a position!

As the economy moves from manufacturing to service (or from primary to tertiary and quarternary employment, in the terminology of futurist H. Kahn), we can expect more jobs with associated consumption standards. Since future survival is academic unless present survival is assured, and since most of us depend upon jobs for survival, there is every reason to expect, regardless of the possible negative effect on our psyches, that the economic requirements of the production mechanism will pre-empt the human need for future planning. All one has to do to remain Free for the present or the future is . . . work. . . .

Our alternative to savings by chance is savings by design through expansion of the Social Security system. Since the current maximum benefits hover at the officially defined poverty level and diminish at a confiscatory rate as the beneficiary's earned income rises, one can only assume that the end goals of the system are three fold: 1) to minimize publicly distasteful starvation, 2) to encourage private investment (since only unearned income can be received without a reduction of benefits), and 3) to encourage a reduction in older workers to make room for younger workers entering the economy.

Neither of the first two goals has met with much success. The first has been approximated by the creation and expansion of numerous state and local welfare agencies which supplement the meager provisions of Social Security payments, while the second, though increased, has been considerably attenuated by pressures to consume.

The third goal is positive only to the degree that the first and second are met, thereby eliminating the deprivation that would result from elimination from the work force. Although this final goal has met with substantial success, it has done so at the expense of the living standards of those forcefully retired.

If the Social Security system were expanded to include more of the working population, proportionately greater income coverage for death, disability, or retirement, as well as allowances for education and re-education costs, it would need substantially more revenues than it currently receives. Existing financial institutions would suddenly find themselves cut off from their normal supply of funds. Life, casualty, and medical insurance companies would be hard-pressed to generate new business because their services would be essentially redundant. The indignation at government interference would swell the public press with letters and advertisements "in the public interest" signed by austere, concerned, and prudent executives from insurance companies and savings banks. The indignation would be exceeded only by the volume of insinuations threatening creeping socialism, welfare statism, and the apocalyptic arrival of the Last Great Congressional Pork Barrel.

While the finality of the awesome power that would then accrue to central government is anxiety-provoking in even the most rabidly liberal hearts, we must also admit that the arguments of the suddenly disempowered insurance and bank executives all rest on the sanctity of the proposition that Profits, like Motherhood, are inherently Good. Unfortunately, the real world disallows such simplistic truisms: Motherhood is best when wanted; as the reader has seen in the preceding chapters, the forced marriage of the consumer and the insurance and investment industries is troubled at best, and based on dubious legitimacy.

Though the preceding vague proposal is far milder than Robert Theobald's proposals for Guaranteed Annual Income and Committed Spending, the rage and indignation that would be ranged against it would come from the same source and draw on the same moral position. Since that moral position happens to be largely identical with middle-class values, the majority of the middle class, particularly the most silent segments, could be expected to align with the sanctity of Free Enterprise and Profits. We protect Free Enterprise and Profits not only because its implicit value system is deterministic, like our own, but also because we are protecting what we believe to be our own *future* interest.

Though our budgets and psyches would benefit immensely by relief from the responsibility of anticipating the future, we tend to view *others* as the ultimate beneficiaries of such a system. So, with righteous indignation against slackers, ne'er-do-wells, and grasshoppers, we opt against Planning and for Profits. God helps those who help themselves.

But who pays the bill when public suffering threatens the es-tablished order and decorum? Who pays the bill to rectify the defeat of Planning? Is it the insurance company that lobbies for maintaining its Profits? The securities and investment business? The savings and loan associations? Hardly; the bill is passed on to the voters who defeated Planning, the middle class. Compassion and reason somehow always seem to get lost in the shuffle of vituperation, retribution, and "I told you so's" that follow.

As individuals, we are powerfully disposed to both operate in and perceive our world as determinist. Our industry, however, increasingly operates in a probabilistic framework while wishing to be *seen* in a determinist framework. The reason for this split is simple: profits can be maximized most effectively by main-taining the determinist fiction.

The technological environment is rapidly moving toward mak-ing the maintenance of this determinist fiction both unwise and impossible; to maintain the profit system, industry will have to discard a fiction no longer useful.

It may prove somewhat harder to discard the middle-class value system. . . . To date, middle-class support of the industrial sys-tem and values has been based on two main assumptions: 1) that scarcity rules the world, and 2) that I, too, will eventually partic-ipate in the Profits.

Both assumptions have proven vulnerable to the changing technological environment. Both are essentially untrue.

10

GLORIOUS
DESTINY:
CASTRATED
CAPITALISM

Some errors are harder to trace than others because they lie not in the plan of action but in the assumptions that led us to create the plan. An error in basic assumptions, undetected, may condemn us to endless tinkering with the machinery required to manifest our basic assumptions.

To complicate matters further, a set of assumptions that is valid at one time, may become invalid as the plan of action changes the justifying environment. Horace Mann's assumptions that education should be geared to local needs led to a highly developed and mobile society. Thus his initial assumptions became invalid.

Our assumptions about our social relations and our relation to the world are less than clearly visible. Tightly wrapped in myth and homilies, if not religion,[1] our basic assumptions are seldom discussed, let alone evaluated.

The Horatio Alger series presents us with a complete romantic framework for the American Dream. Not only do we learn the glory of the basic assumptions, but we are provided with a concrete Plan of Action with guaranteed Success. One need only be daring, resourceful, and hard-working.

Both the assumptions and the plan of action are in doubt these days, but we still *believe,* in our hearts. Intellectually, we are more inclined to cheer for *A Cool Million,* the late Nathanael West's *parody* of the Horatio Alger series. West's ill-fated protagonist, Lemuel Pitkin, suffers a slow and picaresque dismenberment, culminating in his assassination.

I am convinced that were West alive and writing now, the story would involve the gradual and cautious accumulation of mutual fund shares and the final unplugging of the artificial kidney at the redemption of the last share. Lemuel's new fate is attuned to the present because it is more subdued and slightly anesthetized.

Whatever the environment, the true American Dream still remains one of Wealth, Power, and Independence. While most of us will rationally admit that there is little accord between the dream and the limits of reality, we preserve in our hearts a favored corner for contemplation of the prizes that will be ours at the end of the race. It is the existence of these secret preserves that clouds most discussion.

Critical interpretations of our economic system may be classified in two main camps—one revolutionary and one reformist.

The first camp: Our Visible Enemy, The Establishment Pig

The enemy is a system that enables a small group of people to control the fate of most Americans. This small group, less than 2% of the population, has working control of the American Economy. They control employment, the media by way of ownership of advertising revenues, and politics through donations, corporate law offices, etc. The general welfare of Americans is a secondary consideration to the continued aggrandizement of this small and special group.

Baran and Sweezy, authors of *Monopoly Capital,* elaborate on the means of control and manipulation by illustrating how the gigantic industrial enterprises controlled by this small group of capitalists have bypassed the effective control of the marketplace. Given that a few firms have virtual control of most major markets, it is possible for them to control both supply and demand; promote planned obsolescence, inferior quality, and sensory overload; and, generally, to manipulate the American worker/consumer in such a way as to maximize the benefits that accrue to the few in control.

In essence, though we live in an environment that seems to

burden us with an excessive number of choices, freedoms, and powers, we have, in actual fact, very little power or choice, because *all the important choices have already been made.*

The necessity of employment mutes much protest. It also creates a pattern of consumption; the choice one exercises in deciding to buy a dishwasher or a disposal is effectively meaningless, because both options are for *increased consumption* and the extension of the existing system of production and distribution. The same empty-choice thesis applies to the precious power of the polling booth; there is no real choice.

Pig or hog? It's all the same. Jest the fixin's tha's dif'ren'.

The Second Camp:
The New Industrial Malaise

The firing of Mr. Knudsen by Mr. Ford, Chairman of the Ford Motor Company, would be taken by members of the first camp as proof that the Owners, distant though they may seem, still hold all the trump cards in the Power Game.

Gabriel Hauge, President of Manufacturers Hanover Trust Company in New York, did public lip service to the same notion of power in disavowing any intentions of leaving for the Chairmanship of the Federal Reserve Board. Hauge said, "The Lord and the board (of directors) willing . . . I plan to spend the next ten years right here." Note that Company directors representing ownership occupy a position second only to God.

J. K. Galbraith, the most popular spokesman for the second camp, would dismiss these two items as being either exceptional or public lip service to a largely defunct but still useful deity.

In this camp it is admitted that wealth is very concentrated, but that ownership is separated from management hence from working control. The corporation is given a life of its own such that it acts to serve its own "needs," which are generated deep within the enterprise rather than monolithically imposed by the entrepreneur owner. The difference, it is argued, biases the modern corporation toward a longer-term and less anti-social view than that of the entrepreneurial capitalist.

The corporate imperatives under this scheme are: 1) a level of profits sufficient to preserve the internal autonomy of the enterprise, 2) continued growth, and 3) some control of market to facilitate planning and technological development. These imperatives necessitate the creation and control of consumer demand. This is accomplished through advertising and a complicated relationship with government in which consumer demand is regulated by tax cuts (increases), government spending on space and weapons, etc.

Both camps agree that the Dream lacks credibility; their comments tend to prompt feelings of discomfort and paranoia. Both camps question the doctrine of scarcity and the equitable distribution of those benefits that are produced by the system. They question, in other words, the two basic economic assumptions that define middle-class values.

Some of the more lenient and reform-minded observers see in the advancing diffusion and internalization of corporate power the genesis of the Soulful Corporation, a highly concerned and ethical body politic whose interest in profits is secondary to more-lofty goals. Profits, in this view, are useful as an indicator of operating efficiency. Any inequities and wrongs will be solved by what is obviously a painful "period to adjustment." Many pious ads in our national publications attest to the same altruism.

Viewed in this light, the corporation enjoys a certain philosophical sanctity. The updated Passion Play would involve the crucifixion of, say, Roger Blough of U. S. Steel, with the late President Kennedy in the role of Pontius Pilate. Such is the nature of contemporary tragedy that Blough survives. Other views are more malignant.

The proof of any idea, however, is not so much in its delicacy, elegance, or the completeness of its internal consistency—but in the tools it provides. Whatever critical position we adopt, it remains that we will *experience* all positions as identical or, at least, indistinguishable.

To most of us it would make little difference whether our daughter were ravished and tied to a railroad track by a single ogre with a black cape and long mustache or a committee of men in gray flannel suits. What matters is the ultimate arrival of the train and the fact that she was ravished!

It would be an emotional convenience if the crime were committed by one ogre with a black cape. Not only is it far more satisfying to concentrate our rage on one ogre rather than some amorphous committee, but we must also admit, as a practical matter, that while many ogres have been hanged, very few committees have suffered any such punishment.

Even our moral response to our experience is colored by the simple allure of the Dream. Ogres and heroes do battle at Armageddon, not committees! However gregarious we are in fact, however much our behavior is influenced by the opinions of our peers, it remains that the battle between Good and Evil is a solitary one, fought by monsters and saints. Armageddon escapes the inevitable dullness of war only by intense characterization of the actors. The far Left and Right both find their origins and power in the seductive appeal of this intensity. You know where you stand with the American Nazi Party, the KKK, and the Minutemen. And you know where you stand with the Weathermen. *Their* enemies have names and faces. *They* have a plan of action! Interestingly, they are far more adept at dealing with *techniques* than with *ideas*. Just as our deepest dreams influence our critical thoughts, our response to those thoughts is often the slave of another dream, a dream that all problems have *technical* solutions.

In the end, most of us feel confused. We feel inept, and suffer from a constant, nagging sense that when we packed our bags for life's great trip, we forgot something. Life is more disordered and sloppy than anything else. Acts are not Good or Evil, but . . . confused.

Regardless of how we read the theory—or what dimensions our alarm and discomfort assume—we can see some "hard" results. We can perceive a system *bias,* and we can see that this bias ultimately affects the quality of our life.

The origin of the bias lies in the relations of our economic institutions. Whether it is in the service of entrepreneurial ogres or faceless committees within the "technostructure,"[2] it has become obvious that the modern large industrial corporation has transcended the marketplace economy. We have further learned that one of the prime functions of government is the stabilization of *demand* for corporate products. The capital investment required for much of our industrial production is such that the erratic action of the marketplace is too great a risk: advertising is the first line of defense in transcending the market; government stimulation is the second.

Those readers who are in business or who have suffered the anxieties attendant on the recent business downturn are likely to feel that this is a distorted view. It is, but in a peculiar way. While we can accurately state that four or five major companies control 80% of sales in most major markets, and that large shifts in market share between these companies are rare and that they, therefore, control their markets and prices, induce demand, etc., it remains true that to observe is not to experience. Careers are broken and jobs are lost over far-more-trivial events than minuscule shifts in market share. As producers we *experience* economic life directly, particularly, not *actuarially* as economists and academics observe it. As consumers we experience what economists and academics observe.

Unfortunately, *the free market was the last and most pragmatic right of recall the individual consumer/citizen had.* It was his decision in the marketplace that determined the future of an enterprise. While some freedom of decision still exists, these decisions have little to do with the ability of the corporation to plan and make profits. Moreover, the individual who boycotts the marketplace does so at his own peril, for his employment is dependent upon its continued operation regardless of the products it offers. Because the marketplace economy is assessed as too risk-laden, it no longer acts as the final arbiter of what is produced and what is not produced. A marketplace controlled by the dollar votes of individuals can no longer change or redirect the momentum of the industrial system, because the marketplace itself has been transcended.

In controlling both products and prices in the marketplace, the modern corporation is more of a *tax-collecting* agency than a *tax-paying* body. Though small business can be adversely affected by a change in tax policy, our large corporations strive to achieve the maximum practicable return on invested capital. Taxes are passed on to the consumer as a direct cost.

The passage of the tax-reform bill reducing the oil depletion allowance from 27½% to 22%, has already produced rumblings from Dallas to the effect that prices will be increased. The industry intends to recoup the $235 million increase in its tax bill. The same threatened increase in prices is cited as a possible response to tampering with the oil-import quota system.

The oil industry isn't the only industry capable of revising its prices to maintain its return on investment. In an economy truly controlled by the marketplace, such changes would be diluted by competition.

We are all aware of how much employment depends upon adequate demand. As cited earlier, it has been an act of highest patriotism to consume. At one time, it was possible to identify a person's philosophical predisposition by whether or not he "lived to eat" or "ate to live"; one may require the other, but it is still possible to determine a priority. The same applies to the consumer/producer—does he consume to produce or produce to consume? Again, each requires the other: terror pushes, need pulls.

The cycle is strongly coercive, because employment is all-or-none. One either works full time or not at all. Increased productivity is translated into increased production, not less production time.

Although industrial productivity has more than doubled since 1940, the average work week has remained the same. The decision has been for *more things, not more time.* The work week for professionals has actually tended to expand. Although there are some options in the kind of work one does, there are no options as to the *amount* of work one does in a given *kind* of work. To question the supreme value of Work is to question the entire system. You either believe and participate or you don't believe . . . and you don't participate.

Our power, then, is only to consume *more.*

In an environment that is dominated by scarcity, the goal of greater consumption is a positive good. Ironically, it is the efficiency of our production apparatus that has given us a vision of choice. A man who is starving will likely view a machine that doubles the production of bread as a positive event; one who is not starving will likely ask about quality and the taste of the bread, and ponder whether or not it might be time to start building tables to put the bread on.

This difference in perspective consititutes a large measure of the "generation gap." A man who has experienced hunger is unlikely to feel enthusiasm for a hunger strike. The situation is very much like the one in which two people describe the contents of a glass. One says it is "half empty"; the other says it is "half full": the descriptions tell us more about the predispositions of the viewers than the contents of the glass. The man who has experienced "empty glass" is likely to use that experience as his basis of measurement; it is never 99% full—it is 1% empty. Emptiness is his basic existential position; hence the imperative to produce. The quality of Béarnaise sauce is irrelevant to those who have never eaten steak.

Abundance reduces the credibility of our singular imperative to produce More. *If some experience basic scarcity, then we must question the basic distributing mechanisms.*

Ironically, we find that while government has stepped in to guarantee some markets and buttress demand to enable long-range corporate capital planning, this very certainty has eliminated the poor as potential consumers.

Why should the farmer or food-products marketer worry about whether or not every American is eating well if the government underwrites the bottom of his market? Few Americans realize that the productivity of the American agricultural system has been underwritten by the government. Primary benefits for this assumed responsibility were given to the producers and profit makers. Secondary and sometimes dubious benefits (e.g., price stability) were given to the general consumer, and distinct *disbenefits* were provided for the poor. The very act of underwriting greater farm capitalization and productivity eliminated the need to penetrate all consumer markets; at the same time, government policy did not acknowledge the responsibility for having violated the market mechanism. Food for the poor is called charity; actually it is a by-product for a controlled market and should be supported by its primary beneficiaries—the food industry—as an overhead cost.

The same, though somewhat more complicated, process applies to the housing, oil, and automobile industries.

In each case, the producing consumer bears not only the cost of providing a bottom (i.e., a guaranteed minimum return) for the industrialized market but also the cost for whatever secondary distribution system the government establishes to guarantee subsistence for the poor. The latter get short shrift, of course, because action follows political power. The power hierarchy serves special interests first; producer/consumers second, and the poor last, if at all. With a regularity that suggests Liturgy, special-interest groups maintain that without this or that government support of their market, *employment* will be threatened: i.e., hamburger is still better than beans: the specter of joining the jobless poor awaits all those who protest the inevitable pre-eminence of special interests. In this manner, income redistribution occurs not between high- and low-income groups but between low and middle, impeding social change.

If there is a man behind us with a whip forcefully urging us to keep moving and stop grumbling, there are also some positive rewards ahead. Someday we might participate in the profits of the system. We might hold the whip.

Anyone can do it. If you don't start your own business, you can always invest your savings. As the reader has already seen in previous chapters, however, most savings-investment avenues lead to returns that barely support life, let alone increasing opulence.

Aside from the fact that most Americans are stimulated to want more than they can afford, it is virtually impossible to accumulate a large amount of capital under anything less than extraordinary circumstances. *The industrial economy is biased against such accumulation, for the simple reason that it can more effectively utilize the profits from increased consumption.*

What has developed is specialization on a gigantic scale; the corporation exists as an efficient enterprise for investment and production, while the individual serves as a highly efficient consumer.

In essence, an unwritten contract exists between the production apparatus and the consumer. We agree to the goal of More. We work and consume our way toward that goal, hoping that the apparatus will reward our skill and loyalty. To avoid the contract is to face an eternal damnation of conflict in the form of advertising and conforming pressure. Most of us choose to take our chances with the apparatus rather than swim against the consuming tide. In doing so, we commit our fate to the planning capability and social conscience of the production apparatus.

The terms of this unwritten contract would hardly be called favorable to the individual. We agree to do our best for the system, but the system commits itself to very little, if anything, in return. Even our methods of investment have been turned into consumer items.

Do we invest our savings in mutual funds or consume them? The mutual fund (read syndication, real-estate trust, investment company, etc.) is really an ideal product; it is the capon of the investment world. Possessed of all the economic benefits of participation in the growth of the economy, *the mutual fund holder is by legal definition totally divorced from the possession of any power whatsoever.* His power, if any, lies entirely in whether or not he decides to consume mutual funds or bread.

Since Regulated Investment Companies are constituted so as to prevent any *management* of the companies invested in, and expressions of enthusiasm or distaste for a particular enterprise are manifested by either a buy or a sell order, the investor is several times removed from any meaningful exercise of power.

Except for the entrepreneurial few who will form new enterprises and survive growth and conglomeration, those who expect to reap investment rewards beyond mediocrity are doomed to disappointment. Castrated capitalism is the ultimate consumer product; what few benefits that accrue cannot be measured in terms of character or power. The benefits take the form of bread. And more bread.

Yet those who view the apparatus of production and distribution with doubt or misgiving are viewed as potentially dangerous eccentrics or subversives. If faith is shaken by some embarrassing event such as the destruction of children's minds by TV radiation, much care is given to the delicacy of the system. The God of Production, we are told, works his wonders in unfathomable ways and requires an occasional human sacrifice. In the grand scale of things, the cost is trifling.

Silent complicity is evoked by repetition of numerous trusted adages:

"Don't Rock the Boat" summarizes that approach which states in one-syllable words that we live in a highly complex society that must be run by experts, not novices. If one presses, we learn that an occasional human sacrifice produced our breakfast.

"Don't Bite the Hand That Feeds You" admonishes the malcontent to silence by implying, more directly than the previous homily, that he is beholden to someone or something. Both adages reduce the importance of the individual; in each instance, he is smaller than the boat or hand he is declared dependent on.

"Never Look a Gift Horse in the Mouth"; though this saying can be used as an alternative to Don't Rock the Boat, its uses are potentially far richer and laden with deeper meanings. At the far extreme, one recalls Tiresias' admonitions to the searching Oedipus and remembers his horrible discovery.

Whatever the aphorism, those who question are swept aside as eccentrics or subversives, and we must admit a long-term indenture, if not slavery, to the primacy of Production. Children who question are reminded of the Depression. Those who are older should know better.

The voices of dissent, however, grow constantly louder, and we must all bear painful witness to the death of a dream. Our dream has been the end of responsibility.

In the world of chance—the world that preceded the world of technology, specialization, and production—each individual was largely self-sufficient. Once we dreamed of infinite riches and omnipotence! *Popular Science* and *Popular Mechanics* still do. So do most of our Sunday supplements. The day of the Electronic Eden is at hand. We have only to close our eyes and dream on.

Unfortunately, reality is a little more demanding. Life in the Electronic Eden requires an extended responsibility and leaves no role for chance.

As technology collapses time and space, the causal network that joins one human being to another becomes more dense and complicated. Though we may still debate the quantification of the system, we are beginning to perceive its dimensions. They indicate that any approach to abundance must be taken with a tremendous increase in social responsibility. We must all be our brothers' keepers, and we are all brothers. As the causal network increases, it becomes more difficult for any individual to remove himself, to declare that his welfare is the product of his own work and intrinsic worth . . . or even the gratuitous hand of God.

Our welfare is inextricably connected with the welfare of our fellows. We view the marvel of individuality across an abyss of interdependence. Rather than see the abyss and understand its meaning, many cling to the myths of the past—to the Horatio Alger legends—by viewing their own acts with an increasingly blind narcissism.

The crisis of our institutions and social order is mounting so rapidly, however, that it will soon be necessary to close one's mind completely to avoid realizing our complete interdependence and the contradictory imperatives of our present system.

Regardless of whether we see our production system as operated by capitalist ogres or faceless technocrats, it remains that we find ourselves in a position of silent complicity, with few viable avenues of correction.

11

AN ACCOUNTANT'S NIGHTMARE: THE ROLE OF GOVERNMENT

"Ethical standards in industry are distressingly
low. We're always hearing about 'crime in the
streets' today but crime in the executive conference room affects far more Americans"
—RALPH NADER

Fear of waste and corruption in government is part of the
American political tradition. It is difficult to avoid the suspicion
that some of our representatives consider their first elective mandate to be the confirmation of our worst fears. If many Americans
assume a distasteful and righteous stance toward the inevitable
moral corruption of government, it may prove instructive to see
who benefits from maintaining such a tradition of belief.

Is it the public? The benefits that accrue to such attitudes are
small at best. Moral indignation that is not followed by a serious
effort to rectify the wrong is nothing better than vanity . . . or a
shoddy rationalization for cheating on last year's income tax.
Only by succumbing to utter cynicism can we believe that those
in government enjoy or find utility in the suspicion directed
toward them. If congressmen and senators at the state and national levels enjoy the exercise of power, we must consider that
their power comes dearly priced. Life for most elective public
servants is a constant round of long evening meetings, longer

conferences, and even longer committee harangues, all seasoned by the regular flow of hate mail from illiterate constituents.

If neither the public nor those in government benefit from such attitudes, then who does? What other group is there? Again we find that whether one projects visions of capitalist ogres or technocrat committees, the result is the same: the intense organization of our productive machinery creates a constituency with very specific and definable interests. These interests are most efficiently served when government is viewed as an evil of dubious necessity.

In the most general sense, the interests of industry are continued maximum growth and profits. Maximum production is most efficiently achieved by maximizing individual consumption of products. Those products which serve groups of people (families, towns, etc.) are poor consumption increases, because they offer economies of scale. It is far more profitable to promote the ownership of private automobiles than it is to promote efficient and comfortable public transportation.

While it is something of a problem to put more than one turkey in each stomach, it is distinctly possible to urge the consumption of four personal TVs rather than one family TV. The same applies to sinks, toilets, swimming pools, portable radios, and a multitude of products that constitute the American Standard of Living.

Redundance, given enough advertising, is an adequate and profitable substitute for imagination.

Mass markets, however, require mass planning and massive investments. Ironically, government support is necessary. Our historic bias for private rather than public works has been supported by a tradition of belief in the inherent corruption of government. The concerned but confused citizen is then presented with a choice between the inefficiency and waste of redundant but righteous *private* production and the inefficiency and waste of corrupt government. Inevitably, we cling to our Puritan Traditions and choose private production. In this manner, Americans accept Righteous Indignation in lieu of real government services.

One concrete example of this relationship among producer, government, and consumer is the automobile industry. While federal and state taxation on income, gasoline, and road use financed the construction of a national network of superhighways and thereby subsidized the automobile and trucking industries, public and private group transportation languished.

Those who defend the continued glut of automobiles like to point out that Americans prefer personal transportation and are prejudiced against public transportation. Government inattention to public transportation, however, has produced this prejudice. Moreover, since automobiles are expensive, not all individuals can afford to support their prejudice.

We can imagine the relation between public and private transportation as being a kind of reversible reaction:

XI-A
Public-and-Private-Sector Relationship

Public⇌Private
Gov.

Government plays a role as a catalyst. Had the automobile companies been forced to foot some of the bill for highway construction, the direct price of automobiles would have been considerably higher, the market consequently smaller, and their utility limited. The individual consumer would have been in a position to make a clear and uncoerced decision between public and private transportation. The decision was (and is) coerced, however, because government policy has reduced the direct costs of private ownership by devoting tax dollars to the completion and expansion of the necessary road system. Since we have limited control over the direction of tax revenues, the net effect is to force the consumer to buy an automobile for traveling on the roads he has built with his taxes.

Government forced the consumer decision to favor automobiles. The rationalization most commonly offered is that though the decision was coerced, government support of the auto industry indirectly provided the impetus for large increases in production. The construction, building materials, oil, steel, glass, rubber, and other industries were given greater markets. Government support meant more and better jobs for more people.[1]

Those of us who are middle class now look upon our automobiles with misgivings as we ponder the time wasted in transit from city to suburb. We might also resent the increasing cost of gasoline, insurance, and repairs.

Some of the costs, however, are indirect. A recent study[2] of public transportation in Nassau County, New York, revealed that the inadequacy of the network was one of the major causes of unemployment among underskilled workers, who, unable to demand a living wage, found transportation to work (when available) prohibitively expensive. In spite of this, New York City increases its subway fares. In a city where living costs are among the highest in the world and 30% of the labor force earns less than $90 a week, fare increases can be the straw that breaks the camel's back. A difference of $1.00 a week may cause some marginal working families to decide that welfare benefits are better than working.[3] A decision to increase the fare without a subsidy sometimes only worsens the problem of financing public transportation, because more people opt for private transportation as the fare increases; i.e., higher fares=fewer fares=no change in total revenue=continuing deficit. The problem of balancing the public-transportation budget still remains, but more people have been forced off the subway and, perhaps, onto welfare or into their automobiles. Some, like the elderly, are forced to stay at home.

The lowest *net* system cost may lie in providing a healthy subsidy to public transportation. *The cost of the subsidy is only one of many ways for allocating the true costs of an exceedingly complex social organization.* The tax increase to pay the transportation subsidy must be weighed against decreased costs of public welfare, decreased demand for road and parking space (and hence increased revenues from productive property), decreased automobile insurance and repair bills as smaller traffic volume reduces accidents, decreased city operating expenses as fewer traffic patrolmen are needed, decreased cleaning expenses as automobile pollutants diminish, etc. The list of areas in which *real dollar costs* may be reduced is enormous. The *social* benefits that would grow from such a subsidy are harder to account for in dollar terms, but surely the increased mobility of the poor and the aged is worth something! Surely the decrease in emphysema, nervous tension, and physical injuries is worth considering.

Whatever the decision, the cost is borne by the consumer. Many people insist that each of our institutions must be self-supporting, failing to realize that any social organization has certain costs. What does not appear as a cost in one way may appear as a cost in a dozen other ways. Those who insist on viewing each institution as completely isolated rather than as part of a complex social organization are supporting a system of belief at the expense of more-rational allocation of our economic resources. This insistence is the source of many of our self-fulfilling prophesies. The poor remain poor because they remain immobile and undereducated. Dollars not allocated to indigent school systems now are allocated threefold to welfare programs later. Righteous belief is supported at tragic human expense.

One of industry's Sacred Cows is the precious nature of consumer freedom. Regular advertisements in the media inform us that under some other economic system the consumer might never have the opportunity to decide between fourteen brands of hair dryers. Public services are derided as "socialism" and tools to centralize bureaucratic power. They rob the individual of his freedom of choice in the marketplace. The street, however, is remarkably one way. Just as Henry Ford once said that car buyers could have whatever color they wanted, so long as it was black, industry seldom protests government policies that restrict consumer choices by forcing the consumer to buy services from private industry. The consumer can have whatever he wants so long as it is *More*.

The auto industry is far from exhausted as a case history. The reader, however, may have noted that there is a family resemblance between the decision equation above and the examples of system environments in the discussion of the value of money in chapter 2.

Both illustrations are means of indicating that if we analyze our social organization as a system composed of competing elements and forces, we must ultimately find that the system will have a *bias*. The bias in most situations can be traced to those with capital. Return on invested capital is a priority claim. The graduated income tax has a multitude of loopholes which favor capital income over earned income.[4]

Most of us, with our identities rooted in the idea of freedom and independence, would prefer to believe that all decisions are firm and isolated events. Our interdependence has increased to such a degree, however, that no single decision is without ramifications. Each primary decision poses secondary and tertiary decisions. Subway fares can change welfare rolls, property taxes, and the concentration of sulphur dioxide in the air. A city full of leaky faucets and toilets can cause the eventual inundation of a valley town hundreds of miles away. Implications end only at the limits of comprehension.

Limits can be selected to favor different ends; within a given set of limitations, an industry can argue with force, vigor, and complete logic for a decision that can have entirely negative net results in a larger environment set.

Setting limits and allocating costs presents a real problem to the legislator. A young and highly respected member of the Massachusetts House of Representatives, one of the few who does not moonlight as a lawyer or run a business in his "spare time," once commented that of the seven-thousand-odd bills he was required to vote on in the preceding year, he had had time to explore the long-term implications and meaning of no more than thirty!

When we further consider that the interests of the oil, utilities, steel, and automobile industries are rather clear and deliciously quantifiable when compared to such vague and haplessly benign notions as the "general interest" or "the general welfare," Nader's statement develops an ominous tone. It would seem likely that the best even the most agonizingly conscientious individual can do is appear confused and "soft" in a world that favors "hard" answers.

Those who trust to Good Conscience and the growth of the Soulful Corporation to end such problems may wait a long time for their trust to bear fruit. Some examples of recent corporate behavior ranging from the sympathetically understandable to the positively malignant should serve to illustrate.

1) Paper companies along the Hudson River have been large contributors to the pollution of that once scenic river. With amazing constancy, the companies have pumped dyes, acid by-products, and wood-pulp fibers into the river, killing some plant and animal life outright and beginning the eutrophication

process, which eventually kills all animal life but the few forms of bacteria, maggots, and slugs that inhabit the fiber-matted riverbed.[5]

When pressures to install pollution-control equipment were mounted against the paper manufacturers, some mills announced that they already had programs well underway. Most, however, urged "further study." A few companies flatly refused to install the equipment, threatening to close down if they were forced. Such threats, now virtually traditional in industry that assumes the pre-eminence of production, reduce the effective power of state agencies because the agencies must weigh the long-term benefits of cleaning the river against the immediate pressure from local governments whose tax base and employment will be threatened by the closing of the plant.

Although the tactics of industry in avoiding the issue are pigheaded and shortsighted, at best, something more than sympathy for this view must be forthcoming from regional and national government. Some industries, paper among them, operate on such a low margin and return on investment that the transition period from uncontrolled to controlled production threatens their capital base. In some instances, the increase in prices necessitated by pollution-control equipment would price the manufactured material out of the market in relation to competing materials.

2) The oil industry, through the National Import Quota Act, has used its power to further extend its already extensive influence on government. The act serves to provide a totally artificial price support for oil. Senator Ed Muskie estimates that the cost to the average New England family, a high-consumption area, is at least $150 a year in artificially maintained prices. The same artificial market has made the exploitation of the Alaskan oil fields a commercial possibility: if the quota system did not exist, Alaskan oil would not be competitive.[6] The ensludgement of Santa Barbara has resulted in damage or destruction of marine life and a loss in property values. Complex technology is used to remove oil from the earth—but the methods of clean-up consist largely of spreading straw. While the Union Oil Company continues drilling and pumping, oil continues to seep from the channel bed, and the only solution to the problem

seems to be the drilling of more oil wells "to relieve pressure."
In a *Ramparts* article the process of relieving the pressure is
estimated to take upward of fifty years.

3) Perhaps the most malignant and gratuitous exception to the
Soulful Corporation is the organized action of lumber companies
to remove all valuable redwoods. The Sierra Club set out to
mark stands of significant and large Sequoias that should be preserved. A stand of record trees was found near the Nevada bor-
der. The trees were marked. When a survey party returned a
month later to determine the exact location of the site, all the
trees were *gone*. The lumber companies, as part of a deliberate
policy of undermining the power of the conservation groups,
have been cutting down the redwoods as fast as they are iden-
tified, so that there will be few, if any, to protect, when and
if the conservation groups ever get enough power in the California
legislature to protect the remaining trees. Such actions are distinctly malicious, lacking any qualities that even resemble soulfulness. . . .

The daily press provides an ongoing parade of stories about
corporations defiling the environment. But, then, it isn't necessary to read a newspaper. We have only to look around us.

If we look back now to our old notions about private goods
being better than public goods, we find that the issue has
changed. We no longer see struggling, upstanding, and independent corporations fighting the parasitic tentacles of corrupt
government. Now we see ruthless corporations reaping private
profits at the expense of the public environment on the one
hand, and the stultifying, inefficient, and corrupt agencies of
government on the other hand. Even in this most cynical light,
it is obvious that we must re-evaluate the role of government
and question the pre-eminence of private over public goods. If
we cannot have greater goods, we can at least strive for lesser
evils.

The industrial system progresses by manupulating and creating
consumer demand. Ultimate control of demand is placed in the
hands of government. We have consented to this manipulation
and control because we all believe in the primacy of production.
Naïvely, we have believed that whatever problems we had would
be solved by the wondrous machine of Production. Centuries of
history lend credibility to this idea. While our single-minded pur-

suit of Production has produced technological wonders, it has also produced a warped and tyrannical value system.

The system we need is one in which production and distribution are covariables of equal importance, maximized within the limits of our physical resources. A responsibility such as this cannot be relegated to the vagaries of the marketplace or delegated to the soulfulness of corporations. It must be the role of government. The marketplace economy seldom considers the secondary and tertiary effects of a transaction. Government can and must be concerned with such effects. It is the sum total of these effects that determines the quality of our lives.

Government that does not treat production and distribution as equally valued covariables is serving the production system alone. One further example should illustrate the absurdity that follows from our prejudice for private goods.

General Electric, Honeywell, and Westinghouse would be delighted to produce 200 million air cleaners rather than cope with the costs of keeping the air clean in the first place. If our usual reasoning holds, however, we would keep the chore of cleaning the air away from the inefficient and corrupt hands of government and entrust the job to efficient and ingenious industry.

Air would become an ideal product. Demand could be plotted against contamination and population. Senators could brag that unemployment had decreased due to increased production of air cleaners and that per-capita income had risen so that an air cleaner was within the reach of every American family. Or would be if they could hold out another five years. The approach would be lauded as the triumph of American ingenuity and industry, because it increased profits, production, employment, per-capita income, and the GNP.

The reader who thinks this fantasy unlikely should consider the present circumstances in Tokyo. Burdened with countless motorbikes and small cars and umbrellaed by frequent temperature inversions, Tokyo often has air conditions that are close to asphyxiating. The suffocating wayfarer is offered respite by the small stands offering a whiff of pure oxygen to clear the lungs. At a price, of course.

If we were to attempt to quantify our problem (a project this writer will leave to those whose election will soon depend upon it), we would plot, say, Life Support Systems vs. GNP. A more-poetic notation would be "Nature vs. Industrialization," but the phrasing invites arguments. Not everyone would agree that Virgin Nature is desirable. Our curve would look like this:

FIGURE XI-B

Life Support Systems vs. GNP

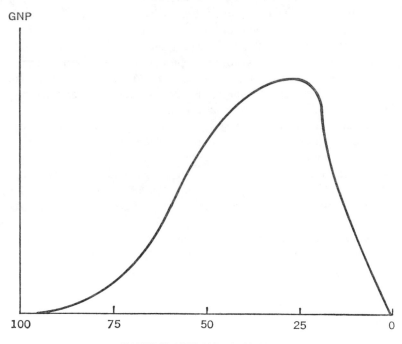

NATURAL LIFE SUPPORT SYSTEMS

The shape of the curve is determined by the technology available, and represents the limits of production with that technology. On the curve above, LSS begins to deteriorate rapidly if production attempts to exceed N. Since most production plants are less than totally modernized, we could expect that the GNP/LSS would lie within the given line rather than upon it.

We must also set two guidelines. The first is an estimation of how low the LSS can go and still provide for human survival.

Approaching and beyond this point, the rate of increase of GNP will diminish to zero and then become negative as human illness (death) and increased material costs reduce production.

Measurements such as those proposed above have ultimate relevance to the world after industrialization has reached some indeterminate critical point. A primitive society without industrialization lacks the production leverage to interfere significantly with the environment. Nature necessarily overpowered all acts of preindustrial man. We are now in a position, however, in which our technological leverage threatens the normal processes of nature.

The second is a Standard Life Support System line that reflects some technical judgment which maximizes life expectancy and allows a maximum diversity of life-styles.

Our graph now looks like this:

FIGURE XI-c
Life Support Systems vs. GNP with Standard and Minimum

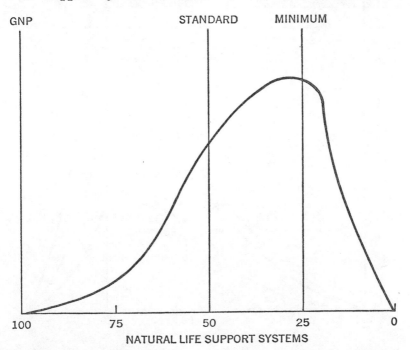

GNP   STANDARD   MINIMUM

100   75   50   25   0

NATURAL LIFE SUPPORT SYSTEMS

Since technology changes over time, we would have a family of curves, each curve representing the limits of technology in a particular period.

The GNP difference between the minimum and the standard LSS illustrates the difference between optimum human needs and the imperatives of the industrial system. Given the primacy of growth and production for the system, its goals are directed

FIGURE XI-D

Life Support Systems vs. GNP for Different States of Technological Development

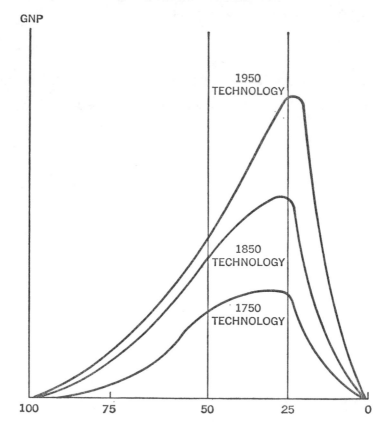

to maximum GNP, *a point reached considerably after human freedom of choice has been pre-empted.*[7]

The plight of the American Indian is an interesting example of this coercion of choice.[8] Confined to reservations on which neither the quantity nor the quality of the land can support the life-style of traditional Indian culture, the Indian must accept an alien industrial culture—ours—or perish. All differing value systems and cultures must give way to Industrial Man.

Although we cannot quantify the LSS, we can begin to assemble some of the elements that would compose it. Some readers, under the guise of scientific rigor, might protest that these elements are not quantified and are, therefore, impossible to put into a meaningful perspective. Such arguments usually mean, "How much is that in dollars?" To some vague degree, air, water, and land pollution can be reduced to terms of economic loss or costs.[9] But to rely on economic expressions of loss is to have missed a larger point.

Even in terms of the elements above, however, it is palpably obvious that if a line were drawn on the graph to show the LSS vs. GNP over a period of time, it would be below the standard LSS and dropping.

In effect, the gap between our decaying environment and the LSS standard is a form of taxation. The cost has accrued to the individual, not to the industrial system. Public pollution has enhanced someone's private profits.

The gap, measured by the change in GNP, is a measure of the rate at which we are converting the environment into dollars. There is a limit to this process. We may all face that embarrassing moment when the entire environment has been converted into purely economic values. You cannot breathe economic values. Surely that is not a world to look forward to.

How we perceive the system depends on where we stand in line for the distribution of benefits. For the moment, let us assume that we are all well placed in the line. Those economic costs from overreaching industrialization which are not deferred to the indefinite future are paid out of surplus earnings, and glibly accounted for as part of the cost of earning a living. Costs that are not specifically and directly translatable into economic terms, such as the loss of starlight and sunsets, are recompensed in proper division-of-labor terms by the mechanism of the vacation. Though we are slow to realize it, even our capacity to enjoy our natural surroundings is at first limited, then packaged and sold as an economic product.

Whether one views it in demonic, SDS terms or a more benign framework, our industrial system has clearly overreached its proper limits. It has done so, choosing the most benign viewpoint, because of our naïve enthusiasm for the wonders of technology and our innocent assumption that the endless resources of the world would eventually provide a bounty for everyone. Production is the cornerstone of our belief in the Ultimate Good of mankind; it has become a kind of Eternal Verity.

Those who question its pre-eminence are ranked with sodomists, mother haters, and fey lepidopterists, as representing either malignant forces of evil or "soft" visions of an unattainable world.

The upper-middle class, the largest beneficiary of the system in number and the group rewarded not only with the products of the system but also the means to temporarily escape the destruction it has wrought on the environment, is most given to questioning the ultimate value of the system. The middle and lower-middle class, still working to achieve and still feeling large unsatisfied material wants, is in the position of a man who is just learning to play poker well when the man who has won all the chips for the evening declares the game is really a bore and decides to go home. Is he right or is he just trying to keep his winnings? Cynicism will prevail in a framework dominated by want.

The problem of perceiving the necessary changes is complicated by the fact that those who have seen the need generally suffer from a kind of culture shock at having lost a dependable verity. Some compensate for this loss with the revivalist fervor of the recent convert. The god most hated is that which has most recently fallen.

Stated rationally, our historic scarcity has led us to a faith in production that cannot be sustained by reality. Our faith that equitable distribution will follow the imperatives of increased production has proven naïve. What we must change is not production itself, but its pre-eminence over all other values.

We can see the necessity for this change more clearly when we realize that production is not just a point on a chart but a shape representing the distribution of goods and services:

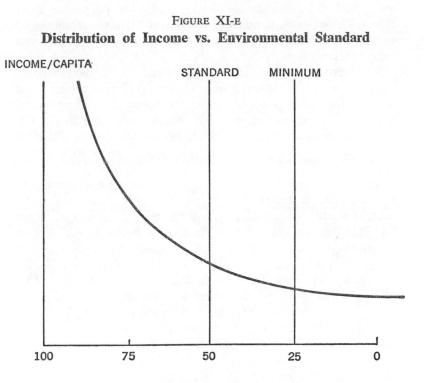

Figure XI-e
Distribution of Income vs. Environmental Standard

Each shape represents the distribution of goods and services over the population for a given technological period. Not only are the poor increasingly separated from the post-industrial capital-intensive society, they are also more dependent on it for their very sustenance, including the air they breathe.

The industrial system's power over the environment gives it ever greater power over our decisions. In a world where the very quality of the air we breathe and the water we drink is a product of technology, one has little choice about participating in the system; you do, or you don't breathe. Though posing the relationship in such an all-or-none manner may seem extreme to some readers, we have only to look about us. It was the non-productive elderly who died in the 1952 smog calamity in London. . . . It will be the unhealthy and unproductive poor and elderly who die first in the increasing air pollution of our cities. Those most necessary to the production system enjoy commutation distance as a reward . . . or a well-air-conditioned apartment.

To return to a more traditional, capital vs. labor viewpoint, we could view the overreaching of the industrial system as a form of regressive taxation. Profits and growth have been maximized at the expense of the environment, thus extending a diffused tax to the general population. Worse, the profits allow the beneficiaries to escape or diminish the negative effects of the environment.

These costs are incurred not only in the present but in the future. When it comes time to pay the postponed cost of industrial waste and pollution, it will be painfully leveraged. Since the industrial system controls prices and demand, the cost of pollution-reduction equipment will be capitalized and added to the price of products. The Harvard Center for Population Studies estimates that air-and-water-pollution control will cost $13.5 billion a year.[10] Since the price of reversing the damage increases geometrically with time and population, we can ill afford delay. Yet the bill for starting the cleanup amounts to a full 34% of our current real growth in GNP!

If we assume that return on invested capital is to be maintained, then the cost for this program will be levied in taxes against the producer/consumer—the middle class—and it will be assessed at a time when the average industrial worker has experienced no increase in net purchasing power for a full five years. Since the middle road of the Nixon administration will most likely dictate a play-off between direct tax costs and inflation, the net effects will be divided between the middle class and the poor, with the poor absorbing the larger part of the burden. Many who find their appetites stimulated by clean air will not have the means to fully satisfy their hunger. . . .

The barriers to change are nothing less than formidable. The tactical problems posed in setting limits on industry while preserving or easing the change in the market system and the priority of products are enormous. *But the change required in our attitudes is even greater.* Production must join the ranks of gods forgotten, remembered only as in childhood.

The philosophically inclined may fear the loss of individualism implicit in the necessary changes. They might cite that the power of centralized government is more dangerous than the power of special interests, that all actions intended for the collective good are achieved at the expense of individual freedom. Such problems are real, but they do not confront the basic issue, which is that our social system is a failure as it stands. Many experience poverty from birth to death. Many, many more walk a grim treadmill of desperation throughout their lives, only to sink into poverty in their old age. We live with the constant irony that mediocrity in the game of life is defined as a full house, while most players draw no better than a pair. Such inconsistencies will not be tolerated forever.

Looking at the "hard" side of our situation, it remains problematic how long America, comprising no more than 6% of the world population, can pre-empt almost 50% of the world's resources.[11] If we have not already reached the tolerance limits of our biological resources, we may soon reach the tolerance limits of our neighbors.

A system that we fail to modify of our own accord will inevitably be destroyed.

12

HOW GROSS IS OUR NATIONAL PRODUCT?

"A good society is a means to a good life for those who compose it; not something having a kind of excellence on its own account."
—BERTRAND RUSSELL

When last measured, our national product had achieved a grossness in excess of a trillion dollars. An important aspect of the GNP and those who deal with it is that the facile discussion and manipulation of figures followed by six or more zeros tends to silence embarrassing questions from common mortals. Sheer quantity lends a transcendent quality to all discussion. It is important to understand that such sums are subject to interpretation.

For all the vastness of the sums involved, our economic archangels do a good deal of bickering about how it should be added. Many of our shiny Knights of National Grossness are really Bob Cratchets in disguise. Any gathering of economists is guaranteed to produce such disagreement about the consideration of the GNP as an event, that one can't help but think of it as a kind of quantitative *Rashomon*. All of them are lying . . . or some of them are lying . . . or none of them are lying. The answer lies not only in the economic perceivers, but in the perceivers of the perceivers. The answer, the final accounting, in other words, is nowhere. Even if we agreed not to argue with the accounting procedures that go into the sum, we would still have communication problems.

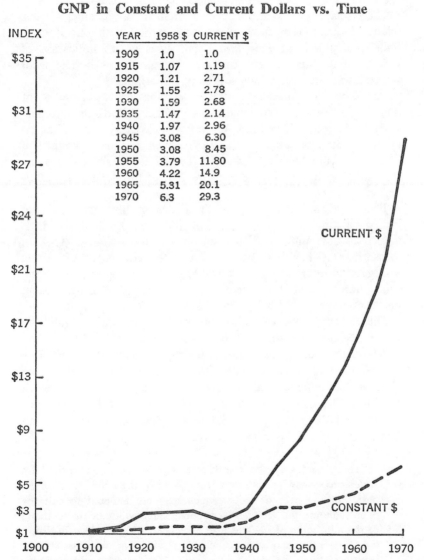

Figure XII-a
GNP in Constant and Current Dollars vs. Time

YEAR	1958 $	CURRENT $
1909	1.0	1.0
1915	1.07	1.19
1920	1.21	2.71
1925	1.55	2.78
1930	1.59	2.68
1935	1.47	2.14
1940	1.97	2.96
1945	3.08	6.30
1950	3.08	8.45
1955	3.79	11.80
1960	4.22	14.9
1965	5.31	20.1
1970	6.3	29.3

Should we, for instance, talk in current or constant dollars? The preceding graph shows two measurements of the growth of the GNP, one in real dollars, one in current dollars.

The "real," or "constant," measurement is a much better relative indication of how much we can buy with our dollars. Still, it only tells us *how much,* but gives us no indication of *what* we buy. Since more guns tends to mean less butter, *what* we buy with our real dollars is very important.

The GNP, no matter how it is summated, is an index of dollars, not an index of benefits. To some, this distinction may seem obvious and important. Others would rightly argue that no matter what was done to the GNP, even the most ungrateful anarchist would have to agree that the GNP has served as some indication of the continuing improvement of the American Standard of Living.

The occasional past value of the indicator, however, does not justify its continued use. The best that can be said for it is that it is an antiquated instrument; to use it as a tool in measuring the health of the nation is the equivalent of asking a surgeon to operate with a Bowie knife. The economic operation gains drama when it is performed with the GNP Bowie knife, but finer tools would minimize the danger to the patient.

The industrial worker who has watched his real purchasing power decline over the past five years while the GNP climbed to new highs, current and real, is inclined to doubt the credibility of doctors who operate with Bowie knives. Not only is the GNP an inadequate tool, its use predisposes us to a view of economic life that is simplistic at best and potentially sinister.

The GNP is a tool that belongs to what economist Kenneth Boulding calls the "cowboy economy":

> "The closed earth of the future requires economic principles which are somewhat different from those of the open earth of the past. For the sake of picturesqueness, I am tempted to call the open economy the "cowboy economy," the cowboy being symbolic of the illimitable plains and also associated with reckless, exploitative, romantic, and violent behavior, which is characteristic of open societies. The closed economy of the future might similarly be called the "spaceman" economy, in which the earth has be-

come a single spaceship, without unlimited reservoirs of anything, either for extraction or for pollution, and in which, therefore, man must find his place in a cyclical ecological system which is capable of continuous reproduction of material form even though it cannot escape having inputs of energy."[1]

The notion of a closed economy or closed system is distasteful to many, because it seems to put finite boundaries on our aspirations. This, as we shall see shortly, isn't necessarily so.

But before we can discuss the differences between open and closed systems, we must provide some evidence that the assumption underlying the necessity of closure—limited resources —is true.

Since the early nineteenth century, there have been predictions that we would consume all our natural resources. A presidential commission appointed in 1909 predicted that we would very likely have no oil by the year 1935. Similarly, it has been predicted that we would have no natural gas, no lumber, no coal, and no steel in periods of time ranging from yesterday to just the turn of the new millennium.

The bearded, billboard-bearing freak who has read signs of doom in the spread of facial warts and the disappearance of the nickel cigar is a familiar object of ridicule and humor. Increasingly, the prophet is not a freak but a scientist.

Scientists may be more respectable than mystics, but they seldom prove to be much better as prophets. Most predictions of an end to resources have been, and must be, based on projections of past consumption into the future, a technique that is just as prone to failure in the estimation of resources as it has proved to be in investments. The public bias is on the optimistic side because large corporations are in the habit of providing free documentary films to the public schools telling our children of the Wonders of Science and how man has always managed to find a substitute material for one that is scarce because of his Incredible Ingenuity and the Incentives of the Free Enterprise System.

Undoubtedly, there is some truth in these notions. It should be pointed out, however, that the skeptical optimist who uses the historical inadequacy of historically based predictions is skating on the very thinnest of logical ice. Besides, while it may be industrially possible to invent a substitute for scarce natural rubber or a material economically competitve with steel, a scarcity of air for lungs presents technological problems of a different order.

If we were to schematize our economic system, it would look something like an hourglass. Our production apparatus lies in the structure of the glass, pumping processed natural resources from one bulb to the other. Resources become products and pollution. Both are eventually consumed.

We eat corn, fish, and beef, and absorb DDT, dieldrin, and a host of other, obscure but deadly, poisons. We drink water and absorb esoteric but deadly radioactive material. We drive our cars at superhighway speeds to accomplish all the necessary chores of modern existence, leaving a trail of noxious gases behind that must be diluted with 60 million liters of fresh air per minute before it is safe to breathe. In one minute the car usurps air that 10 million human beings would breathe in the same time.[2] Put another way, each hour of turnpike driving consumes the *lifetime* breathing of ten people! One need not ponder long to realized that the dollar increase in production is a hopelessly narrow measure of benefits.

FIGURE XII-B

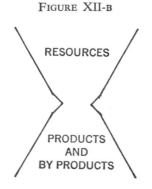

RESOURCES

PRODUCTS
AND
BY PRODUCTS

Economic parameters such as the GNP measure the *speed* of the productive pump at converting resources into products.[3]

If resources are infinite because of our technological virtuosity (a proposition yet to be proved), we must still be concerned with the amount of pollution we can produce along with our products. If the capacity of the planet to supply resources and absorb waste is infinite, then we need feel no concern. The planet's capacity to absorb pollution and waste, however, is all too palpably finite. Many lakes, streams, and rivers are already biologically dead. An increasing concentration of DDT in the world's water supply is affecting the ecological balance. DDT lowers the death rate from disease while increasing crop yields, by killing insect pests. While population increases absorb the increased agricultural yield, the increased DDT concentration reduces the fish population of the sea.[4] The net result is more hungry and protein-starved people—and a growing potentially deadly DDT concentration.

A similar relation holds for the increase of nitrates and phosphates in our water supply. Artificial fertilizers increase crop yields, while detergents provide the sanitation necessary in a very densely populated world. Both the fertilizers and the detergents eventually find their way to the world's water supply, encourage the growth of algae, upset the plant/animal balance, and begin the process of eutrophication, which has been most successfully demonstrated in Lake Erie, a body of water devoid of animal life except for some slugs and a mutant carp that feeds on poison. We could find ourselves suffocating in a clean and well-starched shirt.

Daniel Moynihan informed President Nixon that the atmosphere would contain 25% more carbon dioxide by the year 2000 if present conditions continue. The defeated SST promised to pollute the atmosphere with carbon dioxide at high altitude, threatening an acceleration of the "greenhouse" effect, which would raise the temperature of the earth, causing the polar caps to melt and raising the sea level by more than one hundred feet. One consolation in such a disaster is that air traffic would no longer be stacked up for hours over LaGuardia, Kennedy, and Logan airports. . . .

Frightening estimates and projections now appear in the newspapers with regularity. Many are questionable, even suspect, in their accuracy, because scientists as yet have only a limited knowledge of the complex workings of our planetary ecosystem.

To quibble with accuracy or calibration, however, is rather like questioning the sighting of a rifle when the muzzle is at our temple.

Readers who wish to pursue the subject of ecology and technological disaster may begin by reading the daily newspapers. More-organized reading can begin with Rachel Carson's *Silent Spring* and R. Stewart's *Not So Rich As You Think*.

Since the open vs. closed system argument often rests on a system of personal belief, we may expect that movement toward a rational and realistic appraisal of our circumstances will be painfully slow and accompanied by much rhetoric. We might be well advised to examine the consequences of being *wrong* as well as being right.

If the economists and ecologists who argue that we must consider ourselves bound by the resources of a closed system are wrong in their estimation of our circumstances, the worst that can happen is a slowdown and reappraisal of our headlong technological rush. Although a change or slowdown in the pace of technological development might have discomfiting effects for some, there would be some compensation, in that fewer people will suffer from "future shock."[5] In short, we have very little to lose.

If those who insist on perpetual growth based on an open system of infinite resources are wrong, we will all be dead. We can give the Pan Am Building back to those meek anaerobic bacterial forms that will inhabit the earth and let them fight for survival with mutants of the influenza virus. The best we can envision is a series of technological miracles that will provide some compensation for the loss of our natural environment. We would very likely retain our lives at the cost of our souls . . . or at least our freedom.

A society of free enterprise in which the quality of the air we breathe is a function of our individual ability to pay for the machinery to process that air, is far from free: The quality of the air we breathe is determined by our usefulness to the apparatus of production. Those who are skilled and loyal to the concept of industrial growth are rewarded with the best products and air that industrial production can provide. Those who are unskilled but loyal are rewarded with a quantity and quality of air and goods adequate to sustain enough of their existence to prove the charity and essential goodness of those with skills and loyalty. Those who question the concept and lack loyalty are deprived of air. One's capacity to serve the machinery of production determines whether life is pleasant.

This projection isn't necessarily paranoid and extreme: if the example of the air cleaners in the preceding chapter has any credibility, then such tyranny exists as a definite future possibility.

Interestingly, the differences between a capitalist mixed economy and a socialist/communist economy are exceedingly small under this light.[6] Both systems are ranged about the idea of technology and industrial growth; regardless of the political ideology that feeds the system, both require such enormous planning and intensive organization that the life-styles an individual may adopt and still survive are severely limited.

Skeptical readers will be quick to point out that in a primitive society where the average life-span is thirty years, life is a rather bleak experience: an admixture of hardship, misery, and adversity. If nothing else, such skeptics might argue, the industrial economy has managed to prolong human life to a more satisfactory length. Therefore it must be good.

Such reasoning contains an uncomfortable amount of truth. But it is also true that there is a law of diminishing returns.

Again, we must consider *quality* as well as *quantity*. For every Colette, capable of extracting the last bittersweet drops of experience from life's cup, there are hundreds, nay, thousands, not so blessed. And one wonders if that magnificence would have been possible had she spent her last years in the service of an artificial kidney. A tour of the local hospital will be sufficient to make many readers question how long life *really* is, and whether the decaying pale bodies that populate our overcrowded homes for the aged are being served by their medical machines, or vice versa. The quality of such life is low indeed.

In any case, *what bears examination is not so much the facts of our organization but the efficacy of the systems of belief we hold and the imperatives that follow from those systems.* This examination is long overdue. According to some, it may be entirely too late. It is an awesome prospect. We are not talking about forming commissions or study groups to explore a problem, but about asking most of the world to step outside itself, to examine tenets of belief so ingrained, so powerful, that they remain largely invisible because they form the very environment of our culture. *Our task is not to formulate new plans of action but to determine and change the invisible assumptions responsible for our existing plans.*

Returning to the visible world, momentarily, let us believe in the DuPont Company. Let us believe that our material resources, if not infinite, can be indefinitely extended by our technological virtuosity. Even if we can assume this, there is no such guarantee that we can extend our *biological* resources by technological means. In any case, as we have already speculated, a world in which technology has supplanted nature may not be much fun.

Our resources *must* be viewed as a closed system. Even if *some* elements of the system are effectively infinite, the boundaries of the system are determined by the limits of the *single* finite resource. The stranded astronauts will die of whatever resource is scarcest. Ultimately, food is useless without an adequate supply of air or water. Growth, in such circumstances, is negative as well as positive. We can no longer define growth as inherently good without qualification, question, or recourse. Measurement of the GNP and Gross World Product is not enough.

The situation has a rather gross natural analogue: Mothers don't measure their child's health by weighing the amount of excrement passed. They watch to see signs that the child is growing at a healthy rate, that he is bright, active, receptive, and learning. To feed the child excessively leads to nothing better than a fat and sluggish child. There is little pleasure in the growth of a retarded child; his form changes, but his *experience* does not. We shudder slightly when we meet such individuals and are thankful that it is not us or ours.

I am amazed when I watch my son! It isn't his growth that amazes me but the speed with which that growth becomes the tool of his expanding world of experience. I seldom consider how tall he is or how much he weighs, because it is relatively unimportant. What is important is what he does, that he plays longer and more-complicated games, that he walks and runs and climbs the stairs, that he talks and gestures, that he, each day, adds some

new experience to his life, a new expansion of his self. Though
he is not yet two, I see and sense his hunger for experience. I
marvel not so much at his growth but at his capacity to exploit
it; his growth, though almost daily palpable, seems no more than
a necessary tool, and that is the miracle that we seem to have
lost—growth that serves experience.

Our growth as a society isn't nearly so healthy. We grow in
dimension, in size, but not in experience. We wait, enthralled by
the cancer of our haphazard growth, as though some mysterious
increment of size would change the entire basis of our experience, would liberate us from our grotesque condition.

But our experience does not change. We panic at the realiza-
tion of our self-destructive power run amok in a universe with
which we refuse to communicate.

Liberals often join with conservatives in the acceptance of
growth as an article of faith. Economic Growth, the article says,
allows for increases in material wealth that will ease the redress
of social injustice. Liberals and conservatives then unite to criti-
cize government agencies for failing to plan adequately. The object of the planning, however, is not the weighing of ends, pro-
portions, and possible goods balanced against potential evils, but
the adjustment of a machine so that it functions *efficiently*. Operational efficiency is an inherent good, and the search for that
efficiency should be the call (our newspapers often declare) to
non-partisan arms. We never question the machine of economic
growth itself; we nag the means and ignore the ends, assuming
that somehow everything will work out for the best.

As Thomas J. Watson, Jr., chairman of IBM, suggested in an
often-quoted speech, what we need is a set of national goals:

> Watson, who served on the Commission on National Goals in
> the late years of the Eisenhower administration, said the first
> realization of the commission was that "this country has no very
> specific goals set down on paper." . . . And "No matter what
> goals we choose, there was practically no mechanism in govern-
> ment to methodically implement them and there isn't now."

Mr. Watson isn't entirely right. We *do* have a set of national
goals. They may be a bit "soft" for the technicians of the econ-

omy to handle, but they are real. Our national goals are "life, liberty, and the pursuit of happiness."

Not a very "hard" set of goals, and a bit vague. Certainly subject to some variety in interpretation. But if we cannot be sure of the means for implementing the "pursuit of happiness" and "liberty," we can at least be quite certain that the Gross National Product is totally inadequate as a measure of achievement. Wouldn't it be lovely if those words—those goals—inspired more than rhetoric from the Amvets and assorted Rotarians.

Troubling circumstances evoke a desire for action. If we can, we reduce our imperatives to directives that eliminate the need for continuing thought. It would be wonderful if all problems could be solved by a refusal to collect Green Stamps, the mock burial of a new car on the Berkeley campus, the dutiful return of garden pesticides to some central collecting point, moderation (or immoderation) in one's habits of thought or speech, a regular contribution to the United Fund, or even an occasional spirited riot.

But they can't. There are no simple directives.

We do have one imperative, however, and that is to overcome the differentiation of human beings that our industrial system has wrought. We seldom actually *see* half the people in our existence. At least we don't see them as people. Human intercourse is dividing between poles of intimacy and hostility; *community* dissipates between the two poles. Whatever the future holds, only a sense of community, of interdependence, of renewed responsibility, of—in fact—a rewritten Social Contract, will be enough to make it possible.

Most of our economic thought has been guided by a belief in the value of competition. Companies compete, and we assume that this competition will result in better products for consumers. As individuals, we compete every day, consciously or unconsciously, always hoping that we will win, assuming that the entire society derives some net benefit from our competition with our fellows. If there is no net benefit, we are satisfied that there are no alternatives and that if some must lose, we would rather it were someone else.

That was the old game. It was a nice game because it was based on the assumption that all play added to the value of the pot and that all players eventually benefited. It allowed us to believe inwardly that a current small evil would contribute to a future large good.

But it really isn't that way. We are all playing a new game. More of life resembles a zero-sum game every day: Every win requires a loss. The balance is always zero.

We must change not only the form, but the *substance,* of our relations. That perspective which allows a man to view his fellows competitively and his environment opportunistically must cease to exist.

A FINAL WORD

"For the World is a mountain of shit: if it's
going to be moved at all, it's got to be taken by
handfuls."

—A. GINSBERG

Some may disagree with Mr. Ginsberg's assessment of the world's composition—but one thing is clear: Whatever the composition, it must be moved by the handful. It's going to take a long time.

.

FOOTNOTES

INTRODUCTION

1. National Industrial Conference Board, *Economic Almanac* 1967–68, p. 372.
2. Proper scientific method tells us that a theory is only as good as the data it explains. Scientific method, as applied by both the American Right and Left, has a distinctly paranoid tone. Indeed, when one reads of the travails of people such as Eldridge Cleaver or the Chicago Seven, paranoia seems the only *sane* method of operation. In truth, however, operation and theory have different requirements. Paranoia in operation enables us to see a generalized enemy as specific, even embodied. And that generalized enemy is joyously and wantonly making a direct assault on our person. The clear discernment of evil is a joy in itself. We, on the other hand, live in a labyrinth of disembodied shadings. When we grasp the paranoid vision, we are wishing to draw blood from the communion wafer; we exchange clarity of mind for the peace of tribal images, reality for illusory presence.

CHAPTER 1

1. "Good Living Begins at $25,000 a Year," *Fortune*, May 1968.
2. Information of this sort can be found in *This U.S.A.* (Ben J. Wattenberg in collaboration with Richard M. Scammon, Doubleday & Co., Inc., Garden City, 1965), an interesting study of the 1960 Census, in which the statistician-technician uses a conjured humanity to sweep poverty under the Bigelow of the National Conscience and paint a rosy relative picture of life in America. A sample of this false humanistic reasoning is exhibited in requesting cross tabulation of categories to reveal that *some* of those with incomes under $3000 a year may be in the Armed Forces. Aside from the fact that it is horrifying that many Negro youths cannot obtain employment without laying

their life on the line in Vietnam, the writer neglects asking for the same type of cross tabulation in reverse, i.e., how many families with five or six children live on incomes of $3500 or $4000 or $5000?

3. While casual examination of the production/consumption cycle may seem at first to be a restatement of the chicken/egg problem, the late President Eisenhower's 1959 plea to the public to "buy" as a means to end the recession is evidence of the primacy of the consumer in the cycle. The coercive element becomes clear when it is seen that government is stimulating consumption as a prerequisite to maintaining or enhancing production, which will, in turn, maintain or enhance employment. The same regulatory machinery works in the opposite direction when the economy overheats. Unemployment is increased. Perhaps we can see it as the necessary sacrifice of some for the good of all, but the rationale becomes suspect when we consider that the same system that until very recently paid Senator Eastland approximately $300,000 a year to keep his *land* idle, is loath to provide adequate income to *people* who must remain idle.

4. We are also aware of a curious effect strings of zeros have on our minds; mathematically expressed, this effect would read something like this: understanding or inversely related to the number in question, or:
$$U_{llm}(f\ 1/N) = O$$
where N equals such figures as the National Debt, Federal Reserve Board figures, or the National Income.

5. "If you've seen one, you've seen them all"—S. T. Agnew, 1968. Undoubtedly an immortal statement. Perhaps the visual element of ghettos can be cumulated and reduced to a category. But can the Experience? Worse, must Novelty have priority over human need?

6. Ronald Segal, *The Americans: A Conflict of Creed and Reality*, Viking Press, New York, 1968.

7. Ferdinand Lundberg, *The Rich and the Super Rich*, Lyle Stuart, New York, 1968, p. 29.

CHAPTER 2

1. Most small savers are forced to save through the savings banks and savings and loan associations, where the interest rate is likely to be less than 6%. Treasury bills, are now passed in larger, $10,000 denominations to decrease the flow of higher-rate hunters and the consequent drain on the savings and commercial banks.

2. *Consumer Reports* performs just such evaluations.

3. There is a danger in this, of course, and that is that the investment aspects of collecting will overcome and overshadow the aesthetic Service Return aspects. Considerations of profit have taken the fun out of more than a few hobbies. Several years ago, a stock broker spoke to me of his art collection almost entirely in terms of investment; he had, in fact, transferred the whole vocabulary and analytic of his vocation to his avocation. Picasso was a "blue chip."

CHAPTER 3

1. Richard Goode, *The Individual Income Tax*, The Brookings Institution, 1964, p. 3.
2. One doesn't have to be an economic seer to see the absurdities in some of the reform measures.
3. Statistics of the Bureau of Labor Statistics indicate that increased taxes have been a major portion of the increases responsible for the decreasing purchasing power of industrial workers.

CHAPTER 4

1. Norman O. Brown, *Life Against Death*, Vintage Books, p. 238.

The alienated consciousness is correlative with a money economy. Its root is the compulsion to work. This compulsion to work subordinates man to things, producing at the same time confusion in the valuation of things (*Verwertung*) and devaluation of the human body (*Entwertung*). It reduces the drives of the human being to greed and competition (aggressiveness and possessiveness, as in the anal character). The desire for money takes the place of genuinely human needs. Thus the apparent accumulation of wealth is really the impoverishment of human nature, and its appropriate morality is the renunciation of human nature and thus to dehumanize human nature. In this dehumanized human nature man loses contact with his own body, more specifically with his senses, with sensuality and with the pleasure-principle. And this dehumanized human nature produces an inhuman consciousness, whose only currency is abstractions divorced from real life—the industrious, coolly rational, economic, prosaic mind.

CHAPTER 5

1. Recent articles in *Look* and *U.S. News & World Report* (January 1970) voiced the growing concern about the housing shortage. Apartment vacancies in urban areas are practically nil and have resulted in exorbitant rent increases and numerous proposals for rent control.
2. Recent labor contracts providing annual increases in wages in excess of 6% are some indication that comparable housing costs will increase at a rate equal to or faster than inflation. The size of the market is another factor; the market for, say, $80,000 houses is rather thin, because few people can afford the necessary expenses. The sale price then becomes negotiable and dependent on the vagaries of both owner and potential buyer.

3. We should all pray that 4% is higher than it will turn out to be. The prognosis for future inflation is one of those things that changes from commentator to commentator and may ultimately be correlated to the harmonics of the moon or some other absurdity. Most economists feel comfortable in putting their bets on 2% inflation, with luck. A little sloppiness could raise it to 3%. As urbanization continues, however, we can expect to see a greater increase in urban/suburban land and building values. The Phillips curve indicates that industrial societies face intolerable inflation on one hand and intolerable unemployment on the other. The events of the past two years indicate that inflation may very well run at an annual rate of 4%.

CHAPTER 6

1. *The Consumers Union Report on Life Insurance,* published by Consumers Union, distributed by Harper & Row, New York, Evanston, and London. The clearest book available on the subject.
2. Your particular benefits are a matter of complex calculation related to your earnings history. Any insurance planning should be done with up-to-date information on your Social Security account. This information may be obtained by sending a "Request for Statement of Earnings" postcard from your local S.S. office and mailing it to:
   Social Security Administration
   Baltimore, Maryland 21235.
   Your account credits determine the benefits your family is eligible for in the event of your death or disability. The local S.S. office can detail these benefits, given your statement of earnings.
3. Relative life expectancy has begun to fall in some of the industrialized countries. A United Nations study found that Americans a decade ago ranked seventeenth in life expectancy, but now rank twenty-fifth. In the past, insurance companies have reaped enormous profits from the extension of life expectancy. A reversal, which has been projected by some ecologists, may be in the offing.
4. We can avoid this by buying renewable 5-year term. Most term policies are renewable. Since they may be extended to age 65 with no medical examination, they are "permanent" for all intents and purposes.
5. Estimate from James Gollin, *Pay Now, Die Later,* Random House, 1966.

CHAPTER 7

1. Winthrop Knowlton's *Growth Opportunities in Common Stocks* (Harper & Row, 1965) is a direct and relatively accessible book on the subject of security analysis. Highly recommended.
2. Interestingly, savings interest does not enjoy the $100 income-tax ex-

clusion on dividends; an inequity of the tax system, since only one American in five owns any stock at all, while many save.

3. Worse, it's high enough to draw money out of banks and into treasury notes and commercial paper, reducing money available to non-corporate borrowers drastically.

4. For a more-detailed analysis of the interrelation of S.S. and investments, see Chapter 8.

5. Based on an average commission of 1% and assuming the broker receives 35% of the commission. A fairly standard arrangement in brokerage houses.

6. Since this was written, Performance Systems has encountered substantial troubles.

7. I personally fear that a day will come when it will be impossible to eat an entire meal at one sitting; when one will have to go from franchise to franchise, collecting individual packets, paper plates, and plastic utensils.

8. *Journal of Finance*, Vol. XXIII, May 1968, #2. "Problems in Selection of Security Portfolios. The Performance of Mutual Funds in the Period 1945–64."

9. Smoking a pack a day costs more than $100/yr., also . . .

10. Mutual funds reduce risk by diversification of investments; they are so diversified, in fact (and so regulated), that they seldom own more than 3% of the outstanding stock of a particular company and never involve themselves in company management. The type of company they invest in is a function of the philosophy of the fund's management. In a sense, mutual funds are the passive counterparts of some of our more broadly based diversified industrial companies.

Another word comes to mind here—conglomerates. Yet there is a difference between a diversified industrial company and a conglomerate. In the former, the range and depth of the company's production has expanded in response to the vagaries and insecurities of the marketplace (i.e., defensively), and the company management commits its major energies to increasing *internal* company growth; in the latter, management energy is committed to expansion through acquisition (i.e., aggressively). By virtue of its energy commitments, the managements of conglomerate companies tend toward more-varied and sophisticated financings (sometimes referred to as Chinese money) and have managed to arouse investor distrust of late.

Whatever the form or philosophy of the company, however, all are dedicated to the same object: adequate return on investment. Polaroid, regardless of the size of its capital pool, is a one-product company, in no way resembling a mutual fund. AT&T, however, closely resembles an income fund. Similarly, IT&T resembles a growth fund.

11. At the time of the investor's death the property would be evaluated and placed in his estate. While the estate would be liable for taxes on the current value of the property, no capital-gains tax would be due, and his heirs would own the property at its new evaluation base.

12. The Tax Reform bill of 1969 has closed or tightened many of the more egregious loopholes. By reducing the top marginal tax rate from 70% to 50% (by 1972), however, the same tax bill removed or at least substantially reduced the driving impetus that created and developed such loopholes.
13. Which serve to pool the capital of multiple investors, protect them against liability beyond original investment, and pass on tax losses at favorable personal, rather than corporate, income-tax rates.

CHAPTER 8

1. While some allowance must be made for the fact that some young families will eventually accumulate a significant amount of stock although they own little now, the fact remains that only the very smallest minority of Americans invest in common stocks.

   Most Americans put their savings into . . . savings. They earn interest on their capital, not dividends or capital appreciation. Since the return on fixed dollar investments is noticeably lower than that on common stocks and that required to retire with adequate capital to replace one's income, we must assume that many of those few Americans who do save adequate portions of their incomes receive an inadequate rate of return on their investments, restoring much of our formerly mitigated gloom. Perhaps the most tragic past example of such instances is the investment millions of patriotic Americans made in War Bonds during World War II. Heavily advertised and promoted, coercively pressed on laborers and white-collar workers, these bonds constitute the backbone of many families' retirement plans. These patriotic, hard-working, and believing workers, who are now retiring, discover that their $25 War Bonds have a purchasing power of less than $15, an amount less than what they originally paid for the bonds, and before consideration of the tax liabilities that will accrue when the bonds are liquidated.
2. Pensions have definitely come of age: private and non-private plans combined now serve some 42 million Americans and control some 260 billion dolllars in assets. There are, however, some 95 million workers in the American labor force. Moreover, inclusion in some form of non-contributory pension (80% of those covered) does not guarantee adequate coverage. Indeed, in some cases there may be *no* coverage, because the plan isn't a vested plan (giving full, irrevocable pension rights after a predetermined number of years' service) and the worker has lost rights as he changes jobs. Many young—and not so young—professionals are in this position. Only 76% of the existing pension plans allow vesting—which may require ten or fifteen years' service. Only a careful reading of the contract can determine whether or not the pension will produce an adequate income to maintain your

standard of living after retirement. The problem is of such a magnitude that many in the field consider it necessary that private systems be merged with the Social Security system.

CHAPTER 9

1. Most readers of this book will find themselves incapable of imagining that employment will not always exist for them. Many professionals are overemployed. While electricians work thirty-hour weeks in New York, doctors and lawyers, and other professionals, increasingly find that their work week runs to sixty hours and tends to expand rather than contract. Indeed, no relief is in sight for the professional for at least a decade, perhaps until the end of the century.

CHAPTER 10

1. Read Lynn White, Jr., "The Historical Roots of Our Ecologic Crisis," in *The Environmental Handbook*. Ballantine/Friends of the Earth, 1970.
2. J. K. Galbraith's word describing the apparatus from which the "Soulful Corporation" may eventually evolve. Readers interested in pursuing this line of thought are urged to read *The Affluent Society* and *The New Industrial State*. Capitalism isn't alone in being enamored with the notion of Perpetual Material Progress to the Electronic Eden. We have now reached a point where communism (and certainly socialism) can be viewed as no more than pantywaisted Revisionism, because they are concerned with little more than variations on techniques for the allocation and distribution of resources and production. In the light of what may be a necessary Cultural Revolution, such changes in political process are mere dabbling and crass temporizing.

CHAPTER 11

1. Historically, "more and better jobs" has been one of the prime determinants of justice. California citrus growers, whose crops were repeatedly damaged by land erosion caused by hydraulic gold mining, failed to win damages in litigation until they developed a public constituency. This constituency was developed, in part, because people saw that hydraulic mining was declining in economic importance while citrus farming was growing.
2. New York *Times*, study by Organization for Social and Technical Innovation.
3. New York *Times*, December 1969.

4. The Tax Reform bill of 1969 does little if anything to mitigate the inequity of our tax structure.
5. *The Wall Street Journal*, December 18, 1969.
6. *Ramparts*, January 1970, "Raping Alaska," by Barry Weisberg.
7. Jay W. Forrester's *World Dynamics*, Wright-Allen Press, 1971, examines this subject in detail.
8. Joint Economic Committee Report, *Toward Economic Development for Native American Communities.*
9. Some elements with economic components follow:
    1) Air pollution: cleaning; damage to buildings, exposed objects, etc; economic loss from increased sickness, death, created demand for medical services, created demand for air filters, etc.
    2) Water pollution: increased consumer costs for preliminary purification, economic loss to fisheries, artificially inflated fish-product prices to consumers, medical costs, increased travel costs for vacationers.
    3) Land pollution; increased shelter costs in urban areas due to primacy of roadways, increased transportation costs for disposal of waste matter, excess product packaging, bone and organ damage from toxic DDT and strontium 90 concentrations.
    4) Noise pollution: accidents, irritability, mental illness, damage to structures, productivity lost for lack of sleep, etc.
    The preceding list is, by no means, exhaustive. It exists only to make a point. Skeptical readers who would like to pursue the matter are advised to contact their local Sierra Club or Audubon Society for a virtually endless statement of industrial ramifications ranging from the mundane to the transcendental.
10. Newsweek, January 26, 1970.
11. Ehrlich, Paul, *The Population Bomb*, Ballantine.

CHAPTER 12

1. Boulding, Kenneth, *Beyond Economics*, University of Michigan, 1968, "The Economics of the Coming Spaceship Earth," p. 281.
2. Chase, Stuart, *The Most Probable World*, Penguin Books, 1969, p. 60.
3. Kenneth Boulding considers that a more realistic model of our economic acts would be based on the mechanics of the bathtub. We must not only question how much water we pour into the tub but also measure the amount of water that drains *out*, for our real progress is measured by the water that remains in the tub. "It is not the increase of consumption or production which makes us rich, but the increase in capital, and any invention which enables us to enjoy a given capital stock with a smaller amount of consumption and production, out-go or income, is so much gain."
    —"Income or Welfare?" Kenneth E. Boulding, *Review of Economic Studies*, XVII (2) 1949–50 ⅜43 pp. 79–80.

4. An article in *Ramparts* estimates that had the *Torrey Canyon* been loaded with hydrocarbon poisons such as DDT, the disaster would have virtually annihilated all marine life in the North Sea. Many of the major oil companies are contemplating transporting these materials by tanker.

5. Coined by sociologist Eric Toffler in reference to the accelerating changes in our culture and environment. In 1950, E. B. White estimated that the generation cycle was down to ten years. Some sociologists think it is now down to less than four years. Skeptical readers are urged to read the papers and view the experiential void via the media that separate a ten-year-old from a fourteen-year-old. . . .

6. Both economies are based on a system of belief that may be expressed as follows: Our experience is a closed system. Our resources are an open system. The means to escape the necessary limitations of our closed system of experience is the open system of material resources. Rather than confront the difficulties of our system of experience, we divert our energies to an essentially impossible task.

APPENDIX A

Understanding the relation of money to our future involves recognition of the *time value* of money. Whether we are discussing insurance, annuities, or investments, a crucial consideration is what money is worth over time.

We might build our idea from the notion that "A bird in the hand is worth two in the bush"—i.e. a dollar now is worth more than a dollar delivered five or ten years from now.

Suppose someone promises to deliver $1 ten years from now. How much should I be willing to pay for that contract? $1? No! If money is worth 4% per yr. I know that I should not pay more than $.675 for the contract, because I could have $1 ten years from now by saving that amount.

Such contracts for future delivery of money are the heart of both life insurance and economic planning.

The tables that follow offer a quantitative method for determining what sums of money will produce what income "streams" assuming different rates of return.

I. PRESENT VALUE A

To find out how much money you need *now* to provide an *annual* income for T years multiply the income by a number in the row numbered with the appropriate T. Use the 4% figure when capitalizing the Social Security figures.

TABLE A
Present Value Factors for Annual Incomes Received in Monthly Installments for Various Rates of Return

T/R	3	4	5	6	7	8	9	%
1	.98	.98	.98	.97	.97	.96	.96	
2	1.94	1.92	1.91	1.89	1.87	1.85	1.84	
3	2.87	2.83	2.79	2.75	2.71	2.68	2.64	
4	3.77	3.70	3.64	3.57	3.50	3.44	3.38	
5	4.65	4.54	4.44	4.34	4.24	4.15	4.06	
6	5.50	5.35	5.20	5.06	4.93	4.80	4.68	
7	6.32	6.12	5.93	5.75	5.57	5.41	5.25	
8	7.12	6.87	6.62	6.39	6.18	5.97	5.78	
9	7.90	7.58	7.28	7.00	6.74	6.49	6.26	
10	8.66	8.27	7.91	7.58	7.27	6.97	6.70	
11	9.39	8.93	8.51	8.12	7.76	7.42	7.10	
12	10.10	9.57	9.08	8.63	8.22	7.83	7.47	
13	10.79	10.18	9.63	9.11	8.65	8.22	7.82	
14	11.46	10.77	10.14	9.57	9.05	8.57	8.13	
15	12.12	11.33	10.64	10.00	9.42	8.89	8.42	
16	12.75	11.88	11.10	10.40	9.97	9.20	8.68	
17	13.36	12.41	11.55	10.79	10.10	9.48	8.92	
18	13.96	12.91	11.98	11.15	10.40	9.74	9.14	
19	14.54	13.39	12.38	11.49	10.69	9.98	9.35	
20	15.10	13.86	12.77	11.81	10.96	10.20	9.53	
21	15.64	14.31	13.14	12.11	11.21	10.41	9.70	
22	16.17	14.74	13.49	12.40	11.44	10.60	9.86	
23	16.69	15.15	13.82	12.67	11.66	10.78	10.00	
24	17.19	15.55	14.14	12.92	11.87	10.94	10.13	
25	17.67	15.93	14.44	13.16	12.05	11.09	10.25	
26	18.14	16.30	14.73	13.39	12.23	11.24	10.36	
27	18.60	16.65	15.00	13.60	12.40	11.36	10.47	
28	19.04	16.99	15.27	13.80	12.56	11.48	10.56	
29	19.47	17.32	15.52	13.99	12.70	11.60	10.65	
30	19.89	17.64	15.75	14.17	12.83	11.70	10.72	
31	20.30	17.94	15.98	14.34	12.96	11.79	10.80	
32	20.69	18.23	16.19	14.50	13.08	11.89	10.86	
33	21.07	18.51	16.40	14.65	13.19	11.97	10.93	
34	21.45	18.78	16.59	14.79	13.30	12.04	10.98	
35	21.81	19.03	16.78	14.93	13.39	12.11	11.03	
36	22.16	19.24	16.96	15.05	13.48	12.18	11.08	
37	22.50	19.52	17.13	15.17	13.57	12.24	11.12	
38	22.83	19.75	17.28	15.29	13.65	12.29	11.16	
39	23.15	19.97	17.44	15.39	13.72	12.34	11.20	
40	23.46	20.19	17.58	15.49	13.79	12.39	11.23	

PRESENT VALUE B

Some sums of money will not be necessary immediately. In the example of insurance, some needs may not be realized for five, ten, twenty, or even forty years. To account for the time difference, we discount the sum needed.

Although we could discount sums needed in the future by 8% or 9% if we invest in common stocks, it would be unwise to do so, because the dollar is constantly decreasing in value as a result of inflation. A 6% or 7% discount rate is reasonable, however.

TABLE B

Present Value of $1 for Various Rates of Return

YR	3	4	5	6	7	8	9	%
1	.97	.96	.95	.94	.93	.93	.92	
2	.94	.92	.91	.89	.87	.86	.84	
3	.91	.89	.86	.84	.81	.79	.77	
4	.89	.85	.82	.79	.76	.73	.71	
5	.86	.82	.78	.75	.71	.68	.65	
6	.84	.79	.75	.70	.67	.63	.60	
7	.81	.76	.71	.66	.62	.58	.55	
8	.79	.73	.68	.63	.58	.54	.50	
9	.77	.70	.64	.59	.54	.50	.46	
10	.74	.66	.61	.56	.50	.46	.42	
11	.72	.65	.58	.53	.47	.43	.39	
12	.70	.62	.56	.50	.44	.40	.36	
13	.68	.60	.53	.47	.41	.37	.33	
14	.66	.58	.50	.44	.39	.34	.30	
15	.64	.56	.48	.42	.36	.31	.27	
16	.62	.53	.46	.39	.34	.29	.25	
17	.60	.51	.44	.37	.32	.27	.23	
18	.59	.49	.42	.35	.30	.25	.22	
19	.57	.47	.40	.33	.28	.23	.19	
20	.55	.46	.38	.31	.26	.21	.18	
21	.54	.44	.36	.29	.24	.20	.16	
22	.52	.42	.34	.28	.22	.18	.15	
23	.51	.41	.33	.26	.21	.17	.14	
24	.49	.39	.31	.25	.20	.16	.13	
25	.48	.38	.29	.23	.18	.15	.12	
26	.46	.36	.28	.22	.17	.14	.11	
27	.45	.35	.27	.21	.16	.12	.10	
28	.44	.33	.25	.20	.15	.12	.09	
29	.42	.32	.24	.18	.14	.11	.08	
30	.41	.31	.23	.17	.13	.10	.07	
31	.40	.30	.22	.16	.12	.09	.07	
32	.39	.29	.21	.15	.11	.09	.06	
33	.38	.27	.20	.15	.11	.08	.06	
34	.37	.26	.19	.14	.10	.07	.05	
35	.35	.25	.18	.13	.09	.07	.05	
36	.34	.24	.17	.12	.09	.06	.04	
37	.33	.23	.16	.12	.08	.06	.04	
38	.32	.22	.16	.11	.08	.05	.04	
39	.31	.22	.15	.10	.07	.05	.03	
40	.31	.21	.14	.09	.07	.05	.03	

II. HOW TO CALCULATE YOUR INSURANCE NEEDS

We start our calculations with your current income. This is what you must replace. If you own a home with a mortgage, decreasing term insurance is the least-expensive form of coverage.

Period I
Current Income
    minus Social Security payments, insurance, and investments
    less Mort. pmts. Decreasing term to cover home mort.
Net income 4% value factor
    for n years, n being number of years until your child reaches maturity.
    less S.S. value n factor×income/child
    less S.S. value of survivors' benefits for n years, n being determined by age of youngest child.
Net $ required for Period I

Period II
Duration 62 minus age at end of Period I; income required on 4% value factor discounted by duration of Period I @ 5, 6, or 7%

Period III
(Income required less S.S. benefits) ×annuity factor 16

    Period I
    Period II
    Period III————————Total insurance income needs
                   Decreasing term insurance

The figure above will provide for all your family's major needs except education and what might be called the "closing expenses" on your existence. The latter can be calculated easily and added on; the former involves a good deal of speculation on just what tuition and peripheral school expenses are going to involve when your children reach college age.

To arrive at this figure you should pick a number from the air . . . say, $4000 a year; multiply it by the present value of that dollar at 4% and then discount the resulting amount by the number of years between the present and metriculation.

Let's go through that again, only with an imaginary family. John and

Priscilla Wombat, at twenty-five and twenty-four, respectively: they have two children (ages one and two); John earns $12,000 a year as a widget engineer.

$12,000
— 1,200 (10% allowance for savings, investments, life insurance
_____
$10,800
— 2,000 (Mortgage payments on 24M @ 7% for 25 yrs.) 24M d.t. ins. pol.
_____
$ 8,800 Net income to be replaced

Period I
Duration 20 years, factor 13.86=$122,000, less capitalized Social Security benefits of:
1 yr. old, 20 yrs. @ $1500=factor 13.86 equiv. $20,800
2-yr.-old, 19 yrs. @   1500= in   13.39   "   20,000
Mother, 19 yrs. @ 1400=Table 13.39   "   18,700
                           A   _____
                                          $59,500
Net Required, Period I=$62,500

Period II
Duration 18 years, factor 12.9=$113,500
                     ×   .319 (6%, 30-yr.-discount factor)
                    _____
                    $ 34,500   Table B

Period III
Income $8,800
  — 1,600 S.S. benefits
  _____
  $7,200 Net Required×annuity payout (factor 16)
         $115,000
         ×   .109 (6%, 20-yr.-discount factor)
         _____
         $ 12,700   Table B

Total term required, periods I, II, and III=$106,700
                                 +   24,000 d.t. ins.

At this point, the reader has probably noticed quite painfully that although we have yet to make any provision for education costs, the total amount of coverage needed is $130,000. By squeezing Period

I and eliminating Period II, we could lower the amount required substantially, thus reducing the burden of premiums. The amount still remains rather large, however, and this points out the inadequacy of the "ordinary," or "straight," life-insurance policy—the annual premiums for such coverage would be substantially higher than the 10% allotted to insurance, savings, and investments.

The fact that we will be pressed to provide complete income replacement within our budget, using less-expensive, term insurance, not only points out the dangers of "ordinary" insurance but necessitates a good hard look at our insurance priorities. It does not make sense to insure your wife or children at the expense of the family's most pressing insurance need—income protection. If you die and are inadequately insured, annuities, endowment policies, etc., will lapse, because there will not be enough money to keep up the premiums. If a child dies, funeral expenses will compound the family grief but it will not endanger the economic future of the entire family. The same goes for your wife, though as McCall's is wont to point out, her economic value is not to be underestimated.

SAMPLE FORMS

Gross income $
children: ✕, age
wife: age

less:
S.S. payments,
insurance, investments,
―――――――mortgage payments 1 d.t.
TOTAL

―――――――NET INCOME TO BE REPLACED

Period I—capitalize n.i. @ 4% for duration of period.
    period =21—age of youngest child

―――――――×Discount factor (see factor in Table A)

Less capitalized S.S. benefits:
  (a) benefits/child capitalized Discount Factor$_4$ (Table A)
  (b) benefits/mother capitalized Discount Factor$_4$ (Table A)
    (alt=max family allowance on n yrs. (Table A)
                         ―――――――total

    net――――――(2) renewable 5-yr term

Period II—Duration=62−(current age of wife+P)
        ―――――――×Discount Factor$_4$×Discount Factor$_6$
  (Table A) (Table B) (3) renewable 5 yr. term

Amount is discounted or carried in present value because it is not required immediately, i.e., Period II will not commence until x years following death. A smaller amount of money now will produce the requisite amount when invested. The same reasoning applies to Period III.

Period III—Income

$$-\frac{\text{S.S. benefits}}{\text{Net} \times \text{annuity factor}} =$$

$$\times \text{discount}$$ (table B)

(4) renewable 5 yr. term————
Education fund

$$= \text{future cost}$$

$$\frac{\text{————discount (Table B)}}{5 \text{ net cost/child}}$$

Total insurance needs
 1 Decreasing term
 2 5 yrs. renewable convertible term
 3   ″
 4   ″
Decreasing term

III. INVESTMENT GROWTH RATE TABLES

Use Table C to calculate how much a given sum will grow in a given period of time.

TABLE C
Compound Interest Rate

T/R	3	4	5	6	7	8	9	10
1	1.03	1.04	1.05	1.06	1.07	1.08	1.09	1.10
2	1.06	1.08	1.10	1.12	1.14	1.16	1.19	1.21
3	1.09	1.12	1.15	1.19	1.23	1.26	1.29	1.33
4	1.13	1.17	1.21	1.26	1.31	1.36	1.41	1.46
5	1.16	1.22	1.28	1.34	1.40	1.47	1.54	1.61
6	1.19	1.26	1.34	1.42	1.50	1.59	1.68	1.77
7	1.23	1.32	1.41	1.50	1.60	1.71	1.83	1.95
8	1.27	1.37	1.48	1.59	1.72	1.85	1.99	2.14
9	1.30	1.42	1.55	1.69	1.84	2.00	2.17	2.35
10	1.34	1.48	1.63	1.79	1.97	2.16	2.37	2.59
15	1.56	1.80	2.08	2.39	2.75	3.17	3.64	4.18
20	1.80	2.19	2.65	3.21	3.87	4.66	5.60	6.73
25	2.09	2.66	3.39	4.29	5.43	6.85	8.62	10.83
30	2.43	3.24	4.32	5.74	7.61	10.06	13.27	17.45
35	2.81	3.95	5.51	7.68	10.68	14.75	20.41	28.10
40	3.26	4.80	7.04	10.29	14.97	21.17	31.41	45.26

Use Table D to calculate how much a given sum will amount to when it is invested every year.

TABLE D
Compound Interest Rate

T/R	3	4	5	6	7	8	9	10
1	1.01	1.02	1.02	1.03	1.03	1.04	1.04	1.05
2	2.06	2.08	2.10	2.12	2.14	2.16	2.18	2.20
3	3.14	3.18	3.23	3.27	3.32	3.37	3.42	3.47
4	4.25	4.33	4.41	4.50	4.59	4.68	4.78	4.87
5	5.39	5.52	5.66	5.80	5.95	6.10	6.25	6.41
6	6.56	6.76	6.97	7.18	7.40	7.63	7.86	8.09
7	7.78	8.05	8.34	8.64	8.95	9.27	9.61	9.95
8	9.02	9.39	9.78	10.19	10.61	11.05	11.52	12.00
9	10.31	10.79	11.30	11.83	12.39	12.98	13.60	14.25
10	11.63	12.24	12.89	13.57	14.29	15.06	15.87	16.72
15	18.88	20.42	22.11	23.97	26.00	28.22	30.66	33.34
20	27.27	30.37	33.88	37.88	42.41	47.57	53.43	60.09
25	37.00	42.47	48.91	56.49	65.44	75.99	88.46	103.19
30	48.28	57.20	68.00	81.40	97.73	117.76	142.35	172.59
35	61.36	75.11	92.56	114.75	143.02	179.12	225.28	284.36
40	76.53	96.91	123.80	159.36	206.54	269.29	352.87	464.37

APPENDIX B

Ordinary life insurance policies, annuities, and mutual funds are sold as investment vehicles that allow one to prepare for retirement. Proper consideration of this problem demands some exploration of its mathematical dimensions.

We can determine the amount of capital we will need by estimating the income we will require and multiplying it by the reciprocal of our predetermined withdrawal rate from the capital sum, i.e.

$$\text{capital} = \text{income} \times 1/\text{withdrawal rate (as \% capital)}$$

We will assume that the withdrawal rate will approximate 7% or 1/15, approximately what most annuities produce.

We know that the amount of capital we can accumulate will be determined by a) the amount we save, b) the return on our investment, and c) the number of years given for investment, i.e.

$$\text{capital} = \text{savings (as \% income)} \times \text{growth rate}^N,$$
$$\text{where } N = \text{investment period.}$$

Putting the two halves of the equation together, we have:

$$S_i \times G^N = I \times 1/_W \text{ or}$$
$$G^N = 1/S_i \times 1/_W$$

We have now accounted for everything except inflation. To compensate for purchasing power lost to inflation, we must assume a likely inflation rate and adjust our equation.

$$G^N = 1/SW \times 1/(1-i)^N, \text{ where } i = \text{inflation rate.}$$

In the calculations that follow, we are assuming a moderate, 2% inflation rate.

For a given savings rate, we can now determine the growth rate (return on investment) required to complete our investment project for a variety of periods.

If we save 10% of our anticipated retirement income needs,

AGE	N	s=10%	s=20%	
25	40	9	6+	
30	35	10+	7+	% required growth rates
35	30	12+	9	
40	25	16	11+	

To translate this into living terms, let us assume that you conclude that you will need only 40% of your current income for retirement. Social Security benefits, imputed rental income from your paid-for house, and other items have served to reduce the requirement to this amount. You can reach this goal by saving *no less than 8%* of your income from age thirty on to retirement! Other savings projects will absorb more of your income, and it will be necessary to invest all your dollars in stocks rather than fixed dollar investments.

APPENDIX C

Providing for a college education is a simpler problem than retirement at least in calculation.

$$\frac{A \times 1/1 - i^n}{Growth\ F^{10}} = \$/child/year\ to\ be\ saved$$

where: A=amount estimated presently necessary for college education

$1/1 - i^n$=inflation adjustment factor; i=rate, n=years to matriculation.

Growth F=amount to which \$1 savings will accumulate, given a compound rate of return on investment.

More concretely, let us assume that we are going to begin an investment program as each of our children is born and that our goal is to accumulate enough money to pay for the child's education. If we assume that each child will matriculate at eighteen, that inflation will progress at 2% a year, that we will obtain a net compound rate of return on our savings of 6%, and that we are allowing \$2000 (constant dollars) per year for college expenses, we arrive at the following figure:

$$\frac{(Amount\ Needed) \times (inflation\ adjustment)}{amount\ to\ which\ \$1\ will\ accumulate\ at\ 6\%\ interest\ in\ 18\ years}$$

$$\frac{(\$2000 \times 4) \times 1/.70}{32} = \$360/yr/child$$

The figure above is a rather rosy one in that it assumes a 2% inflation rate and only \$2000 per year for expenses. Though it may not be the last word, the figure does give some idea of the minimum dimensions required for an educational program. Expressed in terms of income, a father must devote 2–4% of his income per child to education.

APPENDIX D

Present value of mortgage payments net after taxes for a variety of interest rates per thousand dollars borrowed

R/TAX BRACKET	0	19	25	40	52	61	70
3	1412	1335	1310	1245	1195	1160	1124
5	1366	1247	1209	1115	1039	982	926
6	1339	1205	1162	1057	975	909	846
7	1326	1177	1130	1013	919	849	778
8	1309	1149	1098	971	869	793	716